Four Corners

Jack C. Richards · David Bohlke

1

Student's Book

CAMBRIDGE
UNIVERSITY PRESS

CAMBRIDGE UNIVERSITY PRESS
Cambridge, New York, Melbourne, Madrid, Cape Town, Singapore, São Paulo, Delhi, Dubai, Tokyo, Mexico City

Cambridge University Press
32 Avenue of the Americas, New York, NY 10013-2473, USA

www.cambridge.org
Information on this title: www.cambridge.org/9780521126342

First published 2012

Printed in Hong Kong, China, by Golden Cup Printing Company Limited

A catalog record for this publication is available from the British Library.

ISBN 978-0-521-12634-2 Full Contact 1 with Self-study CD-ROM
ISBN 978-0-521-12646-5 Teacher's Edition 1 with Assessment Audio CD / CD-ROM
ISBN 978-0-521-12640-3 Class Audio CDs 1
ISBN 978-0-521-12619-9 Classware 1
ISBN 978-0-521-12638-0 DVD 1

For a full list of components, visit www.cambridge.org/fourcorners

Art direction, book design, photo research, and layout services: Adventure House, NYC
Audio production: CityVox, NYC
Video production: Steadman Productions

Authors' acknowledgments

Many people contributed to the development of *Four Corners*. The authors and publisher would like to particularly thank the following **reviewers**:

Nele Noe, **Academy for Educational Development, Qatar Independent Secondary School for Girls**, Doha, Qatar; Yuan-hsun Chuang, **Soo Chow University**, Taipei, Taiwan; Celso Frade and Sonia Maria Baccari de Godoy, **Associaçao Alumni**, São Paulo, Brazil; Pablo Stucchi, **Antonio Raimondi School** and **Instituto San Ignacio de Loyola**, Lima, Peru; Kari Miller, **Binational Center**, Quito, Ecuador; Alex K. Oliveira, **Boston University**, Boston, MA, USA; Elisabeth Blom, **Casa Thomas Jefferson**, Brasilia, Brazil; Henry Grant, **CCBEU – Campinas**, Campinas, Brazil; Maria do Rosário, **CCBEU – Franca**, Franca, Brazil; Ane Cibele Palma, **CCBEU Inter Americano**, Curitiba, Brazil; Elen Flavia Penques da Costa, **Centro de Cultura Idiomas – Taubate**, Taubate, Brazil; Inara Lúcia Castillo Couto, **CEL LEP – São Paulo**, São Paulo, Brazil; Geysa de Azevedo Moreira, **Centro Cultural Brasil Estados Unidos (CCBEU Belém)**, Belém, Brazil; Sonia Patricia Cardoso, **Centro de Idiomas Universidad Manuela Beltrán**, Barrio Cedritos, Colombia; Geraldine Itiago Losada, **Centro Universitario Grupo Sol (Musali)**, Mexico City, Mexico; Nick Hilmers, **DePaul University**, Chicago, IL, USA; Monica L. Montemayor Menchaca, **EDIMSA**, Metepec, Mexico; Angela Whitby, **Edu-Idiomas Language School**, Cholula, Puebla, Mexico; Mary Segovia, **El Monte Rosemead Adult School**, Rosemead, CA, USA; Dr. Deborah Aldred, **ELS Language Centers, Middle East Region**, Abu Dhabi, United Arab Emirates; Leslie Lott, **Embassy CES**, Ft. Lauderdale, FL, USA; M. Martha Lengeling, **Escuela de Idiomas**, Guanajuato, Mexico; Pablo Frias, **Escuela de Idiomas UNAPEC**, Santo Domingo, Dominican Republic; Tracy Vanderhoek, **ESL Language Center**, Toronto, Canada; Kris Vicca and Michael McCollister, **Feng Chia University**, Taichung, Taiwan; Flávia Patricia do Nascimento Martins, **First Idiomas**, Sorocaba, Brazil; Andrea Taylor, **Florida State University in Panama**, Panamá, Panama; Carlos Lizárraga González, **Groupo Educativo Angloamericano**, Mexico City, Mexico; Dr. Martin Endley, **Hanyang University**, Seoul, Korea; Mauro Luiz Pinheiro, **IBEU Ceará**, Ceará, Brazil; Ana Lúcia da Costa Maia de Almeida, **IBEU Copacabana**, Copacabana, Brazil; Ana Lucia Almeida, Elisa Borges, **IBEU Rio**, Rio de Janeiro, Brazil; Maristela Silva, **ICBEU Manaus**, Manaus, Brazil; Magaly Mendes Lemos, **ICBEU São José dos Campos**, São José dos Campos, Brazil; Augusto Pelligrini Filho, **ICBEU São Luis**, São Luis, Brazil; Leonardo Mercado, **ICPNA**, Lima, Peru; Lucia Rangel Lugo, **Instituto Tecnológico de San Luis Potosí**, San Luis Potosí, Mexico; Maria Guadalupe Hernández Lozada, **Instituto Tecnológico de Tlalnepantla**, Tlalnepantla de Baz, Mexico; Greg Jankunis, **International Education Service**, Tokyo, Japan; Karen Stewart, **International House Veracruz**, Veracruz, Mexico; George Truscott, **Kinki University**, Osaka, Japan; Bo-Kyung Lee, **Hankuk University of Foreign Studies**, Seoul, Korea; Andy Burki, **Korea University, International Foreign Language School**, Seoul, Korea; Jinseo Noh, **Kwangwoon University**, Seoul, Korea; Nadezhda Nazarenko, **Lone Star College**, Houston, TX, USA; Carolyn Ho, **Lone Star College-Cy-Fair**, Cypress, TX, USA; Alice Ya-fen Chou, **National Taiwan University of Science and Technology**, Taipei, Taiwan; Gregory Hadley, **Niigata University of International and Information Studies, Department of Information Culture**, Niigata-shi, Japan; Raymond Dreyer, **Northern Essex Community College**, Lawrence, MA, USA; Mary Keter Terzian Megale, **One Way Línguas-Suzano**, São Paulo, Brazil; Jason Moser, **Osaka Shoin Joshi University**, Kashiba-shi, Japan; Bonnie Cheeseman, **Pasadena Community College** and **UCLA American Language Center**, Los Angeles, CA, USA; Simon Banha, **Phil Young's English School**, Curitiba, Brazil; Oh Jun Il, **Pukyong National University**, Busan, Korea; Carmen Gehrke, **Quatrum English Schools**, Porto Alegre, Brazil; Atsuko K. Yamazaki, **Shibaura Institute of Technology**, Saitama, Japan; Wen hsiang Su, **Shi Chien University, Kaohsiung Campus**, Kaohsiung, Taiwan; Richmond Stroupe, **Soka University, World Language Center**, Hachioji, Tokyo, Japan; Lynne Kim, **Sun Moon University (Institute for Language Education)**, Cheon An City, Chung Nam, Korea; Hiroko Nishikage, **Taisho University**, Tokyo, Japan; Diaña Peña Munoz and Zaira Kuri, **The Anglo**, Mexico City, Mexico; Alistair Campbell, **Tokyo University of Technology**, Tokyo, Japan; Song-won Kim, **TTI (Teacher's Training Institute)**, Seoul, Korea; Nancy Alarcón, **UNAM FES Zaragoza Language Center**, Mexico City, Mexico; Laura Emilia Fierro López, **Universidad Autónoma de Baja California**, Mexicali, Mexico; María del Rocío Domíngeuz Gaona, **Universidad Autónoma de Baja California**, Tijuana, Mexico; Saul Santos Garcia, **Universidad Autónoma de Nayarit**, Nayarit, Mexico; Christian Meléndez, **Universidad Católica de El Salvador**, San Salvador, El Salvador; Irasema Mora Pablo, **Universidad de Guanajuato**, Guanajuato, Mexico; Alberto Peto, **Universidad de Oxaca**, Tehuantepec, Mexico; Carolina Rodriguez Beltan, **Universidad Manuela Beltrán, Centro Colombo Americano**, and **Universidad Jorge Tadeo Lozano**, Bogotá, Colombia; Nidia Milena Molina Rodriguez, **Universidad Manuela Beltrán** and **Universidad Militar Nueva Granada**, Bogotá, Colombia; Yolima Perez Arias, **Universidad Nacional de Colombia**, Bogota, Colombia; Héctor Vázquez García, **Universidad Nacional Autónoma de Mexico**, Mexico City, Mexico; Pilar Barrera, **Universidad Técnica de Ambato**, Ambato, Ecuador; Deborah Hulston, **University of Regina**, Regina, Canada; Rebecca J. Shelton, **Valparaiso University, Interlink Language Center**, Valparaiso, IN, USA; Tae Lee, **Yonsei University**, Seodaemun-gu, Seoul, Korea; Claudia Thereza Nascimento Mendes, **York Language Institute**, Rio de Janeiro, Brazil; Jamila Jenny Hakam, **ELT Consultant**, Muscat, Oman; Stephanie Smith, **ELT Consultant**, Austin, TX, USA.

The authors would also like to thank the Four Corners editorial, production, and new media teams, as well as the Cambridge University Press staff and advisors around the world for their contributions and tireless commitment to quality.

Scope and sequence

LEVEL 1	Learning outcomes	Grammar	Vocabulary
Welcome Unit Pages 2–3 **Classroom language** Page 4	**Students can . . .** ☑ introduce themselves and others ☑ say hello and good-bye		
Unit 1 Pages 5–14			
New friends **A** *What's your name?* **B** *How do you spell it?* **C** *Are you a student?* **D** *Names and jobs*	**Students can . . .** ☑ ask for and say names ☑ spell names ☑ talk about where people are from and what they do ☑ discuss people's names and jobs	The verb *be* Possessive adjectives Subject pronouns *Yes / no* questions with *be*	Names and titles Interesting jobs
Unit 2 Pages 15–24			
People and places **A** *Where are you from?* **B** *What's your email address?* **C** *Family* **D** *Family and friends*	**Students can . . .** ☑ ask for and say people's nationalities ☑ ask for and give phone numbers and email addresses ☑ identify family members and give their ages ☑ give information about family and friends	Plural subject pronouns Questions with *be* *Who* and *How old* with *be*	Nationalities Family members Numbers 0–101
Unit 3 Pages 25–34			
What's that? **A** *Is this your notebook?* **B** *What's this called in English?* **C** *Clothing* **D** *Favorite things*	**Students can . . .** ☑ ask about and identify everyday items ☑ ask what something is called in English ☑ talk about clothes and possessions ☑ describe favorite possessions	Demonstratives Articles *a* and *an* Plurals Possessive pronouns *Whose* *'s* and *s'*	Everyday items Clothes and colors
Unit 4 Pages 35–44			
Daily life **A** *Getting around* **B** *What time is it?* **C** *My routine* **D** *My weekend*	**Students can . . .** ☑ describe how people get around ☑ ask for and tell the time ☑ ask and answer questions about routines ☑ describe the things they do on weekends	Simple present statements Simple present *yes / no* questions	Ways of getting around Days of the week and routines
Unit 5 Pages 45–54			
Free time **A** *Online habits* **B** *How much is it?* **C** *What do you do for fun?* **D** *Online fun*	**Students can . . .** ☑ talk about their online habits ☑ accept and decline help ☑ ask and answer questions about leisure activities ☑ discuss how they use technology	Adverbs of frequency Simple present *Wh-* questions with *do*	Online activities Leisure activities and places
Unit 6 Pages 55–64			
Work and play **A** *What does she do?* **B** *Can I speak to . . . ?* **C** *Can you sing?* **D** *Work and study*	**Students can . . .** ☑ identify and talk about jobs ☑ ask for someone on the telephone ☑ have someone wait ☑ describe their talents and abilities ☑ talk about study and work programs	Simple present *Wh-* questions with *does* *Can* for ability *And*, *but*, and *or*	Jobs Abilities

Functional language	Listening and Pronunciation	Reading and Writing	Speaking
Interactions: Saying hello Saying good-bye			• Introductions • Greetings
Interactions: Asking for spelling	**Listening:** Spelling names **Pronunciation:** Contractions	**Reading:** "Famous Names" An article **Writing:** My name	• Class introductions and greetings • *Keep talking:* Name circle • Class name list • Guessing game about famous people • *Keep talking:* "Find the differences" activity about jobs and cities • Quiz about celebrities
Interactions: Asking for someone's phone number Asking for someone's email address	**Listening:** Directory Assistance calls Information forms People I know **Pronunciation:** Word stress	**Reading:** "People in My Life" Photo captions **Writing:** My friends	• True and false information about people • *Keep talking:* Interviews with new identities • Class survey for new contact information • Information exchange about family members • *Keep talking:* Family trees • Presentation about friends
Interactions: Asking what something is	**Listening:** Things around the classroom Favorite things **Pronunciation:** Plurals	**Reading:** "What's your favorite item of clothing?" A webpage **Writing:** My favorite thing	• Questions and answers about personal items • *Keep talking:* Things in the closet • Memory game about everyday items • Personal items and their owners • *Keep talking:* "Find the differences" activity about clothing colors • Presentation of favorite things
Interactions: Asking the time	**Listening:** Times of different events Angela's routine **Pronunciation:** Reduction of *to*	**Reading:** "What's your favorite day of the week?" A message board **Writing:** About my weekend	• Survey about getting to school and work • *Keep talking:* Transportation facts • Interview about the times of specific events • Interview about routines • *Keep talking:* "Find someone who" activity about routines • Survey about busy weekends
Interactions: Declining help Accepting help	**Listening:** Shopping Favorite websites **Pronunciation:** Stress in numbers	**Reading:** "Fun Online Activities" An article **Writing:** Let's chat	• Comparison of online habits • *Keep talking:* Interview about online habits • Role play of a shopping situation • Interview about leisure activities • *Keep talking:* Interviews about fun activities • Discussion about favorite websites
Interactions: Asking for someone on the phone Having someone wait	**Listening:** Telephone calls Ads for overseas programs **Pronunciation:** *Can* and *can't*	**Reading:** "Overseas Opportunities" A magazine article **Writing:** My abilities	• "Find someone who" activity about jobs • *Keep talking:* Memory game about jobs • Role play of a phone call • Interview about abilities • *Keep talking:* Board game about abilities • Discussion about study and work programs

LEVEL 1	Learning outcomes	Grammar	Vocabulary
Unit 7 Pages 65–74			
Food **A** *Breakfast, lunch, and dinner* **B** *I like Chinese food!* **C** *Meals* **D** *Favorite food*	**Students can . . .** ☑ say what meals they eat ☑ say what they like and dislike ☑ talk about their eating habits ☑ talk about their favorite food	Count and noncount nouns *Some* and *any* *How often* Time expressions	Food More food
Unit 8 Pages 75–84			
In the neighborhood **A** *Around town* **B** *How do I get to . . . ?* **C** *Fun in the city* **D** *A great place to visit*	**Students can . . .** ☑ give the locations of neighborhood places ☑ ask for and give directions ☑ talk about interesting places in their towns ☑ give a presentation on a city attraction	Prepositions of location *There is, there are*	Places in the neighborhood Places to visit
Unit 9 Pages 85–94			
What are you doing? **A** *I'm looking for you.* **B** *I can't talk right now.* **C** *These days* **D** *What's new?*	**Students can . . .** ☑ describe what people are doing right now ☑ ask if someone can talk now ☑ explain why they can't talk on the telephone ☑ describe what people are doing these days ☑ discuss what people are doing	Present continuous statements Present continuous questions	Actions and prepositions Activities
Unit 10 Pages 95–104			
Past experiences **A** *Last weekend* **B** *You're kidding!* **C** *Did you make dinner last night?* **D** *I saw a great movie.*	**Students can . . .** ☑ say what they did last weekend ☑ show that they're listening ☑ express surprise ☑ talk about routine events in the past ☑ talk about past activities	Simple past regular verbs Simple past irregular verbs *Yes / no* questions	Weekend activities Things to do
Unit 11 Pages 105–114			
Getting away **A** *Where were you?* **B** *That's great!* **C** *My vacation* **D** *Travel experiences*	**Students can . . .** ☑ describe where they were in the past ☑ react to news ☑ talk about their last vacation ☑ describe a vacation	Past of *be* Simple past *Wh-* questions	Adjectives Vacation activities
Unit 12 Pages 115–124			
Time to celebrate **A** *I'm going to get married.* **B** *Sure. I'd love to.* **C** *Planning a party* **D** *Birthdays*	**Students can . . .** ☑ talk about their plans for specific dates ☑ accept or decline an invitation ☑ discuss and agree on plans ☑ describe birthday traditions in their cultures	*Be going to* *Yes / no* questions *Wh-* questions with *be going to* Object pronouns	Months and dates Party checklist

Functional language	Listening and Pronunciation	Reading and Writing	Speaking
Interactions: Expressing dislikes Expressing likes	**Listening:** Food preferences A typical Swedish meal **Pronunciation:** Word stress	**Reading:** "My Favorite Food" An article **Writing:** A typical meal	• Survey about meals • *Keep talking:* Recipes • Information exchange about food preferences • Comparison of eating habits • *Keep talking:* Discussion about eating habits • Interview about favorite food
Interactions: Asking for directions	**Listening:** GPS directions Tourist information **Pronunciation:** Word stress	**Reading:** "Monterey Bay Aquarium" A poster **Writing:** Group poster	• Information exchange with maps • *Keep talking:* Information gap activity with neighborhood maps • Role play about directions • Interview about places in town • *Keep talking:* Description of an unusual zoo • Presentation about a city attraction
Interactions: Asking if someone can talk now Explaining that you can't talk now	**Listening:** Sound effects Telephone calls **Pronunciation:** Intonation in questions	**Reading:** "Status Updates" A micro-blog **Writing:** My status update	• Guessing game about people's actions • *Keep talking:* Interpretations of actions • Role play of a phone call • "Find someone who" activity about things people are doing these days • *Keep talking:* Guessing game about who's doing what • Speculations about someone's activities
Interactions: Showing that you're listening Expressing surprise	**Listening:** Diana's week Matt's busy week **Pronunciation:** Simple past *-ed* endings	**Reading:** "Matt's Movie Reviews" Blog posts **Writing:** A blog post	• Information exchange about last weekend • *Keep talking:* Picture story • Role play of surprising conversations • Interview about routine events in the past • *Keep talking:* Memories • "Find someone who" activity about past activities
Interactions: Reacting to good news Reacting to bad news	**Listening:** A short trip Three vacations **Pronunciation:** Reduction of *did you*	**Reading:** "Travel Tales" Blog posts **Writing:** A postcard	• Interview about where you were • *Keep talking:* Interview about school trips • Class exchange of personal news • Information exchange about vacations • *Keep talking:* Speculations about a vacation • Presentation of postcards
Interactions: Declining an invitation Accepting an invitation	**Listening:** Invitations A "Sweet 16" birthday party **Pronunciation:** Reduction of *going to*	**Reading:** "Birthday Traditions" An article **Writing:** A thank-you note	• Information exchange about special days • *Keep talking:* Weekend plans • Class invitations • Discussion of plans for three scenarios • *Keep talking:* Plan for a party • Discussion about birthday traditions

Welcome

1 Introducing yourself

A Listen and practice.

Simon: Hello. I'm Simon.
Chen: Hi, Simon. My name is Chen. Nice to meet you.
Simon: Nice to meet you, too.

B Pair work Introduce yourselves.

2 Introducing someone else

A Listen and practice.

Simon: Chen, this is my friend Sofia.
Sofia: Hi, Chen. Nice to meet you.
Chen: Nice to meet you, too, Sofia.

B Group work Introduce your partner from Exercise 1 to another classmate.

3 Hi and bye

A Listen and practice.

Simon: Hi, Chen!
Chen: Good morning, Simon! How are you?
Simon: I'm fine, thanks. And you?
Chen: Fine, thank you.

Simon: See you later, Chen!
Chen: Bye, Simon!

B Listen to the expressions. Then practice the conversation again with the new expressions.

Saying hello

Hi.

Hello.

Good morning. 

Good afternoon. 

Good evening. 

Saying good-bye

Bye.

Good-bye.

See you.

See you later.

See you tomorrow.

C Class activity Say hello to your classmates and ask how they are. Then say good-bye.

I can introduce myself and others. ☐

I can say hello and good-bye. ☐

Classroom language

Pair work

Group work

Class activity

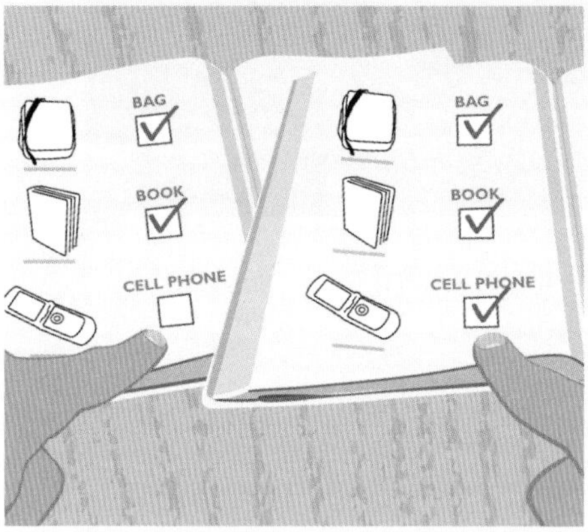

Compare answers.

Cover the picture.

Go to page 12.

Ask and answer questions.

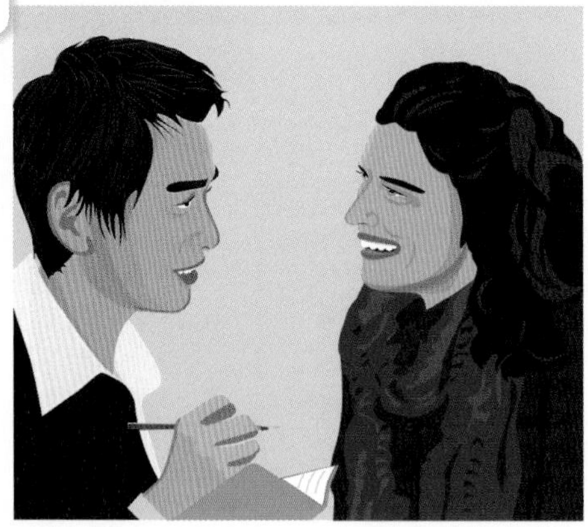

Interview your partner.

Role-play the situation.

New friends

LESSON A	LESSON B	LESSON C	LESSON D
• Names and titles • The verb *be*; possessive adjectives	• Asking for spelling	• Interesting jobs • Subject pronouns; *yes / no* questions with *be*	• Reading: "Famous Names" • Writing: My name

Warm-up

Popular names in the United States

1. Jacob
2. Michael
3. Ethan
4. Joshua
5. Daniel

1. Emma
2. Isabella
3. Emily
4. Madison
5. Ava

Source: www.ssa.gov/OACT/babynames/

A Check (✓) the popular names.

B Say ten popular names in your country.

A What's your name?

1 Language in context First day of class

Listen to Ms. Peters meet her students on the first day of class. Underline the names.

2 Vocabulary Names and titles

A Listen and repeat.

first name — middle name — last / family name

Jennifer Ann Wilson

full name

Miss Gomez = a single woman
Mrs. Chow = a married woman
Ms. Peters = a single or married woman
Mr. Adams = a single or married man

B Pair work Complete the sentences with your own information. Then compare answers.

My first name is ______________________ .
My family name is ____________________ .
My full name is ______________________ .
My teacher's name is __________________ .

3 Grammar — The verb *be*; possessive adjectives

What is (What's)	your name?	**My** name **is** Maria.
	his name?	**His** name **is** Ricardo.
	her name?	**Her** name **is** Yoko.
What are	your names?	**Our** names **are** Maria and Jason.
	their names?	**Their** names **are** Ricardo and Yoko.

A Circle the correct words. Then compare with a partner.

1. Maria is a student. **His** / **Her** last name is Gomez.
2. Ms. Peters **is** / **are** our teacher. **Her** / **Their** first name is Linda.
3. My name is Jason. What's **our** / **your** name?
4. Anna and Bruce **is** / **are** students. **Her** / **Their** teacher is Miss Brown.
5. Their first names **is** / **are** Yoko and Ricardo.
6. Hello, everyone. I'm Miss Diaz. What are **your** / **his** names?

B Complete the conversation with the correct words. Then practice in a group.

A: Hello. Welcome to English class.
What ___*is*___ your name, please?
B: ____________ name is Pam.
A: And what's ____________ last name, Pam?
B: My last name ____________ Nelson.
A: OK. And ____________ is *your* name?
C: Ji-ah. ____________ family name is Lee.

4 Speaking My name is . . .

A Class activity Meet your classmates. Say your first and last name.

A: *Hello. My name is Oscar Martinez. What's your name?*
B: *Hi. My name is Susana Harris.*
A: *It's nice to meet you.*
B: *Nice to meet you, too.*

B Share your information.

A: *What's his name?*
B: *His name is Oscar Martinez. What's her name?*
A: *Sorry, I don't know.*

5 Keep talking!

Go to page 125 for more practice.

I can ask for and say names.

B How do you spell it?

1 The alphabet

A Listen and repeat.

A B C D E F G H I J K L M

N O P Q R S T U V W X Y Z

B Pair work Say a letter. Your partner points to it. Take turns.

2 Interactions Spelling names

A Listen and practice.

Donald: Hello. My name is Donald Wang.
Clerk: How do you spell your first name?
Donald: D-O-N-A-L-D.
Clerk: And how do you spell your last name?
Donald: W-A-N-G.

Asking for spelling

How do you spell your first name?
How do you spell your last name?

B Pair work Practice the conversation again with these names.

John Evans Cindy Douglas Antonia Lopez Richard Wu

A: *Hello. My name is John Evans.*
B: *Hello, John. How do you spell your first name?*
A: *J-O-H-N.*
B: *And how do you spell . . . ?*

3 Listening Spell it!

A Listen to four people spell their names. Check (✓) the correct answers.

1. ☑ Steven ☐ Stephen
2. ☐ Dina ☐ Dena
3. ☐ Kelly ☐ Kerry
4. ☐ Bryan ☐ Brian

B Listen to the conversations. Write the names.

1.

2.

3.
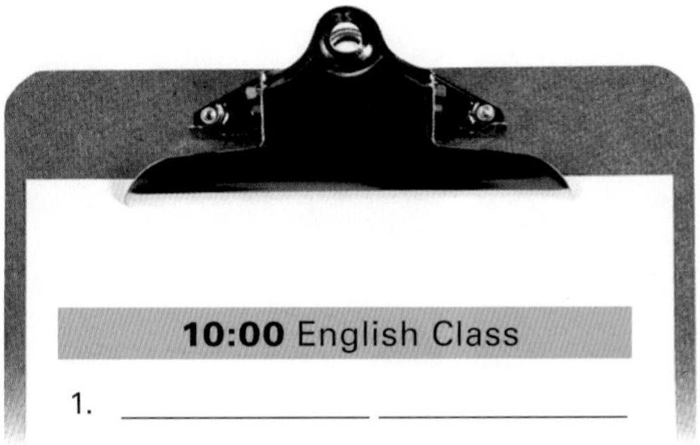

4.
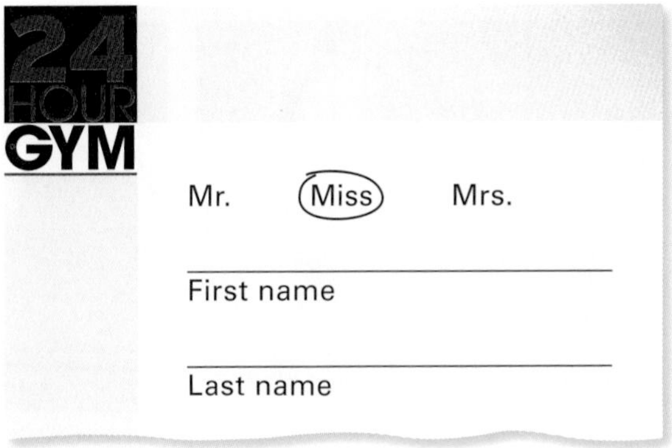

5.
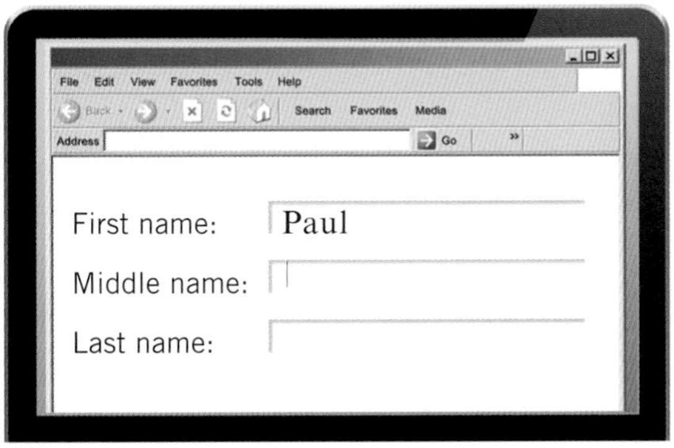

6.

4 Speaking A class list

Class activity Ask your classmates for their names. Make a list.

A: *What's your first name?*
B: *Tyler.*
A: *How do you spell it?*
B: *T-Y-L-E-R.*
A: *And what's your last name?*
B: *Larsen.*

First names	*Last names*
Tyler	*Larsen*
Lindsey	*Fisher*
Marcela	*Perez*
Evan	*Howley*
Dmitri	*Benos*

I can spell names. ☐

C Are you a student?

1 Vocabulary Interesting jobs

A Listen and repeat.

Gael García Bernal is an **actor**. He's from Mexico.

Jeon Do-yeon is an **actress**. She's from South Korea.

Alex Hornest is an **artist**. He's from Brazil.

Brooklyn Decker is a **model**. She's from the United States.

Lang Lang is a **musician**. He's from China.

Diana Krall is a **singer**. She's from Canada.

B Pair work Name other people for each job.

A: *Jet Li is an actor.*
B: *Yes. And Cate Blanchett is an actress.*

2 Conversation My friend the musician

Listen and practice.

Sandy: Hey, Jacob!
Jacob: Oh, hi, Sandy. How's it going?
Sandy: Good, thanks. This is my friend Kevin.
Jacob: Hi. Nice to meet you.
Kevin: Nice to meet you, Jacob.
Jacob: Are you a student here?
Kevin: No, I'm not. I'm a musician.
Sandy: Kevin is from England.
Jacob: Oh? Are you from London?
Kevin: No, I'm not. I'm from Liverpool.

3 Grammar — Subject pronouns; yes / no questions with be

I'm a musician.	**Am I** in your class?
	Yes, **you are.** No, **you're not.** / No, **you aren't.**
You're a student.	**Are you** from London?
	Yes, **I am.** No, **I'm not.**
Kevin **is** from Liverpool.	**Is he** a singer?
He's from Liverpool.	Yes, **he is.** No, **he's not.** / No, **he isn't.**
Sandy **is** a student.	**Is she** from Canada?
She's a student.	Yes, **she is.** No, **she's not.** / No, **she isn't.**
Liverpool **is** in England.	**Is your** name John?
It's in England.	Yes, **it is.** No, **it's not.** / No, **it isn't.**

Contractions I'm = I am you're = you are he's = he is she's = she is it's = it is

A Match the questions and the answers. Then practice with a partner.

1. Is your first name Jacob? _d_
2. Are you from Liverpool? _____
3. Is she from the United States? _____
4. Is she a musician? _____
5. Is Will Smith an actor? _____
6. Is Caracas in Peru? _____

a. No, I'm not. I'm from London.
b. Yes, he is. He's a singer, too.
c. No, she's not. She's an artist.
d. Yes, it is. And my last name is King.
e. No, it's not. It's in Venezuela.
f. Yes, she is. She's from California.

B Complete the conversations with the correct words. Then practice with a partner.

1. A: _____Is_____ your first name Don?
 B: No, _____ not. It's Jeff.
2. A: _____ you from Mexico?
 B: Yes, I _____ . I'm from Mexico City.
3. A: _____ your teacher from England?
 B: No, she _____ .
4. A: _____ you a model?
 B: No, _____ not. I'm a singer.

4 Pronunciation Contractions

Listen and repeat. Notice the reduction of contractions.

I am → I'm he is → he's it is → it's are not → aren't

you are → you're she is → she's is not → isn't

5 Speaking Ten questions

Group work Think of a famous person with a job from Exercise 1. Your group asks ten questions and guesses the name. Take turns.

A: *Is the person a man?*
B: *No, she's not.*
C: *Is she an actress?*

6 Keep talking!

Student A go to page 126 and Student B go to page 128 for more practice.

I can talk about where people are from and what they do. ✓

D Names and jobs

1 Reading

A Look at the pictures. What are their names?

B Read the article. Are they all singers?

★ Famous Names

Actor **Tom Cruise** uses his middle name as his last name. His full name is Thomas Cruise Mapother. Tom is short for Thomas.

Zhang Ziyi is an actress from China. Zhang isn't her first name. It's her family name. In China, family names come first.

Shakira is a singer from Colombia. She uses only her first name. Her full name is Shakira Isabel Mebarak Ripoll.

Jay-Z is a hip-hop singer from the United States. Jay-Z is his nickname. His real name is Shawn Corey Carter.

Kaká is a soccer player from Brazil. His full name is Ricardo Izecson dos Santos Leite. Kaká is his nickname.

Madonna is not a nickname for this singer. It's her first name. Her full name is Madonna Louise Veronica Ciccone.

C Read the article again. Complete the sentences with the correct words.

1. Tom Cruise uses his ___*middle*___ name as his last name.
2. Shakira uses only her ___First___ name.
3. Ricardo Izecson dos Santos Leite's ____________ is Kaká.
4. Ziyi is not Zhang Ziyi's ____________ name.
5. Jay-Z's ___Full___ name is Shawn Corey Carter.
6. Madonna Louise Veronica Ciccone is Madonna's ___First___ name.

D Pair work Tell your partner about another famous person's name.

"Rain is a singer, actor, and model from South Korea. Rain is his nickname. His real name is Jeong Ji-hoon."

2 Writing My name

A Write sentences about your name. Use the model to help you.

My Name

My full name is Anthony Steven Johnson. My nickname is Big Tony. Tony is short for Anthony. My middle name is Steven, and my last name is Johnson.

B Group work Tell your group about your name.

3 Speaking Celebrity quiz

A Pair work Ask and answer the questions about celebrities.

1. He's an actor from Hong Kong. His initials are J. C. What's his name?

   "His name is Jackie Chan."
2. She's an actress from Spain. Her last name is Cruz. What's her first name?
3. He's a soccer player from England. His first name is David. What's his last name?
4. She's an actress and singer. Her nickname is J-Lo. What's her name?
5. He's an actor from Australia. His first name is Russell. What's his last name?
6. She's an actress from the United States. Her last name is Jolie? What's her first name?

B Pair work Create a quiz. Write three sentences about a celebrity.

He's a tennis player.
He's from Switzerland.
His first name is Roger.

C Group work Say your sentences to another pair. They guess the celebrity. Take turns.

A: *He's a tennis player.*
B: *Is he Rafael Nadal?*
A: *No, he isn't. He's from Switzerland.*

I can discuss people's names and jobs.

Wrap-up

1 Quick pair review

Lesson A Do you remember? What are your classmates' last names? Answer with the information you remember. You have two minutes.

A: *Her last name is Fernandes.*
B: *Yes, it is. And his first name is Oscar. What's his last name?*
A: *It's Medina.*

Lesson B Test your partner! Say your full name. Can your partner write it correctly? Check his or her answer. You have two minutes.

First name	Middle name	Last / Family name
____________	____________	____________

Lesson C Brainstorm! Make a list of interesting jobs. How many do you know? You have one minute.

Lesson D Guess! Describe your favorite celebrity, but don't say his or her name! Can your partner guess the name? Take turns. You have two minutes.

A: *He's a singer and a musician. He's from England. He's in Coldplay.*
B: *Is he Chris Martin?*
A: *Yes!*

2 In the real world

What is your favorite movie? Go online and find information in English about five actors or actresses in the movie. Then write about them.

- What are their names?
- Where are they from?

Actors in "Star Wars"
My favorite movie is "Star Wars."
Harrison Ford is an actor in the movie.
He's from the United States . . .

People and places

LESSON A	LESSON B	LESSON C	LESSON D
• Nationalities • Plural subject pronouns; questions with *be*	• Asking for someone's phone number • Asking for someone's email address	• Family members • *Who* and *How old* with *be*	• Reading: "People in My Life" • Writing: My friends

Warm-up

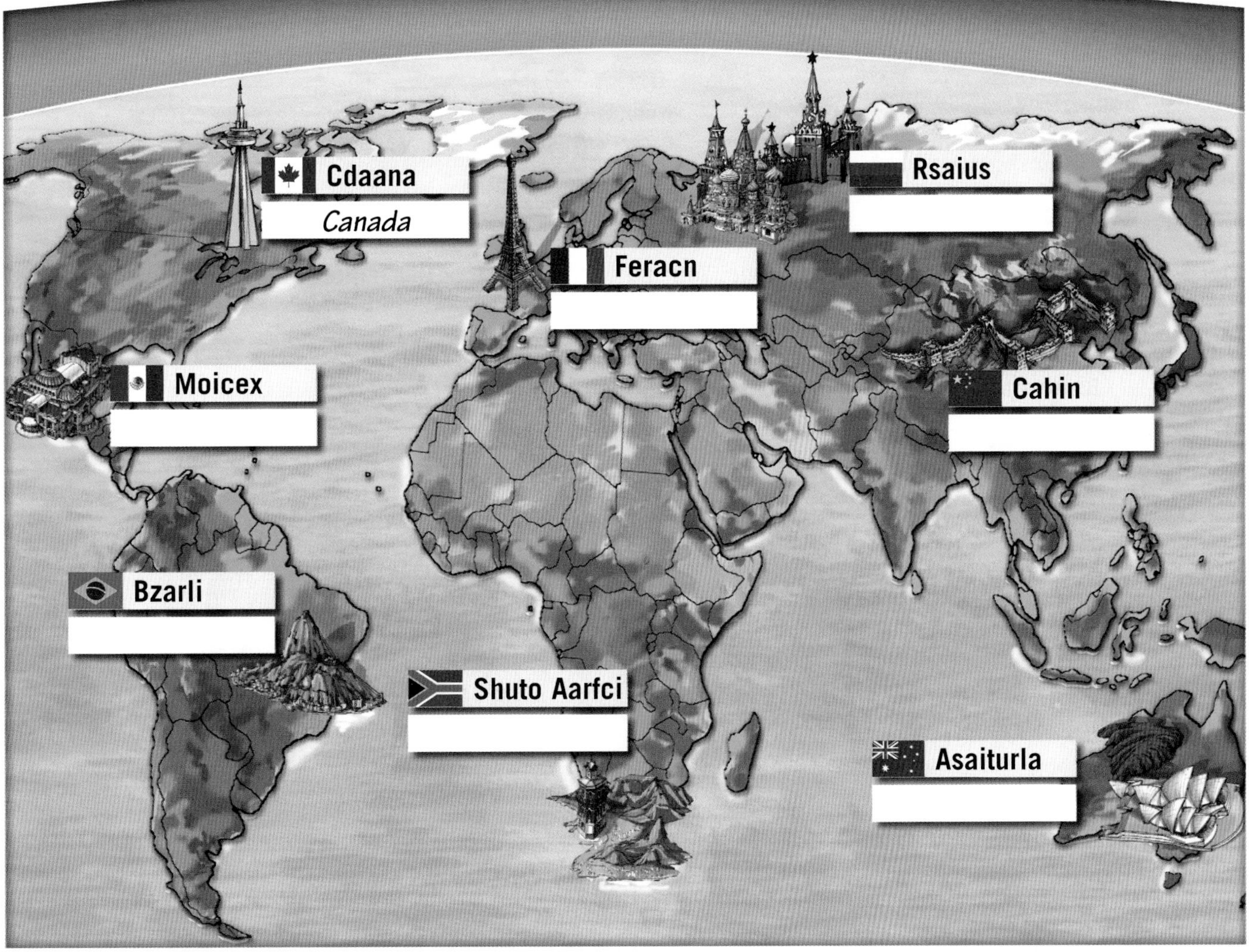

A Write the names of the countries.

B Say the names of five other countries in English.

A Where are you from?

1 Vocabulary Nationalities

A Complete the chart with the correct nationalities. Then listen and check your answers.

Mexican	American	South Korean	Chilean	Greek	Colombian
Spanish	Canadian	Brazilian	Saudi	Peruvian	Japanese
British	Chinese	Turkish	Thai	Ecuadorian	✓Australian

Country	Nationality	Country	Nationality
Australia	*Australian*	Japan	
Brazil		Mexico	
Britain		Peru	
Canada		Saudi Arabia	
Chile		South Korea	
China		Spain	
Colombia		Thailand	
Ecuador		Turkey	
Greece		the United States	

B Pair work Say a famous name. Your partner says his or her nationality. Take turns.

A: *Bill Gates.*
B: *He's from the United States. He's American.*

2 Language in context New neighbors

Listen to Brad and Emily Hill talk about their new neighbors. What are their names?

Brad: Who are they?
Emily: Oh, they're our new neighbors, Carlos and Claudia.
Brad: Are they musicians?
Emily: Yes, they are.
Brad: Where are they from?
Emily: They're from Brazil.
Brad: What city are they from?
Emily: They're from Manaus.

3 Grammar Plural subject pronouns; questions with *be*

Where are you and Sakura from? **We're** from Japan. **What** city are **you** from? **We're** from Osaka. **Are you** Japanese? Yes, **we are**. No, **we're not**. / No, **we aren't**.	**Where** are Carlos and Claudia from? **They're** from Brazil. **What** city are **they** from? **They're** from Manaus. **Are they** Brazilian? Yes, **they are**. No, **they're not**. / No, **they aren't**.
Contractions we're = we are	they're = they are

Complete the conversations with the correct words. Then practice with a partner.

1. **A:** Where are ___*you*___ from?
   B: We're from Mexico.
   A: Oh? ________ city are you from? Are you from Mexico City?
   B: No, we ________ not. ________ from Monterrey.
2. **A:** ________ Jim and Carly American?
   B: No, they ________ . They ________ Canadian.
   A: What city in Canada are ________ from?
   B: They ________ from Toronto.

4 Pronunciation Word stress

A Listen and repeat. Notice the stressed syllables in the nationalities.

●	●•	•●•	•●
Greek	**Brit**ish	Bra**zil**ian	Chi**nese**

B Listen. Underline the stressed syllable in each nationality.

Japa<u>nese</u> Australian Spanish Thai

5 Speaking That's not correct!

A Write three false sentences about people, countries, or nationalities.

B **Group work** Share your sentences. Your group corrects them. Take turns.

A: *Toronto and Vancouver are in Greece.*
B: *No, they aren't. They're in Canada.*

1. *Toronto and Vancouver are in Greece.*
2. *Venus and Serena Williams are Ecuadorian.*
3. *Nicole Kidman and Russell Crowe are British.*

6 Keep talking!

Go to page 127 for more practice.

I can ask for and say people's nationalities.

B What's your email address?

1 Numbers 0 to 10; phone numbers; email addresses

A Listen and repeat.

0	1	2	3	4	5	6	7	8	9	10
zero	one	two	three	four	five	six	seven	eight	nine	ten

B Listen and repeat. Notice that people sometimes say "oh" for "zero" in phone numbers.

281-363-2301 = "two-eight-one, three-six-three, two-three-zero-one"

602-374-4188 = "six-oh-two, three-seven-four, four-one-eight-eight"

C Listen and repeat. Notice the way people say email addresses.

susan8k@cup.org = "susan-eight-K-at-C-U-P-dot-org"

jun_akita@email.com = "jun-underscore-akita-at-email-dot-com"

2 Interactions Phone numbers and email addresses

A Listen and practice.

Stacy: Hey, Emma. What's your phone number?
Emma: It's 309-403-8708.
Stacy: What's your email address?
Emma: It's emma@cup.org.
Stacy: Thanks!

B Listen to the expressions. Then practice the conversation again with the new expressions.

Asking for someone's phone number

What's your phone number?
What's your number?

Asking for someone's email address

What's your email address?
What's your email?

C Pair work Practice the conversation again with the information below.

978-887-8045 ej5@cup.org

604-608-4864 emma_jones@email.com

3 Listening What name, please?

A Listen to four people call Directory Assistance for phone numbers. Check (✓) the correct answers.

1. Carlos Moreno ☐ 333-822-1607 ☑ 323-822-1607
2. Lucy Chang ☐ 662-651-0410 ☐ 662-615-0410
3. Michael Ashcroft ☐ 866-279-9400 ☐ 866-279-9500
4. Beatriz J. Lago ☐ 341-360-7450 ☐ 341-360-4570

B Listen to three people give their names, phone numbers, and email addresses. Complete the forms.

MADISON ENGLISH SCHOOL
REGISTRATION

First name: *Michael*
Middle name: *John*
Last name: ______
Phone: ______
Email: ______

1-2-3 GYM
MEMBERSHIP

First name: ______
Middle initial: *P.*
Last name: ______
Phone: ______
Email: ______

City Library
CARD APPLICATION

First name: ______
Family name: ______
City: *Dallas*
Phone: ______
Email: ______

4 Speaking A new number and email address

A Write a new phone number and email address.

My new phone number: ______ My new email address: ______

B Class activity Ask five classmates for their names, new phone numbers, and new email addresses. Complete the chart with their answers.

	Name	Phone number	Email address
1.			
2.			
3.			
4.			
5.			

C Share your information.

A: *What's her name and phone number?*
B: *Her name is Fatima. Her phone number is 212-691-3239.*
A: *What's her email address?*
B: *Her email is . . .*

I can ask for and give phone numbers and email addresses. ☐

C Family

1 Vocabulary Family members

A Listen and repeat.

B Pair work Ask and answer the questions about the family in Part A.

1. Are Sarah and Roger Mills single?
2. Are Michael and Helen brother and sister?
3. Are Sarah and Roger grandparents?
4. Are Wendy and Jack parents?

2 Conversation Who's that?

Listen and practice.

Lance: Who's that?
Jack: That's my sister. Her name is Wendy.
Lance: How old is she?
Jack: She's seven.
Lance: Is she your only sister?
Jack: Yeah.
Lance: And who are they?
Jack: They're my grandparents.
Lance: Wow. They look young. And who's he?
Jack: That's me!

3 Grammar Who and How old with be

Who's that?	**Who are** they?
That's my sister.	They're my grandparents.
How old is she?	**How old are** they?
She's seven (years old).	They're 70 and 66.

A Read the answers. Write the questions. Then practice with a partner.

A: *Who's that?* ______
B: Oh, that's my brother Ignacio.
A: ______
B: He's ten years old.
A: ______
B: They're my sisters Lucia, Antonia, and Carmen.
A: ______
B: They're 19, 16, and 11.
A: And ______
B: That's my grandfather.
A: ______
B: He's 62.

B Pair work Ask and answer questions about the family in Exercise 1.

A: *Who's that?*
B: *That's Jack Olson.*

Numbers 11–101

11 eleven
12 twelve
13 thirteen
14 fourteen
15 fifteen
16 sixteen
17 seventeen
18 eighteen
19 nineteen
20 twenty
21 twenty-one
22 twenty-two
23 twenty-three
24 twenty-four
25 twenty-five
26 twenty-six
27 twenty-seven
28 twenty-eight
29 twenty-nine
30 thirty
40 forty
50 fifty
60 sixty
70 seventy
80 eighty
90 ninety
100 one hundred
101 one hundred (and) one

4 Speaking My family

A Complete the chart with information about three people in your family.

	Family member	Name	How old . . . ?	Where . . . from?
1.				
2.				
3.				

B Pair work Tell your partner about your family. Ask and answer questions for more information.

A: *Keiko is my grandmother. She's 73.*
B: *Where is she from?*

5 Keep talking!

Go to page 129 for more practice.

I can identify family members and give their ages.

D Family and friends

1 Reading

A Look at the people in Isabel's photos. Who are they? Guess.

B Read the photo descriptions. Who are Isabel's family members? Who are her friends?

People in My Life

I'm with my friends Fernando and Amy. Fernando is on the left. He's from Bogotá, Colombia. Amy is on the right. She's from Perth, Australia. I'm in the middle.

This is my brother Carlos and my sister Julia. Carlos is 18 years old and a good soccer player. Julia is only ten. She's a good tennis player.

This is my grandmother. Her name is Olivia, but her nickname is Nana. She's an artist, and she's 92 years old!

Here's my e-pal Dong-sun. His family name is Choi. He's from Pusan, South Korea. He's 18 years old. His sister is in the photo, too.

C Read the photo descriptions again. Correct the false sentences.

1. Isabel and Amy are ~~sisters.~~ *Isabel and Amy are friends.*
2. Carlos isn't a good soccer player. ______
3. Olivia is 90 years old. ______
4. Isabel and Dong-sun are classmates. ______

D Pair work Ask and answer the questions about Isabel's family and friends.

- Who are Fernando and Amy?
- What's Olivia's nickname?
- How old is Julia?
- What city is Dong-sun from?

2 Listening People I know

A Listen to Gina show some photos to her friend. Who are the people? Check (✓) the correct answers.

1. ☐ friend
   ☑ brother
2. ☐ classmate
   ☐ sister
3. ☐ father
   ☐ grandfather
4. ☐ teacher
   ☐ mother

B Listen again. Answer the questions.

1. How old is Mark? ___*15*___
2. What city is Dominique from? ______________
3. What's the man's name? ______________
4. Is Ms. Parker American? ______________

3 Writing and speaking My friends

A Complete the chart with information about three friends. Then find photos or draw pictures of them.

	Friend 1	Friend 2	Friend 3
Name			
Age			
Nationality			
Other information			

B Write sentences about your friends in the pictures. Use the model and your answers in Part A to help you.

My Friends

My best friend is Samantha. She's 26 years old. She's American. She's a teacher.

Jill is my friend, too. She's . . .

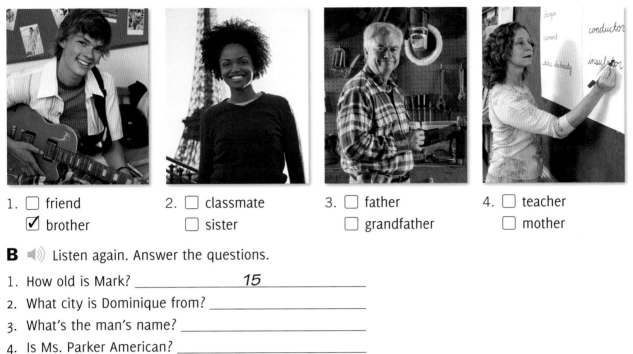

C Group work Share your pictures and sentences. Ask and answer questions for more information.

A: *This is my friend Samantha. She's 26 years old.*
B: *What's her last name?*

I can give information about family and friends. ☐

Wrap-up

1 Quick pair review

Lesson A Guess! Say five countries. Can your partner name the nationalities? Take turns. You have two minutes.

A: *South Korea.*
B: *South Korean.*

Lesson B Test your partner! Write three phone numbers and say them to your partner. Can your partner write them correctly? Check his or her answers. You have two minutes.

My phone numbers	My partner's phone numbers
______________	______________
______________	______________
______________	______________

Lesson C Brainstorm! Make a list of family words. How many do you know? You have one minute.

Lesson D Find out! Are any of your friends or family members from the same cities? You have two minutes.

A: *My father is from Mexico City, and my mother is from Guadalajara.*
B: *My grandmother is from Guadalajara, too!*

2 In the real world

Go online and find information in English about a country from another part of the world. Then write about it.

- What are five cities in the country?
- What are the names and ages of two famous people from the country?

French Cities and People
Paris, Bordeaux, Cannes, Lyon, and Dijon are five cities in France. Marion Cotillard is a famous actress from France. She's . . .

What's that?

LESSON A	LESSON B	LESSON C	LESSON D
• Everyday items • Demonstratives; articles *a* and *an*; plurals	• Asking what something is	• Clothes and colors • Possessive pronouns; *Whose*; *'s* and *s'*	• Reading: "What's your favorite item of clothing?" • Writing: My favorite thing

Warm-up

Year: *1969*

Year: ________

Year: ________

Year: ________

A Label the pictures with the correct years.

✓1969	1978	1986	1994

B Can you name five things in the pictures?

A Is this your notebook?

1 Vocabulary Everyday items

A Listen and repeat.

☐ a bag

☐ a book

☐ a cell phone

☐ a dictionary

☐ an eraser

☐ a key

☐ a laptop

☐ a notebook

☐ a pen

☐ sunglasses

☐ an umbrella

☐ a watch

B **Pair work** Check (✓) the things in your classroom. Then compare answers.

2 Language in context What are those?

Listen to four people talk about everyday items. Circle the items in the conversations.

Pete: Hey, Ling. What's that?
Ling: Oh, it's my dictionary.
Pete: It's nice. What are those?
Ling: They're my English books.

Susie: Are these your sunglasses?
Kyle: No, they're not.
Susie: Is this your notebook?
Kyle: Yes, it is. Thanks.

3 Grammar Demonstratives; articles *a* and *an*; plurals

What's **this**? What's **that**?

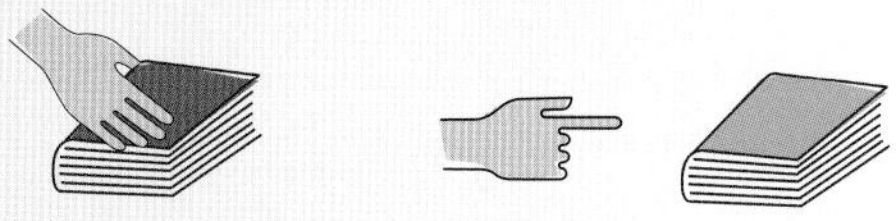

It's my dictionary.
Is **this** your dictionary?
Is **that** your dictionary?
Yes, **it is**. No, **it's not**.

What are **these**? What are **those**?

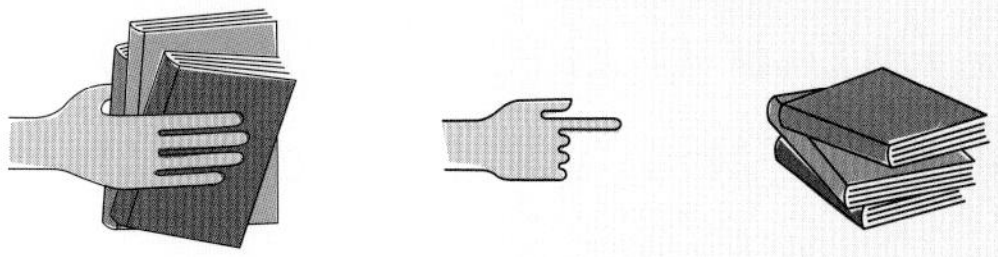

They're my English books.
Are **these** your English books?
Are **those** your English books?
Yes, **they are**. No, **they're not**.

Articles a *and* an

a + consonant sound **a b**ag
an + vowel sound **an e**raser

Plurals

a book → two book**s**
a watch → two watch**es**
a dictionary → two dictionar**ies**
Note: *Sunglasses* and *glasses* are always plural.

A Complete the conversations with the correct words. Then practice with a partner.

A: What*'s this* ?
B: *It's a watch.*

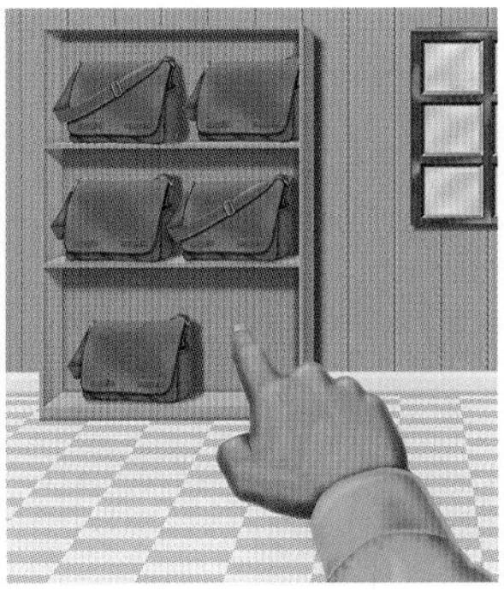

A: What ______ ?
B: ______

A: What ______ ?
B: ______

A: What ______ ?
B: ______

B Pair work Ask and answer questions about everyday items in your classroom.

4 Pronunciation Plurals

Listen and repeat. Notice that some words have an extra syllable in their plural forms.

Same syllables	Extra syllables
eraser / erasers	actress / actress·es
key / keys	address / address·es
laptop / laptops	watch / watch·es

5 Speaking In my bag

Pair work Ask and answer 10 questions about the everyday items in your bags and in the classroom.

A: *Is this your English book?*
B: *No, it's not. It's my dictionary. What are those?*
A: *They're my keys.*

6 Keep talking!

Go to page 130 for more practice.

I can ask about and identify everyday items.

B What's this called in English?

1 Listening Around the classroom

A Listen to Bo and Marta ask about new words in English. Number the pictures from 1 to 5.

☐ an alarm clock ☐ a map ☐ a marker ☐ a poster [1] a remote control

B What things in Part A are in your classroom?

2 Interactions Asking about new words

A Listen and practice.

Alex: Excuse me. What's this called in English?
Lucy: It's a key chain.
Alex: A key chain? How do you spell that?
Lucy: K-E-Y C-H-A-I-N.
Alex: Thanks.

B Listen to the expressions. Then practice the conversation again with the new expressions.

Asking what something is

What's this called in English?
What's the word for this in English?
How do you say this in English?

C Pair work Practice the conversation again with the things in Exercise 1.

A: *Excuse me. What's this called in English?*
B: *It's a map.*
A: *How do you spell that?*

3 Speaking More everyday items

A 🔊 Listen and repeat.

1. a camera
2. a flash drive
3. a hairbrush
4. a newspaper
5. a magazine
6. a comb
7. a coin
8. a wallet

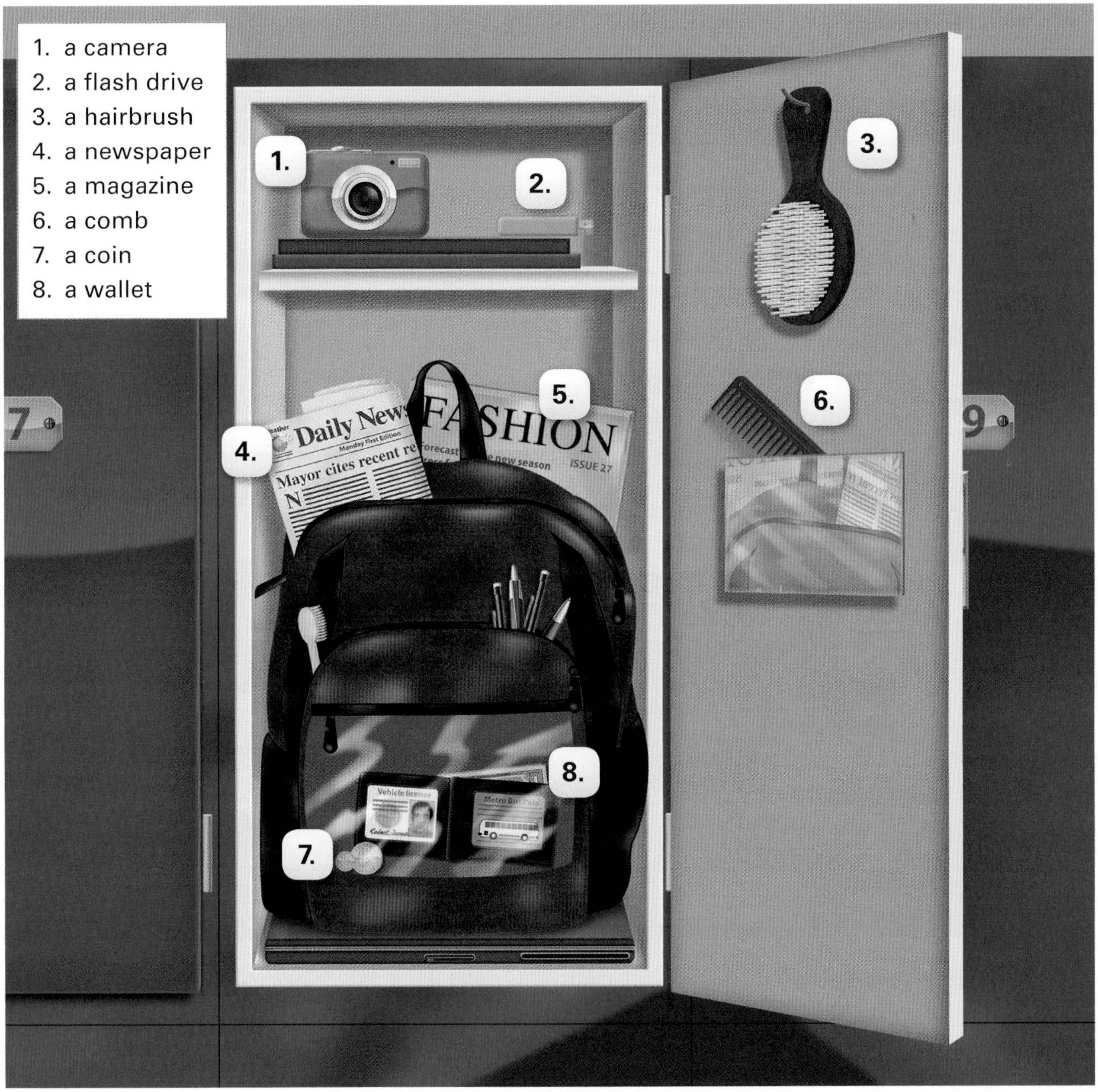

B Pair work Cover the words. What is each thing called? Answer with the information you remember.

A: *What's this called?*
B: *I think it's a . . .*

C Pair work Ask and answer questions about other things in the picture.

A: *What's the word for this in English?*
B: *It's a student I.D.*
A: *What's this called?*
B: *Hmm . . . I don't know. Let's ask the teacher.*

*I can **ask what something is called in English.*** ✓

C Clothing

1 Vocabulary Clothes and colors

A Listen and repeat.

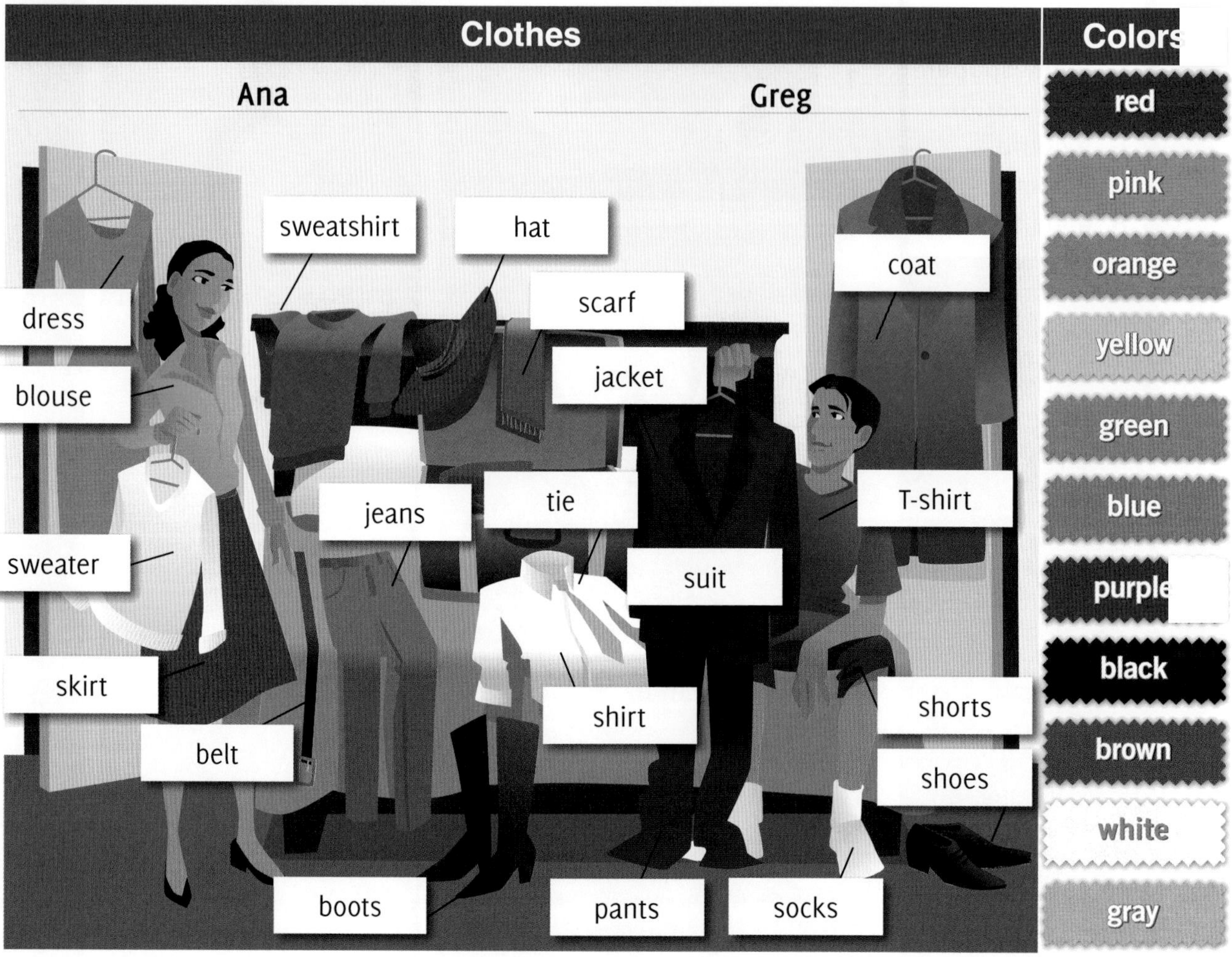

B Pair work Describe a classmate's clothes, but don't say his or her name! Your partner guesses the name. Take turns.

A: *His shoes are brown. His T-shirt is red and green. His pants are gray.*
B: *Is it David?*

2 Conversation Whose bag is it?

Listen and practice.

Greg: Excuse me. I think that's my bag.
Laura: This bag?
Greg: Yes. I think it's mine.
Laura: It is? Oh, yes. This bag is black and yellow. Mine is black and green. I'm very sorry.
Greg: That's OK. Is that bag yours?
Laura: Yes, thank you.
Greg: You're welcome.

3 Grammar Possessive pronouns; *Whose*; *'s* and *s'*

It's my bag. → It's **mine**.
It's your jacket. → It's **yours**.
It's his coat. → It's **his**.
They're her shoes. → They're **hers**.
They're our clothes. → They're **ours**.
It's their bag. → It's **theirs**.

Whose bag is this?
It's Greg**'s** (bag).
Whose bag is that?
It's the student**'s** (bag).
Whose bags are those?
They're the student**s'** (bags).

A Circle the correct words. Then practice with a partner.

1. Whose clothes are these?	They're **your** / **our** / **ours**.
2. Are these Greg's black shoes?	Yes, they're **his** / **hers** / **theirs**.
3. Is this pink scarf Ana's?	No, it's not **his** / **hers** / **theirs**.
4. Are these bags Greg and Ana's?	Yes, they're **his** / **hers** / **theirs**.
5. Whose red socks are these? Are they yours?	Yes, they're **my** / **mine** / **yours**.
6. Is that my sister's skirt?	No, it's not **mine** / **yours** / **hers**.

B **Pair work** Ask and answer questions about the clothing in Exercise 1.

A: *Whose jeans are these?*
B: *They're Ana's. Whose T-shirt is this?*
A: *It's . . .*

4 Speaking Yes, it's mine.

Class activity Put three of your things on a table. Then take three other things and find their owners.

A: *Whose scarf is this?*
B: *I think it's Mary's.*
A: *Is this your scarf, Mary?*
C: *Yes, it's mine.*

5 Keep talking!

Student A go to page 131 and Student B go to page 132 for more practice.

I can talk about clothes and possessions.

D Favorite things

1 Reading

A Look at the pictures. What clothes and colors are they?

B Read the webpage. What countries are the people from?

What's your favorite item of clothing?

SEND US YOUR PICTURES!

This cap is my favorite. It's from my baseball team. Our team colors are blue and white.

– Joe, the U.S.

These boots are my favorite. I think they're from the 1970s. They're red. Red is my favorite color!

– Ariela, Venezuela

Here's a photo of my favorite pants. They're called *salwar*. These are men's pants, and they're from India.

– Sadi, Canada

This dress is my favorite item of clothing. It's called a *hanbok* in Korean. It's my mother's.

– Bin-woo, South Korea

Here's my favorite item of clothing. It's an old shirt. It's from London in the 1980s.

– Ian, the U.K.

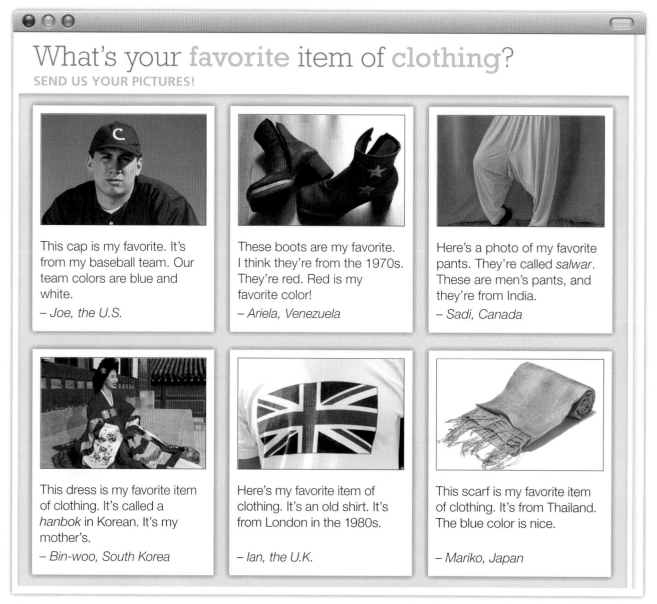

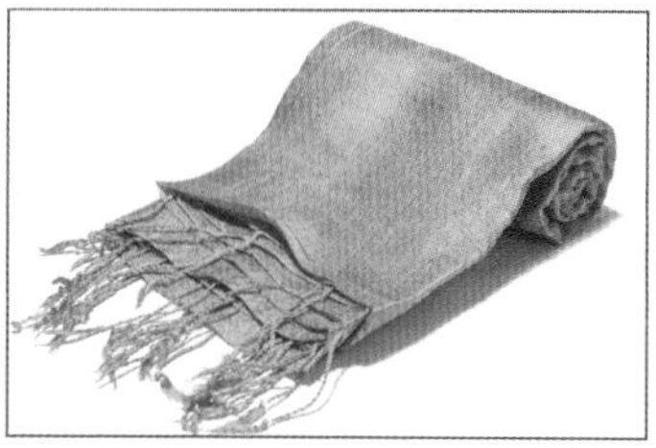

This scarf is my favorite item of clothing. It's from Thailand. The blue color is nice.

– Mariko, Japan

C Read the webpage again. Answer the questions.

1. What's Joe's favorite thing? *His favorite thing is a baseball cap.*
2. What is Ariela's favorite color? ______
3. What are Sadi's pants called? ______
4. What's Bin-woo's favorite item of clothing? ______
5. Where is Ian's shirt from? ______
6. Where is Mariko's scarf from? ______

D Pair work What's your favorite item of clothing? Tell your partner.

"My favorite item of clothing is my blue sweatshirt."

2 Listening It's my favorite.

Listen to four people talk about their favorite things. Check (✓) the things they describe.

1.

a. ☑

b. ☐

2.

a. ☐

b. ☐

3.

a. ☐

b. ☐

4.

a. ☐

b. ☐

3 Writing and speaking My favorite thing

A Draw a picture of your favorite thing. Then answer the questions.

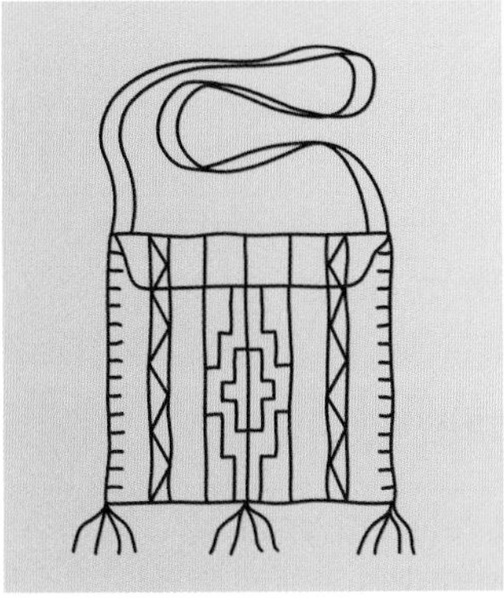

- What is it? ______________________
- Where is it from? ______________________
- How old is it? ______________________
- What color is it? ______________________

B Write about your favorite thing. Use the model and your answers in Part A to help you.

My Favorite Thing

My favorite thing is my bag. It's from Cuzco, Peru. I think it's three or four years old. It's purple, white, and yellow. I love it!

C Group work Share your drawings and your writing. Ask and answer questions for more information.

A: *Here's a picture of my favorite thing.*
B: *What is it?*
A: *It's my bag.*
C: *Where is it from?*
A: *It's from Peru.*

I can *describe my favorite possessions.* ☐

Wrap-up

1 Quick pair review

Lesson A Brainstorm! Make a list of everyday items and the plural forms of the words. How many do you know? You have two minutes.

Lesson B Test your partner! Ask your partner what the things are. You have two minutes.

Student A

Student B

Lesson C Do you remember? Look at your partner's clothes. Then close your eyes and describe them. Take turns. You have two minutes.

"Your shirt is green, and your jeans are blue. I think your socks are white."

Lesson D Find out! What is one thing both you and your partner have in your bags or desks? Find the thing and answer the questions. You have two minutes.

- What color is it?
- How old is it?
- Where is it from?

2 In the real world

What's in style? Find a picture of clothes in a magazine. Then write about them.

- What clothes are in the picture?
- What colors are the clothes?

Clothes in "Style Today"

The woman's sweater in the picture is blue. Her pants are brown, and her shoes are black. Her bag is . . .

Daily life

LESSON A	LESSON B	LESSON C	LESSON D
• Ways of getting around • Simple present statements	• Asking the time	• Days of the week and routines • Simple present *yes / no* questions	• Reading: "What's your favorite day of the week?" • Writing: About my weekend

Warm-up

A Name the things you see in the picture. Use *That's a / an . . .* and *Those are . . . .*

B Say the colors of six things in the picture.

A Getting around

1 Vocabulary Ways of getting around

A Listen and repeat.

drive a car

ride a bicycle / bike

ride a motorcycle

take a taxi / cab

take the bus

take the subway

take the train

walk

B Listen to five ways of getting around. Number them from 1 to 5.

☐ a bicycle [1] a bus ☐ a car ☐ a motorcycle ☐ a train

2 Language in context Going to work and school

A Listen to Mariela describe how she and her family get to work and school. Underline the ways they get around.

I have a car. I drive to work. I don't take the train.
My husband doesn't drive to work. He has a bike, so he rides his bike.
My kids walk to school. They don't take the bus.

B What about you? Check (✓) the ways you get around.

☐ I drive. ☐ I take the bus. ☐ I ride a bike. ☐ I walk.

3 Grammar — Simple present statements

Regular verbs		Irregular verbs	
		I / you / we / they	*he / she / it*
I **drive** to work.	I **don't take** the train.	I **have** a car.	She **has** a car.
You **take** a taxi.	You **don't take** the subway.	You **don't have** a bike.	She **doesn't have** a bike.
He **rides** a bike.	He **doesn't drive** to work.	We **go** to work.	He **goes** to work.
She **drives**.	She **doesn't walk**.	They **don't go** to school.	He **doesn't go** to school.
We **take** the train.	We **don't take** a taxi.		
They **walk** to school.	They **don't take** the bus.		

Contractions don't = do not doesn't = does not

A Complete the sentences with the simple present forms of the verbs. Then compare with a partner.

1. I ___*take*___ (take) the bus to school. I ___*don't walk*___ (not / walk).
2. Jonathan __________ (have) a car. He __________ (drive) to work.
3. My parents __________ (take) the train to work. They __________ (go) to the city.
4. My neighbor __________ (ride) a motorcycle to work.
5. Mei-li ________________ (not / take) the bus. She __________ (walk).
6. We ________________ (not / have) bicycles, and we ________________ (not / drive).

B Pair work Make five sentences about how your family members and friends get to school or work. Tell your partner.

A: *My sister works in a big city. She takes the bus to work.*
B: *My best friend works in a big city, too. He doesn't take the bus. He drives.*

4 Speaking I take the bus.

A Write how you get to school or work in the chart. Add extra information, such as a bus number or a train number.

	Me	Name: _______	Name: _______	Name: _______
To school				
To work				
Extra information				

B Group work Find out how three of your classmates get to school or work. Complete the chart with their information.

A: *I take the bus to school. It's the number 16 bus. How about you?*
B: *I take the bus, too. I take the number 8 bus.*

C Group work Tell another group how your classmates get to school or work.

"Daniel takes the number 8 bus to school."

5 Keep talking!

Go to page 133 for more practice.

I can describe how people get around. ☐

B What time is it?

1 Telling time

A Listen and repeat.

It's twelve o'clock.

It's noon.
It's twelve p.m.

It's midnight.
It's twelve a.m.

It's twelve-oh-five.
It's five after twelve.

It's twelve-fifteen.
It's a quarter after twelve.

It's twelve-thirty.
It's half past twelve.

It's twelve-forty.
It's twenty to one.

It's twelve forty-five.
It's a quarter to one.

B Pair work Say the times in two ways.

9:45   7:30   6:03   1:15   11:40

a.m. = midnight to noon
p.m. = noon to midnight

2 Interactions Time

A Listen and practice.

Joe: What time is it?
Mike: It's 9:15. What time is the bus?
Joe: Nine-twenty. We're early.

Keisha: What's the time?
Emily: It's 9:35. What time is our class?
Keisha: It's at 9:30. We're late!

Asking the time

What time is it?
What's the time?

B Pair work Practice the conversations again with the times below.

4:15 / 4:45   6:20 / 7:00   10:05 / 10:00   5:45 / 5:30

3 Pronunciation Reduction of *to*

A 🔊 Listen and repeat. Notice how *to* is pronounced as /tə/.

/tə/	/tə/	/tə/
It's ten to five.	It's five to two.	It's a quarter to one.

B 🔊 Listen to the conversations. Then practice them. Reduce *to* to /tə/.

A: *Is it five to one?*
B: *No, it's ten to one.*

A: *Is it ten to eight?*
B: *No, it's a quarter to eight.*

A: *Is it a quarter to three?*
B: *No, it's twenty to three.*

4 Listening Am I late?

A 🔊 Listen to five conversations about time. Write the time of each thing.

1. the movie 2. Rod's class 3. the train 4. the bus 5. Susan's class
 __10:00__ _____ _____ _____ _____

B 🔊 Listen again. Are the people early or late? Circle the correct answers.

1. (early) / late 2. early / late 3. early / late 4. early / late 5. early / late

5 Speaking What time is . . . ?

A Pair work Interview your partner. Take notes.

What time is your . . . ?

favorite class lunch break favorite TV show

_____ _____ _____

A: *What time is your favorite class?*
B: *It's at 7:30 a.m. What time is yours?*
A: *Mine is at 8:00 p.m. It's this class!*

B Pair work Tell another classmate about your partner's answers.

"Ji-sung's favorite class is at 7:30 a.m."

> *I can ask for and tell the time.* ✓

C My routine

1 Vocabulary Days of the week and routines

A Listen and repeat.

Weekdays					The weekend	
Monday	Tuesday	Wednesday	Thursday	Friday	Saturday	Sunday

B Listen and repeat.

get up

drink coffee

eat breakfast

read the news

go to school

exercise

cook dinner

study

watch TV

go to bed

C Pair work What is your routine on weekdays? on weekends? Tell your partner.

"I get up and eat breakfast on weekdays. I go to school. I study . . ."

2 Conversation Monday morning

Listen and practice.

Tom: It's Monday morning . . . again!
Liz: Do you get up early on weekdays?
Tom: Yes, I do. I get up at 5:30 a.m.
Liz: Wow! That *is* early!
Tom: And I study all morning and afternoon.
Liz: Do you study in the evenings, too?
Tom: No, I don't. I cook dinner, exercise, and go to bed late, after midnight.
Liz: That's not good. What about on weekends?
Tom: On weekends, I sleep!

3 Grammar — Simple present *yes / no* questions

Do you **go** to school on Mondays?	**Do** you and your friends **watch** TV?
Yes, I **do**. No, I **don't**.	Yes, we **do**. No, we **don't**.
Does Liz **exercise**?	**Do** your friends **study**?
Yes, she **does**. No, she **doesn't**.	Yes, they **do**. No, they **don't**.

A Write *yes* / *no* questions with the information below. Then compare with a partner.

1. (you / get up / 7:00) *Do you get up at 7:00?*
2. (you / read the news / every day) ______
3. (your teacher / drink coffee / in class) ______
4. (your parents / watch TV / in the evening) ______
5. (your friend / exercise / on weekends) ______
6. (you and your friends / study / after midnight) ______

B Pair work Ask and answer the questions in Part A. Answer with your own information.

A: *Do you get up at 7:00?*
B: *No, I don't. I get up at 6:00 on weekdays and 9:30 on weekends.*

Time expressions

on Sunday(s)
on Sunday afternoon(s)
on weekdays
on the weekend
on weekends
in the morning(s)
in the afternoon(s)
in the evening(s)
at noon / midnight
at night
before 7:00
after midnight
every day

4 Speaking Routines

A Pair work Interview your partner. Check (✓) his or her answers.

Do you . . . ?	Yes	No
cook dinner on weekends	☐	☐
drink coffee after 7:00 p.m.	☐	☐
exercise every day	☐	☐
go to bed late on weekdays	☐	☐
get up early on weekdays	☐	☐
read the news in the evening	☐	☐

A: *Do you cook dinner on weekends?*
B: *No, I don't. I cook on weekdays!*

B Pair work Tell another classmate about your partner's routines.

A: *Does Rita cook dinner on weekends?*
B: *No, she doesn't. She cooks on weekdays!*

5 Keep talking!

Go to page 134 for more practice.

I can ask and answer questions about routines.

D My weekend

1 Reading

A Look at the message board question. What's *your* favorite day of the week? Why?

B Read the message board. Whose favorite day is on the weekend?

This week's question:

What's your favorite day of the week?

	busyguy	My favorite day of the week is Saturday. I study from Monday to Friday. On Saturday, I get up late.
	trish06	Not Saturday or Sunday. I work from noon to 4:00 on those days. In the evening, I study. My favorite day is Wednesday, because I don't work on Wednesdays.
	JasonFan	Monday. I watch my favorite TV show every Monday. It has my favorite actor. The show is called "Life with Jason." It's on at 8:00.
	Ricardo	Monday?! No way! Saturday, Saturday, Saturday! We don't go to school on Saturdays.
	SuperDad45	Sunday! I get up late, read the news, and have coffee. Then my son and daughter cook breakfast for my wife and me.
	michiko3	I have two favorite days – Tuesday and Thursday. I have an art class after work on those days, and my teacher is very nice.

C Read the message board again. What's each person's favorite day? Why? Complete the chart.

	Favorite day(s)	Why?
1. busyguy	*Saturday*	*gets up late*
2. trish06		
3. JasonFan		
4. Ricardo		
5. SuperDad45		
6. michiko3		

D Class activity What's your class's favorite day? Vote and discuss your answer.

2 Listening Angela's routine

A Listen to Angela talk about her routine on weekends. Circle the activities she does.

Saturdays		Sundays	
(work)	watch TV	get up late	exercise
go to class	go to bed late	study	cook

B Listen again. Write one more thing Angela does on Saturdays and on Sundays.

On Saturdays: ____________________ On Sundays: ____________________

3 Writing About my weekend

A Complete the chart with information about your weekend routine. Include two activities you do and two activities you don't do.

Saturdays	Sundays
Activities I do:	Activities I do:
• ____________________	• ____________________
• ____________________	• ____________________
Activities I don't do:	Activities I don't do:
• ____________________	• ____________________
• ____________________	• ____________________

My Weekend Routine
On Saturdays, I get up late and watch TV. I don't study, and I don't go to work. On Sundays, . . .

B Write about your weekend routine. Use the model and your answers in Part A to help you.

C Group work Share your writing. Ask and answer questions for more information.

4 Speaking Are you busy?

A Add two questions about routines to the survey. Then circle your answers.

ARE YOU BUSY?	Me		You	
1. Do you study English every weekend?	Yes	No	Yes	No
2. Do you go to work on the weekend?	Yes	No	Yes	No
3. Do you get up before 7:00 on the weekend?	Yes	No	Yes	No
4. Do you exercise on the weekend?	Yes	No	Yes	No
5.	Yes	No	Yes	No
6.	Yes	No	Yes	No

B Pair work Interview your partner. Circle his or her answers. Is your partner busy?

I can describe the things I do on weekends.

Wrap-up

1 Quick pair review

Lesson A Brainstorm! Make a list of ways of getting around. How many do you know? You have one minute.

Lesson B Test your partner! Say four different times. Can your partner write them correctly? Check his or her answers. You have two minutes.

Lesson C Guess! Say a time and a day. Can your partner guess your routine at that time? Take turns. You have two minutes.

A: *Two o'clock on Monday.*
B: *Do you exercise at 2:00 on Monday?*
A: *No.*
B: *Do you study?*
A: *Yes.*

Lesson D Find out! What are three things both you and your partner do on weekends? You have two minutes.

A: *I exercise on Saturday mornings. How about you?*
B: *No, I don't. I go to bed late on Saturdays. How about you?*
A: *Yes, I do!*

2 In the real world

What time is it around the world? Go online and find the local time in these cities.

Beijing	Cairo	Los Angeles	Rio de Janeiro	Tokyo
Buenos Aires	London	Mexico City	Sydney	Toronto

What time is it now?
It is nine o'clock in the evening in Beijing now. In Buenos Aires, it's . . .

Free time

LESSON A	LESSON B	LESSON C	LESSON D
• Online activities • Adverbs of frequency	• Declining help • Accepting help	• Leisure activities and places • Simple present *Wh-* questions with *do*	• Reading: An article • Writing: An online chat

Warm-up

A Look at the pictures. Make two sentences about each one.

B When do you have free time? Write the times.

	Monday	Tuesday	Wednesday	Thursday	Friday	Saturday	Sunday
a.m.							
p.m.							

A Online habits

1 Vocabulary Online activities

A Listen and repeat.

☐ chat with friends

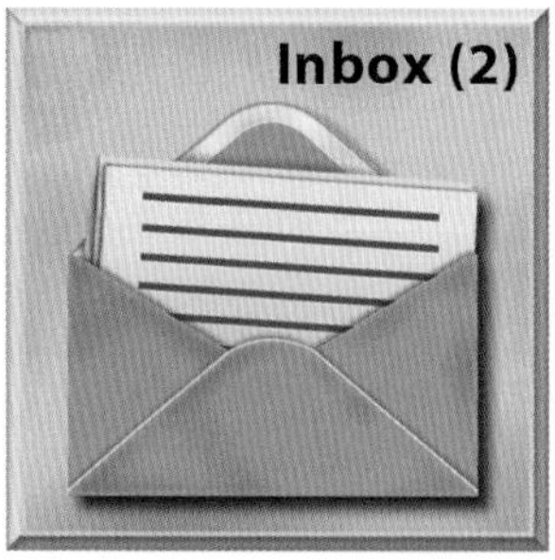

☐ check email

☐ download music

☐ play games

☐ post comments

☐ search the Internet

☐ shop online

☐ upload videos

B **Pair work** Check (✓) the things you do online. Then tell your partner.

"I download music, post comments, and play games. How about you?"

2 Language in context Habits survey

A Read the survey about online habits. Circle the online activities.

Habits survey

1. Do you ever shop online?
- ☑ Yes, I often shop online.
- ☐ Yes, I sometimes shop online.
- ☐ No, I never shop online.

2. Do you ever download music?
- ☐ Yes, I often download music.
- ☑ Yes, I sometimes download music.
- ☐ No, I never download music.

3. Do you ever post comments on blogs?
- ☐ Yes, I often post comments.
- ☐ Yes, I sometimes post comments.
- ☑ No, I never post comments.

B What about you? Do you do the online activities in the survey?

3 Grammar Adverbs of frequency

I	**always** **usually** **often** **sometimes** **hardly ever** **never**	shop online.	100% – 0%	Do you **ever** shop online? Yes, I sometimes shop online. / Yes, I sometimes do. No, I never shop online. / No, I never do.

A Rewrite the conversations with the adverbs of frequency. Then practice with a partner.

1. **A:** Do you download movies? (ever) *Do you ever download movies?*
   B: Yes, I download movies. (often) __________
2. **A:** Do you check email in class? (ever) __________
   B: No, I check email in class. (never) __________
3. **A:** Do you play games online? (ever) __________
   B: Yes, I do. (usually) __________
4. **A:** Do you post comments online? (ever) __________
   B: No, I do that. (hardly ever) __________

B Pair work Ask and answer the questions in Part A. Answer with your own information.

A: *Do you ever download movies?*
B: *Yes, I sometimes do.*

4 Speaking Often, sometimes, or never?

A Complete the chart with information about your online habits. Use the ideas in Exercise 1 and your own ideas.

I often . . .	I sometimes . . .	I never . . .
•	•	•
•	•	•

B Group work Compare your online habits.

A: *I often play games online.*
B: *Oh? I never do that.*
C: *I sometimes do.*

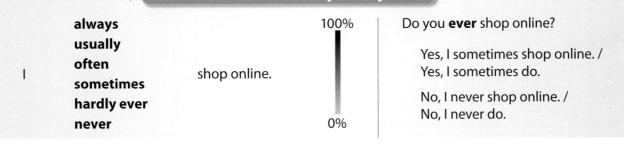

5 Keep talking!

Go to page 135 for more practice.

I can talk about my online habits. ✓

B How much is it?

1 Prices

A Listen and repeat.

$79.00	=	seventy-nine dollars
$79.95	=	seventy-nine dollars and ninety-five cents
	OR	seventy-nine ninety-five
$379.95	=	three hundred seventy-nine dollars and ninety-five cents
	OR	three seventy-nine ninety-five

B Listen and practice.

A: *How much is this?*
B: *It's $54.89.*

A: *How much are these?*
B: *They're $234.99.*

A: *How much is that watch?*
B: *It's only $109.25.*

C Pair work Practice the conversations again. Say the prices in a different way.

2 Interactions At the store

A Listen and practice.

Salesperson: Hello.
Margaret: Hi.
Salesperson: Can I help you?
Margaret: No, thanks. I'm just looking.

Salesperson: Can I help you?
Renato: Yes, please. How much is this camera?
Salesperson: It's $169.50.
Renato: Thanks.

B Listen to the expressions. Then practice the conversations again with the new expressions.

Declining help

No, thanks. I'm just looking.
No. I'm fine, thanks.

Accepting help

Yes, please.
Yes, thanks.

3 Pronunciation Thirteen or thirty?

A Listen and repeat. Notice the difference in stress in the numbers.

Last syllable	First syllable
13 thir**teen**	30 **thir**ty
14 four**teen**	40 **for**ty
15 fif**teen**	50 **fif**ty
16 six**teen**	60 **six**ty
17 seven**teen**	70 **se**venty
18 eigh**teen**	80 **eigh**ty
19 nine**teen**	90 **nine**ty

B Listen to four conversations about prices. Circle the correct prices.

1. $14 / $40
2. $16 / $60
3. $17 / $70
4. $19 / $90

C Pair work Say a number from the chart. Your partner points to it. Take turns.

4 Listening Can I help you?

A Listen to four conversations in a store. Check (✓) the words you hear.

1. ☑ camera ☐ cell phone ☐ laptop
2. ☐ shirts ☐ skirt ☐ T-shirt
3. ☐ bag ☐ bags ☐ belt
4. ☐ scarf ☐ shorts ☐ skirt

B Listen to a salesperson offer help to four customers. Do the customers accept or decline help? Circle the correct answers.

1. accept / decline
2. accept / decline
3. accept / decline
4. accept / decline

5 Speaking Role play

Class activity Role-play the situation. Then change roles.

Group A: You are salespeople. Offer help to the customers. Answer questions about prices.

Group B: You are customers. Decline help three times. Then accept help three times, and ask for the prices of three items.

$168.95

$23.99

$877.50

$40.89

$219.00

$9.25

A: *Can I help you?*
B: *No, thanks. I'm just looking.*

OR

A: *Can I help you?*
B: *Yes, please. How much . . . ?*

I can accept and decline help.

C What do you do for fun?

1 Vocabulary Leisure activities and places

A Listen and repeat.

eat out

go dancing

go shopping

hang out

play soccer

watch movies

B Listen and repeat.

at a club

at a restaurant

at home

at the mall

in / at the park

C Pair work Do you do the activities in Part A? Where? Tell your partner.

A: *I watch movies at home. Do you?*
B: *Yes, I do. I watch movies at the mall, too.*

2 Conversation In our free time

Listen and practice.

Annie: What do you do for fun, Chad?
Chad: Oh, I hang out with friends.
Annie: Yeah? Where do you hang out?
Chad: At the mall. We sometimes watch a movie or go shopping. What about you?
Annie: I play soccer in the park.
Chad: Sounds fun. Who do you play with?
Annie: My brother and his friends. Actually, we need another player. Are you interested?
Chad: Yeah!

3 Grammar Simple present *Wh-* questions with *do*

What do you do for fun?
I hang out.
Where do you hang out?
At the mall.
How do you get there?
We take the bus.

Who do you play soccer with?
My brother and his friends.
When do you usually play soccer?
We usually play on weekends.
Why do you play soccer?
Because it's my favorite sport.

A Read the answers. Write *Wh-* questions. Then practice with a partner.

1. *How do you get to class?* ______ I take the bus to class.
2. ______ I eat out on Friday night.
3. ______ I play sports with my brother.
4. ______ I go shopping at the mall.
5. ______ My friends and I watch movies on Saturday.
6. ______ I sometimes study with my friends.

B Pair work Ask and answer the questions in Part A. Answer with your own information.

A: *How do you get to class?*
B: *I usually walk, but I sometimes take the subway.*

4 Speaking Tell me more!

A Pair work Interview your partner. Take notes.

Questions	Name: ______
1. When do you usually check your email?	
2. What time do you go to bed on Sundays?	
3. When do you chat with friends?	
4. Who do you eat out with? Where do you go?	
5. Where do you go shopping? How do you get there?	
6. What do you do for fun on weekends? Why?	

B Pair work Tell another classmate about your partner's answers. Are any of your partners' answers the same?

A: *Celia usually checks her email at night.*
B: *Luis checks his email at night, too.*

5 Keep talking!

Go to page 136 for more practice.

I can ask and answer questions about leisure activities.

D Online fun

1 Reading

A Look at the pictures in the article. What do you see?

B Read the article. What's the best title? Check (✓) the correct answer.

☐ New Websites ☐ Chat Online ☐ Fun Online Activities

Try one of these activities in your free time.

1 *Buy and Sell*
What do you want? A new video game? A new phone? What *don't* you want? Your old jeans? Your old schoolbooks? Buy and sell things online!

2 ________
Where is your best friend from elementary school now? Does your friend live in your city? Search his or her name, and find your friend.

3 ________
Do you have pictures or movies on your cell phone or camera? Post them! Upload your favorite photos and videos for friends.

4 ________
Tour a museum from your home! Go to the Egyptian Museum in Cairo, Barcelona's Picasso Museum, or Kyoto's National Museum.

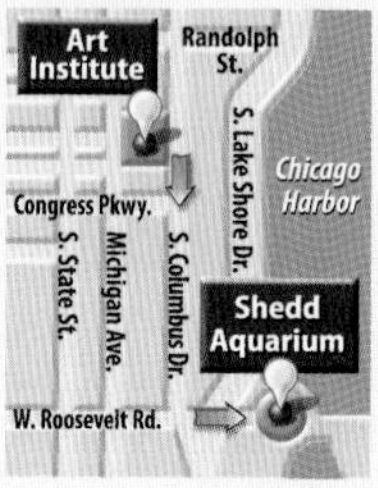

5 ________
Where do you want to go? Search the address and city, and find a map. Get directions to stores, parks, or a new restaurant.

6 ________
Do you want a new album, your favorite song, or a new ringtone for your cell phone? Download it.

C Read the article again. Where do the headings go? Write them in the article.

Map it!	Take a Tour	Share Photos and Videos
Get Music	✓Buy and Sell	Find an Old Friend

D Pair work What activities do you do online? Tell your partner.

"I hardly ever sell things online, but I sometimes buy clothes online."

2 Listening Four websites

A Listen to Allison and James talk about the pictures on four websites. Number the pictures from 1 to 4.

B Listen again. Correct the false sentences.

1. Allison looks at ~~videos~~ *photos* of Lorena Ochoa.
2. The Museum of Modern Art is in Paris.
3. James buys clothes on the website.
4. James often uploads videos.

3 Writing Let's chat!

A Choose a topic for a "chat": free time, online activities, or school. Create a user name. Then write a question about your topic.

B Group work Pass your question to the classmate on your right. Read and answer your classmate's question. Continue to pass, read, and answer all of the questions in your group.

techgirl: *What do you do in your free time?*

jae-min: *I watch TV and play video games. My favorite video game is Soccer Star.*

jramirez: *I hardly ever play video games. I usually watch TV at night. My favorite show is . . .*

C Class activity Tell the class about your chat.

4 Speaking My favorite website

A Group work Add a question about online habits to the list. Then ask and answer the questions.

- What's your favorite website?
- What other websites do you usually go to?
- Where do you upload your photos and videos?
- What news websites do you read?
- What blogs do you read?
- ______________________

B Class activity Share your information. Which websites are popular?

I can discuss how I use technology.

Wrap-up

1 Quick pair review

Lesson A Brainstorm! Make a list of online activities. How many do you know? You have one minute.

Lesson B Test your partner! Write three prices and say them to your partner. Can your partner write them correctly? Check his or her answers. You have two minutes.

My prices	My partner's prices
__________	__________
__________	__________
__________	__________

Lesson C Find out! What are three activities both you and your partner do for fun? You have two minutes.

A: *I play soccer for fun. Do you?*
B: *No, I don't play soccer. Do you go shopping for fun?*
A: *Yes, sometimes.*

Lesson D Do you remember? Complete the sentences with the correct words. You have one minute.

✓Buy	Find	Share	Take

1. ___*Buy*___ and sell online.
2. ____________ photos and videos.
3. ____________ an old friend.
4. ____________ a tour.

2 In the real world

How much are they? Find two different prices for each of these items. Then write about them.

a belt	jeans	a small camera
a downloaded song	a laptop	an umbrella

Different Prices

A black belt is $29.99 at Style Shop. It's $20.00 at Kelly's Accessories. A downloaded song is . . .

Work and play

LESSON A	LESSON B	LESSON C	LESSON D
• **Jobs** • **Simple present *Wh-* questions with *does***	• **Asking for someone on the phone** • **Having someone wait**	• **Abilities** • ***Can* for ability; *and*, *but*, and *or***	• **Reading: "Overseas Opportunities"** • **Writing: My abilities**

Warm-up

A Where do the people usually work? Match the people and the places.

B Do you know any of the jobs in the pictures? Do you know any other jobs?

A What does she do?

1 Vocabulary Jobs

A Match the jobs and the people. Then listen and check your answers.

a. accountant	c. doctor	e. flight attendant	g. pilot	i. receptionist	✓k. waiter
b. cook / chef	d. electrician	f. nurse	h. police officer	j. taxi driver	l. waitress

B Pair work Point to people in the pictures, and ask what their jobs are. Your partner says the jobs. Take turns.

A: *What's his job?*
B: *He's a waiter.*

2 Language in context At work

A Read two job profiles. What are their jobs?

Lucia Ortega works in a hospital from 11:00 p.m. to 7:00 a.m. What does Lucia do? She's a nurse.

Henry Jenkins works in an office. He's an accountant. What company does Henry work for? He works for A1 Accountants.

B What about you? Do you have a job? What is it?

3 Grammar — Simple present *Wh-* questions with *does*

What does Lucia **do**? She's a nurse.	**Where does** Henry **work**? He works in an office.
When does she **work**? She works from 11:00 to 7:00.	**What** company **does** Henry **work** for? He works for A1 Accountants.

A Complete the conversations with the correct words. Then practice with a partner.

1. **A:** *What* does your brother *do* ?
   B: Oh, Tom's a doctor.
   A: Really? ________ does he ________ ?
   B: He works in a hospital.

2. **A:** ________ does Sue ________ ?
   B: On Mondays, Wednesdays, and Fridays.
   A: And ________ company does she ________ for?
   B: She works for Town Bank.

B Pair work Write questions about Mr. Miller, Lisa, and Nicole. Then ask and answer them.

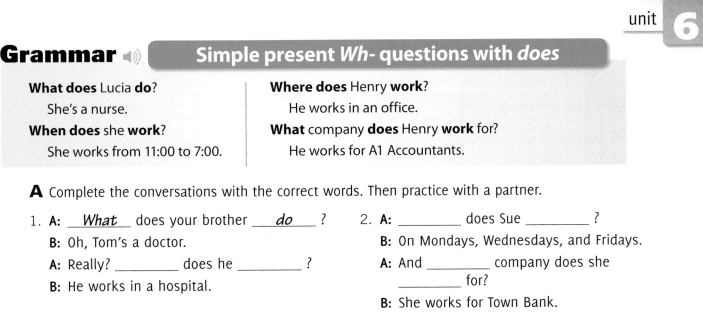

What *does Mr. Miller do* ?
Where ________ ?

What ________ ?
When ________ ?

Where ________ ?
What company ________ ?

A: *What does Mr. Miller do?*
B: *He's an English teacher.*

4 Speaking People's jobs

Class activity Add two jobs to the chart. Then find classmates who know people with those jobs. Ask for more information.

Job	Classmate	Person	Extra information
chef			
nurse			
police officer			
taxi driver			

A: *Do you know a chef?*
B: *Yes. My friend Marco is a chef.*
A: *Where does he work?*
B: *He works at Speedy Sushi.*

5 Keep talking!

Go to page 137 for more practice.

I can identify and talk about jobs.

B Can I speak to . . . ?

1 Interactions On the phone

A Look at the pictures. Where does Ed work?

B Listen and practice.

Ed: Good morning, Ace Accountants.
Ashley: Hello. Can I speak to Laura Reed?
Ed: Who is this, please?
Ashley: It's Ashley Tillman.

Ed: Just a minute, please. . . . Oh, I'm sorry. Ms. Reed is in a meeting.
Ashley: All right. Thank you.

C Listen to the expressions. Then practice the conversation again with the new expressions.

Asking for someone on the phone

Can I speak to . . . ?
Could I please speak to . . . ?
Is . . . there?

Having someone wait

Just a minute, please.
Hold on, please.
One moment, please.

D Pair work Practice the conversation again with the names below.

Gabriela Garcia

Anthony Davis

Kumiko Takahashi

Roberto Santos

A: *Good morning, Ace Accountants.*
B: *Hello. Can I speak to Gabriela Garcia?*
A: *Who is this, please?*

2 Listening A busy woman

A Listen to Kevin call Star Computers on five different days. Where is Ellen Astor each day? Number the pictures from 1 to 5.

at lunch

in a meeting

on another line

on vacation

with a customer

B Listen again. How does Kevin ask to speak to Ellen Astor? Number the questions from 1 to 5.

_____ Is Ms. Astor there?

_____ Could I please speak to . . . ?

__*1*__ Can I please speak to Ellen Astor?

_____ Can I speak to Ellen Astor?

_____ Could I speak to Ms. Astor, please?

3 Speaking Role play

Pair work Role-play the situation. Then change roles.

Student A: You are a receptionist at Sun Travel. Answer the phone. Tell the caller to wait, and then say why the person can't talk.

Student B: Call Sun Travel. Imagine someone you know works there. Ask to speak to the person.

A: *Hello, Sun Travel.*
B: *Hi. Can I please speak to Jackie Miller?*
A: *Of course. Just a minute, please. . . .*
I'm sorry. Jackie's with a customer.
B: *Oh, OK. Thanks.*

I can ask for someone on the telephone.
I can have someone wait.

C Can you sing?

1 Vocabulary Abilities

A Listen and repeat.

dance

draw

fix computers

paint

play the guitar

sing

speak French

swim

B Pair work What things do you sometimes do? Tell your partner.

2 Conversation Top talent?

Listen and practice.

Host: Welcome to *Top Talent*. What's your name, please?
Pamela: Hello. My name is Pamela Wells.
Host: Tell us, can you sing, Pamela?
Pamela: No, I can't sing at all.
Host: Well, can you play an instrument? the guitar? the piano?
Pamela: No, I can't.
Host: You can't sing, and you can't play an instrument. What *can* you do, Pamela?
Pamela: I can dance!
Host: Great! Let's see.

3 Grammar Can for ability; and, but, and or

I		
You		
He	**can**	dance very well.
She	**can't**	sing at all.
We		
They		

Can you sing?
Yes, I **can**. No, I **can't**.
What **can** Pamela do?
She **can** dance, **and** she **can** swim.
She **can** dance, **but** she **can't** sing.
She **can't** sing **or** play an instrument.

A Read the answers. Write the questions. Then practice with a partner.

1. *Can Jenny swim?*	No, Jenny can't swim.
2. ______	Billy can fix computers.
3. ______	Yes, Tom and Jill can sing very well.
4. ______	No, I can't play an instrument.
5. ______	Jay and I can dance and speak French.
6. ______	No, Sally can't paint at all.

B Pair work Make six sentences about Frank with *and*, *but*, or *or*. Tell your partner.

Frank's Abilities		
✓ *draw*	X *sing*	✓ *swim*
X *paint*	X *dance*	✓ *play the guitar*

"Frank can draw, but . . ."

4 Pronunciation *Can* and *can't*

A Listen and repeat. Notice the pronunciation of *can* /kən/ and *can't* /kænt/.

I can draw. I can't paint. I can draw, but I can't paint.

B Listen to the conversations. Do you hear *can* or *can't*? Circle the correct answers.

1. can / (can't) 2. can / can't 3. can / can't 4. can / can't

5 Speaking Can you paint?

A Pair work Add two abilities to the chart. Then interview your partner. Check (✓) the things he or she can do.

Can you . . . ?			
☐ paint	☐ upload a video	☐ sing in English	☐ ride a bicycle
☐ draw	☐ dance	☐ play an instrument	☐
☐ swim	☐ drive	☐ fix a car	☐

B Pair work Tell another classmate about your partner's abilities. Can your partner do something that you can't? What is it?

6 Keep talking!

Go to page 138 for more practice.

I can describe my talents and abilities. ☐

D Work and study

1 Reading

A Look at the pictures. Where do they work? Guess.

B Read the article. Where are Jin-hee, Ramiro, and Aisha now?

OVERSEAS OPPORTUNITIES

FOR STUDENTS

Be an Intern

You work for a short time in a company or an organization. You sometimes get a small salary as an intern.

Jin-hee is from South Korea and has an internship with a publishing company in New York City. The company makes French books. Jin-hee answers the phone and makes photocopies.

Study and Work

In this program, you can study *and* work. You usually study in the morning and work in the afternoon or evening.

Ramiro is from Mexico. He's in Australia now. He studies computer science part-time and works part-time. He takes classes in the morning and fixes computers in the evening. He works 20 hours a week.

Volunteer

Some organizations need extra help. Volunteers usually don't get a salary for their work.

Aisha is from Egypt. She's on a volunteer program in Nigeria at a school for children. She teaches classes, and she helps the children with their schoolwork. She works full-time from Monday to Friday.

C Read the article again. Answer the questions.

1. Do people get a salary as an intern? *They sometimes get a small salary.*
2. What does Jin-hee do as an intern? ______
3. In study and work programs, when do people usually work? ______
4. What does Ramiro study? ______
5. Do volunteers usually get a salary for their work? ______
6. What does Aisha do as a volunteer? ______

D Pair work Do people come to your country from other countries to study or work? What do they do? Discuss your ideas.

2 Listening Exciting opportunities

A 🔊 Listen to two students discuss three advertisements. Number them from 1 to 3.

Volunteer!

Are you interested in animals? Can you swim? _____ with turtles in Costa Rica. Work _____ to Saturday, 6:00 a.m. to _____ p.m. For more information, send an email to **CRVolunteer@cup.edu**

[]

Be an Intern

Are you 18 to _____ years old? Can you speak Chinese, _____, Japanese, or English? Be an intern at a theme _____ in Hong Kong!

Email us at **hongkong@cup.com/intern**

[]

Study and Work

Can you cook? Come to Rome. Study Italian in the morning, and work in a restaurant in the _evening_ . See the city in your _____ time! _____ salary.

Contact us at **study&work@cambridge.org**

[1]

B 🔊 Listen again. Complete the sentences with the correct words.

3 Writing My abilities

A Make lists of things you can and can't do well. Then write a paragraph about your abilities. Use the model and your lists to help you.

> *My Abilities*
> *I can play sports. I can play basketball and tennis very well. My favorite sport is soccer, but I can't play it very well. I can't play golf at all!*

B Pair work Share your paragraphs. Ask and answer questions for more information.

4 Speaking How well can you . . . ?

Group work Discuss the overseas opportunities in Exercise 1, Exercise 2, or your own ideas.

- What abilities do you need in each program?
- How well can you do each thing? (very well? well? not well? not at all?)
- Are any of the programs right for you?

I can talk about study and work programs. ✓

Wrap-up

1 Quick pair review

Lesson A Guess! Describe a job, but don't say what it is. Can your partner guess it? Take turns. You have two minutes.

A: *This person drives a car.*
B: *Is he a police officer?*
A: *No. The car is yellow in New York City.*
B: *Is he a taxi driver?*
A: *Yes.*

Lesson B Brainstorm! Make a list of ways to ask for someone on the phone and have someone wait. You have two minutes.

Lesson C Find out! What are two things both you and your partner can do? What are two things you can't do? You have two minutes.

A: *Can you cook?*
B: *Not really. Can you?*
A: *No, I can't!*

Lesson D Do you remember? Are the sentences true or false? Write T (true) or F (false). You have two minutes.

1. Volunteers usually get a salary. *F*
2. Volunteers always work part-time. ____
3. Interns work for companies or organizations. ____
4. Interns never get a salary. ____

2 In the real world

Go online and find information in English about an overseas program. Then write about it.

- What is the name of the program?
- Where is the program?
- What kind of program is it?
- What do people do in the program?

The Peace Corps

The Peace Corps is an overseas program. Americans volunteer in many countries. They help build things and teach people.

Food

LESSON A
- Food
- Count and noncount nouns; *some* and *any*

LESSON B
- Expressing likes
- Expressing dislikes

LESSON C
- More food
- *How often*; time expressions

LESSON D
- Reading: An article
- Writing: A typical meal

Warm-up

A Match the words and the pictures.

1. Italian food __c__ 2. Mexican food ____ 3. Chinese food ____ 4. Japanese food ____

B Name ten food words you know.

A Breakfast, lunch, and dinner

1 Vocabulary Food

A Match the words and the pictures. Then listen and check your answers.

a. apples	e. carrots	i. eggs	m. pasta
b. bananas	f. cereal	j. fish	n. potatoes
c. beans	✓g. cheese	k. milk	o. rice
d. beef	h. chicken	l. noodles	p. tomatoes

B Pair work Do you ever eat the food in Part A? Tell your partner.

"I often eat apples. I sometimes eat eggs. I never eat noodles."

2 Language in context Favorite meals

A Listen to three people talk about their favorite meals. Underline the food words.

I love breakfast. I usually eat some cereal, but I don't have any milk with it. I also eat an apple.

My favorite meal is lunch. I don't have a lot of time, so I often just get some noodles.

My favorite meal of the day is dinner. A typical dinner for me is rice and beans with some beef.

B What about you? What's your favorite meal of the day? What do you eat?

3 Grammar — Count and noncount nouns; *some* and *any*

Count nouns

an apple  a tomato 

apples  tomatoes 

Do you have **any** apples?
Yes, I have **some** (apples).
No, I don't have **any** (apples).

Noncount nouns

milk  cereal 

Do you have **any** milk?
Yes, I have **some** (milk).
No, I don't have **any** (milk).

A Complete the chart with the food words from Exercise 1. Then compare with a partner.

Count nouns		Noncount nouns	
apples		*milk*	
tomatoes		*cereal*	

B Circle the correct words. Then practice with a partner.

A: What do you want for lunch, Amy?
B: Let's just make **some** / **any** pasta.
A: Good idea. We have **some** / **any** pasta.
B: Let's see. We have **some** / **any** carrots. We don't have **some** / **any** tomatoes.
A: OK, I can get **some** / **any** at the store. What else?
B: Do we have **some** / **any** cheese?
A: No, we don't have **some** / **any**. I can get **some** / **any**.

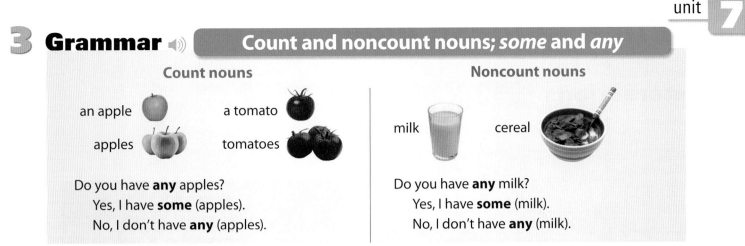

C Pair work Practice the conversation again. Use other food words from Exercise 1.

4 Speaking What do you eat?

A Write your answers to the questions in the chart.

What do you often eat for . . . ?	Me	Name: ________	Name: ________
breakfast			
lunch			
dinner			

B Group work Interview two classmates. Complete the chart with their answers.

5 Keep talking!

Go to page 139 for more practice.

I can say what meals I eat. ✓

B I like Chinese food!

1 Interactions Likes and dislikes

A Look at the pictures. Where are Maria and Tom?

B Listen and practice.

Maria: Do you like pasta?
Tom: No, I don't like Italian food.

Maria: How about Chinese food?
Tom: Good idea. I like Chinese food!

C Listen to the expressions. Then practice the conversation again with the new expressions.

Expressing dislikes

- I don't like . . .
- I don't like . . . at all.
- I hate . . . !

Expressing likes

- I like . . .
- I really like . . .
- I love . . . !

D Pair work Look at Maria's and Tom's likes and dislikes. Are they the same as yours? Tell your partner.

Maria	fish	Mexican food	Japanese food	milk	beans	beef
Tom	cheese	carrots	Chinese food	Italian food	French food	eggs

"Maria loves fish, but I don't like fish at all."

2 Pronunciation Word stress

A Listen and repeat. Notice the stress in the words.

●	●•	•●•
cheese	**ap**ple	ba**na**na
beans	**chic**ken	po**ta**to
beef	**noo**dles	to**ma**to
______	______	______
______	______	

B Listen. Complete the chart with the correct words.

dairy fruit Italian meat pasta

3 Listening I love it!

A Listen to four conversations about food. Check (✓) the words you hear.

1.	2.	3.	4.
☐ beans	☐ cheese	☐ noodles	☐ bananas
☑ beef	☐ chicken	☐ potatoes	☐ carrots
☑ pasta	☐ eggs	☐ tomatoes	☐ cereal

B Listen again. Do the two speakers like the same things?
Circle the correct answers.

1. yes / (no) 2. yes / no 3. yes / no 4. yes / no

4 Speaking What do you like?

A Make a list of food you like and food you don't like.

Food I like		Food I don't like	

B Pair work Tell your partner about the food you like and don't like.
Ask and answer questions for more information.

A: *I really like fish.*
B: *Do you cook fish at home?*
A: *No, I don't. I eat fish in restaurants.*

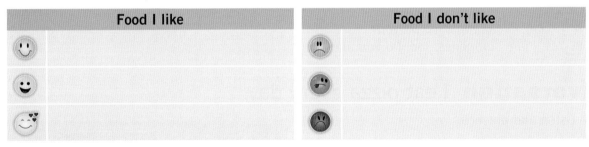

I can say what I like and dislike. ☐

C Meals

1 Vocabulary More food

A Label the pictures with the correct words. Then listen and check your answers.

dumplings	✓hot dogs	pizza	soup	sushi
hamburgers	pancakes	salad	spaghetti	tacos

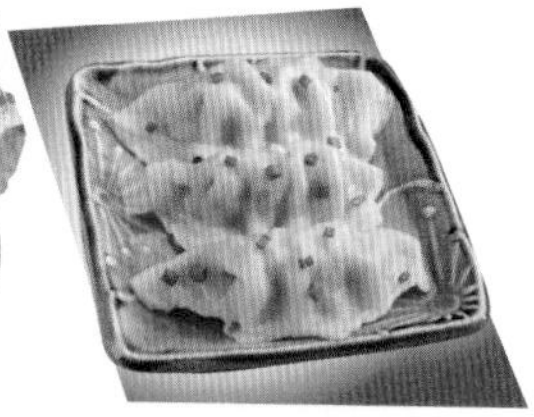

1. *hot dogs* 2. ________ 3. ________ 4. ________ 5. ________

6. ________ 7. ________ 8. ________ 9. ________ 10. ________

B Pair work Which food in Part A do you like? Which food don't you like? Compare your answers.

A: *I really like dumplings. Do you?*
B: *Yes, I like dumplings, too. Do you like . . . ?*

2 Conversation I eat pizza every day.

Listen and practice.

Megan: What is that?
David: Pizza. My father is a pizza chef.
Megan: Really? So how often do you eat pizza?
David: I eat pizza every day. It's my favorite food!
Megan: I don't eat pizza very often, but it looks interesting. What's on it?
David: Cheese, tomatoes, black beans, and fish.
Megan: Black beans and fish on pizza. Yuck!
David: Have some. It's really good.
Megan: No, thanks. I'm not very hungry.

3 Grammar How often; time expressions

How often do you eat pizza?

I eat pizza	**every day**. **once a week**. **twice a month**. **three times a month**. **once in a while**.	I do**n't** eat pizza **very often**. I **never** eat pizza.

A Look at Matt's menu. Answer the questions. Then practice with a partner.

Matt's Menu

	Monday	Tuesday	Wednesday	Thursday	Friday	Saturday	Sunday
Breakfast	cereal	eggs	cereal	eggs	cereal	pancakes	pancakes
Lunch	soup	pizza	soup	sushi	soup	tacos	sushi
Dinner	dumplings	chicken	beef	chicken	pizza	spaghetti	hamburgers

1. How often does Matt eat hamburgers for dinner? *He eats hamburgers once a week.*
2. How often does Matt eat soup for lunch? ____________________
3. How often does Matt eat pancakes? ____________________
4. How often does Matt eat hot dogs? ____________________
5. How often does Matt eat sushi for lunch? ____________________
6. How often does Matt eat dumplings for dinner? ____________________

B Pair work Make six sentences about your eating habits with different time expressions. Tell your partner.

"I eat spaghetti once a month."

4 Speaking Eating habits

A Add three food words to the chart. Then answer the questions.

How often do you eat . . . ?	Me	Name: ____________
hot dogs		
salad		
tacos		

B Pair work Interview your partner. Complete the chart with his or her answers.

C Pair work Compare your information with another partner.

"Kazu eats hot dogs once a week, but I eat them once in a while."

5 Keep talking!

Go to page 140 for more practice.

I can talk about my eating habits. ☐

D Favorite food

1 Reading

A Look at the pictures in the magazine article. Can you name the food?

B Read the article. What's the best title? Check (✓) the correct answer.

☐ Meal Times ☐ My Favorite Food ☐ Dinner Around the World

Letters from our readers

I love nachos. I make them once a week. I just buy some tortilla chips and put cheese, beef, tomatoes, and onions on top. Then I cook it in the microwave.

HEATHER
United States

I like dumplings a lot. You can buy good dumplings in restaurants, but I usually eat my mother's dumplings. They're delicious! I eat them for lunch four or five times a month.

JAE-SUN
South Korea

My wife and I go to our favorite ice-cream shop three times a month. They have many flavors, but we always get chocolate ice cream. It's our favorite.

CARLOS
Argentina

I really like pancakes, but we don't eat them for breakfast. We eat them after dinner. We usually eat them two or three times a month. I like to eat them with jam.

OLGA
Sweden

C Read the article again. Complete the chart with the correct information.

	Favorite food	How often they have it
Heather	*nachos*	*once a week*
Jae-sun		
Carlos		
Olga		

D Pair work Imagine you can have one food in Part A right now. Which food do you want? Why? Tell your partner.

"I want dumplings. I love Korean food. Vegetable dumplings are my favorite."

2 Listening A meal in Sweden

A Listen to Olga describe a typical meal in Sweden. Which meal does she talk about? Check (✓) the correct answer.

☐ breakfast ☐ lunch ☐ dinner

B Listen again. Circle the words you hear.

beans	bread	cheese	fish	milk	pancakes
beef	cereal	eggs	fruit	noodles	potatoes

3 Writing A typical meal

A Think of a typical meal in your country. Answer the questions.

- What do people drink? ____________________
- What do people eat? ____________________
- Do *you* usually eat it? ____________________
- Why or why not? ____________________

B Write about a typical meal in your country. Use the model and your answers in Part A to help you.

C Class activity Post your writing around the room. Read your classmates' writing. Who describes similar meals?

A Japanese Breakfast

People in Japan usually drink green tea for breakfast. They eat fish, rice, soup, salad, and pickles. It's a healthy and delicious breakfast, but I don't eat this. I usually drink orange juice and eat cereal and fruit for breakfast.

4 Speaking What's your favorite meal?

A Pair work Add two questions about food to the chart. Then interview your partner. Take notes.

Questions	Name: ____________
What's your favorite meal?	
What's your favorite kind of food?	
How often do you have it?	
Who makes it?	
Can you cook it?	
What do you drink with it?	

A: *What's your favorite kind of food?*
B: *I love Mexican food.*

B Group work Tell your group about your partner's favorite meal. Do you like that meal, too? Does your group like it?

I can talk about my favorite food. ☐

Wrap-up

1 Quick pair review

Lesson A Brainstorm! Make a list of count and noncount food words. How many do you know? You have one minute.

Lesson B Do you remember? Look at the pictures. Complete the sentences with the correct words. You have one minute.

 I *don't like* fish *at all* .

 I ______ ______ beef.

 I ______ milk!

 I ______ French food.

 I ______ ______ breakfast.

 I ______ carrots!

Lesson C Find out! What is one thing both you and your partner eat every week? eat once in a while? never eat? You have two minutes.

A: *I eat rice every week. Do you?*
B: *Yes, I do.*

Lesson D Guess! Describe your favorite food, but don't say its name! Can your partner guess what it is? Take turns. You have two minutes.

A: *I love this food. It's Italian, and I eat it once in a while. I eat it at home.*
B: *Is it pasta?*
A: *Yes.*

2 In the real world

Go online and find information in English about your favorite movie star's or musician's eating habits. Then write about them.

- What is his or her favorite food?
- How often does he or she usually eat it?

Jack Black's Favorite Food

The American actor Jack Black doesn't have one favorite food. He has two of them! He loves pizza and cheeseburgers.

In the neighborhood

LESSON A	LESSON B	LESSON C	LESSON D
• Places in the neighborhood • Prepositions of location	• Asking for directions	• Places to visit • *There is, there are*	• Reading: "Monterey Bay Aquarium" • Writing: Group poster

Warm-up

A Look at the picture. Make six sentences about it.

B Where can you do these things?

buy glasses	buy some fruit	check email	eat lunch	get a book	see a movie

A Around town

1 Vocabulary Places in the neighborhood

A Match the words and the places. Then listen and check your answers.

a. bank	c. bus stop	e. gas station	✓g. library	i. subway station
b. bookstore	d. coffee shop	f. hotel	h. newsstand	j. supermarket

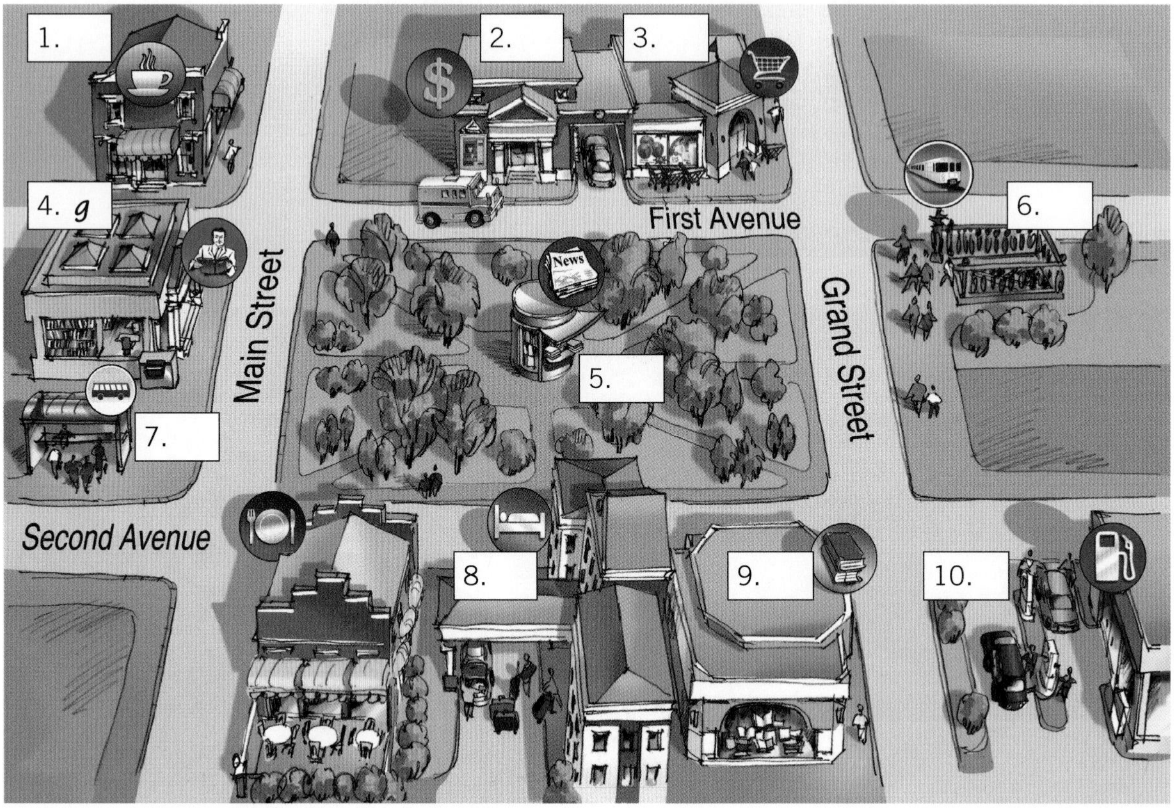

B Pair work Which places are in your school's neighborhood?

"We have a coffee shop, some restaurants, and a . . ."

2 Language in context Ads

A Read three advertisements for places in a neighborhood. What places do they describe?

Mama's Place
Come to Mama's Place for real Italian food.
On Second Avenue
10% off
between 5:30 and 6:30 p.m.

ABC
Supermarket
WE'RE ALWAYS OPEN!
Find everything you need at ABC Supermarket!
New location next to Town Bank

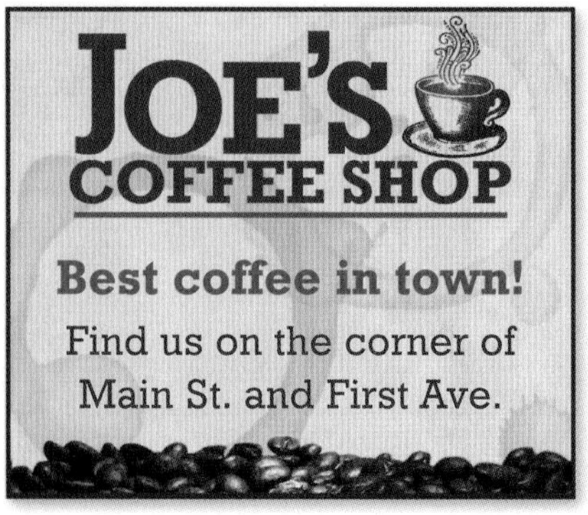

JOE'S
COFFEE SHOP
Best coffee in town!
Find us on the corner of Main St. and First Ave.

B What can you do at each place in Part A?

3 Grammar Prepositions of location

in

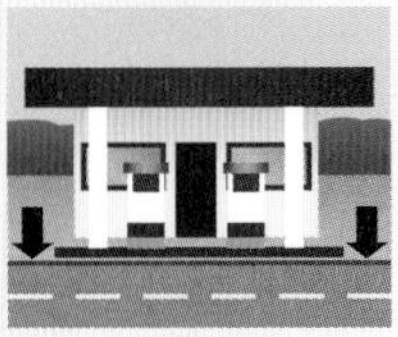
on

next to

across from

between

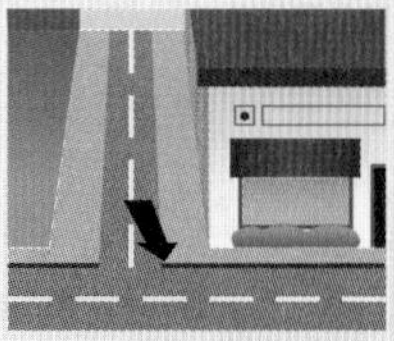
on the corner of

The newsstand is **in** the park.
The gas station is **on** Second Avenue.
The supermarket is **next to** the bank.
The bus stop is **across from** the park.

The hotel is **between** the restaurant and the bookstore.
The coffee shop is **on the corner of** Main Street and First Avenue.

Look at the map in Exercise 1. Complete the sentences with the correct prepositions.

1. The newsstand is ___*in*___ the park.
2. The subway station is ____________ the park.
3. The bookstore is ____________ the hotel.
4. Mama's Place is ____________ Second Avenue.
5. The gas station is ____________ Second Avenue and Grand Street.
6. The library is ____________ the coffee shop and the bus stop.

4 Pronunciation Word stress

Listen and repeat. Notice the stress on the first or last syllable.

●•		•●
bookstore	**news**stand	a**cross**
coffee	**sta**tion	be**tween**
corner	**sub**way	ho**tel**

5 Speaking Where's the drugstore?

A Pair work Add these four places to the map in Exercise 1. Then ask and answer questions about their locations.

drugstore

post office

Internet café

department store

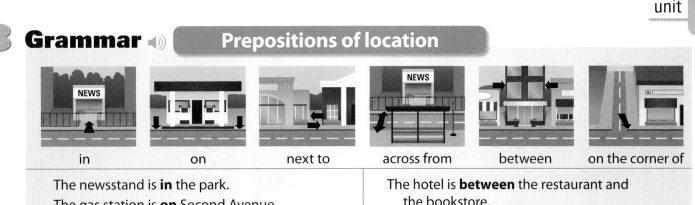

A: *Where's the drugstore on your map?*
B: *It's next to the bank. Where is it on your map?*

B Pair work Where are the places in your town? Tell your partner.

6 Keep talking!

Student A go to page 141 and Student B go to page 142 for more practice.

I can give the locations of neighborhood places.

B How do I get to . . . ?

1 Giving directions

A Listen and repeat.

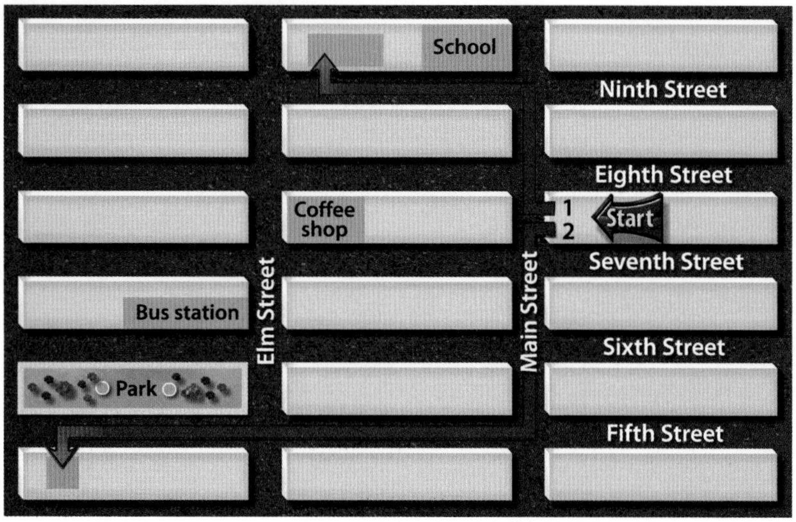

1
Go up Main Street.
Turn left on Ninth Street.
Go one block.
It's **on the right**, next to a school.

2
Walk down Main Street.
Take a right on Fifth Street.
Walk two blocks.
It's **on the left**, across from the park.

B Pair work Give directions from *Start* to the coffee shop and the bus station.

2 Interactions Directions

A Listen and practice.

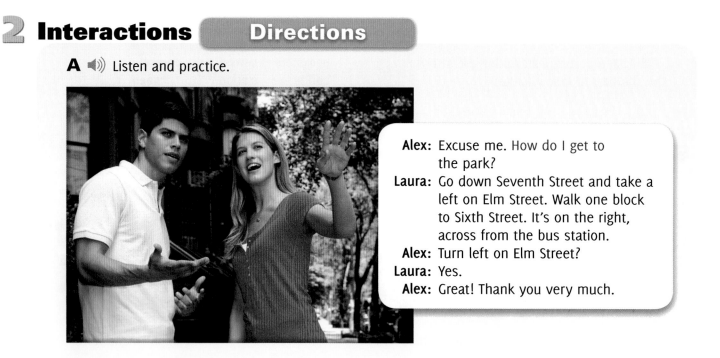

Alex: Excuse me. How do I get to the park?
Laura: Go down Seventh Street and take a left on Elm Street. Walk one block to Sixth Street. It's on the right, across from the bus station.
Alex: Turn left on Elm Street?
Laura: Yes.
Alex: Great! Thank you very much.

B Listen to the expressions. Then practice the conversation again with the new expression.

Asking for directions

How do I get to . . . ?
How can I get to . . . ?

3 Listening Follow the route

A 🔊 Listen to Carl and Alice use their GPS to get from Pioneer Square to the library in Seattle. Follow their route. Then mark an ✗ at the library.

Key
A. Olympic Hotel
B City Hall
C. Smith Tower
D. Pioneer Square
E. Qwest Field

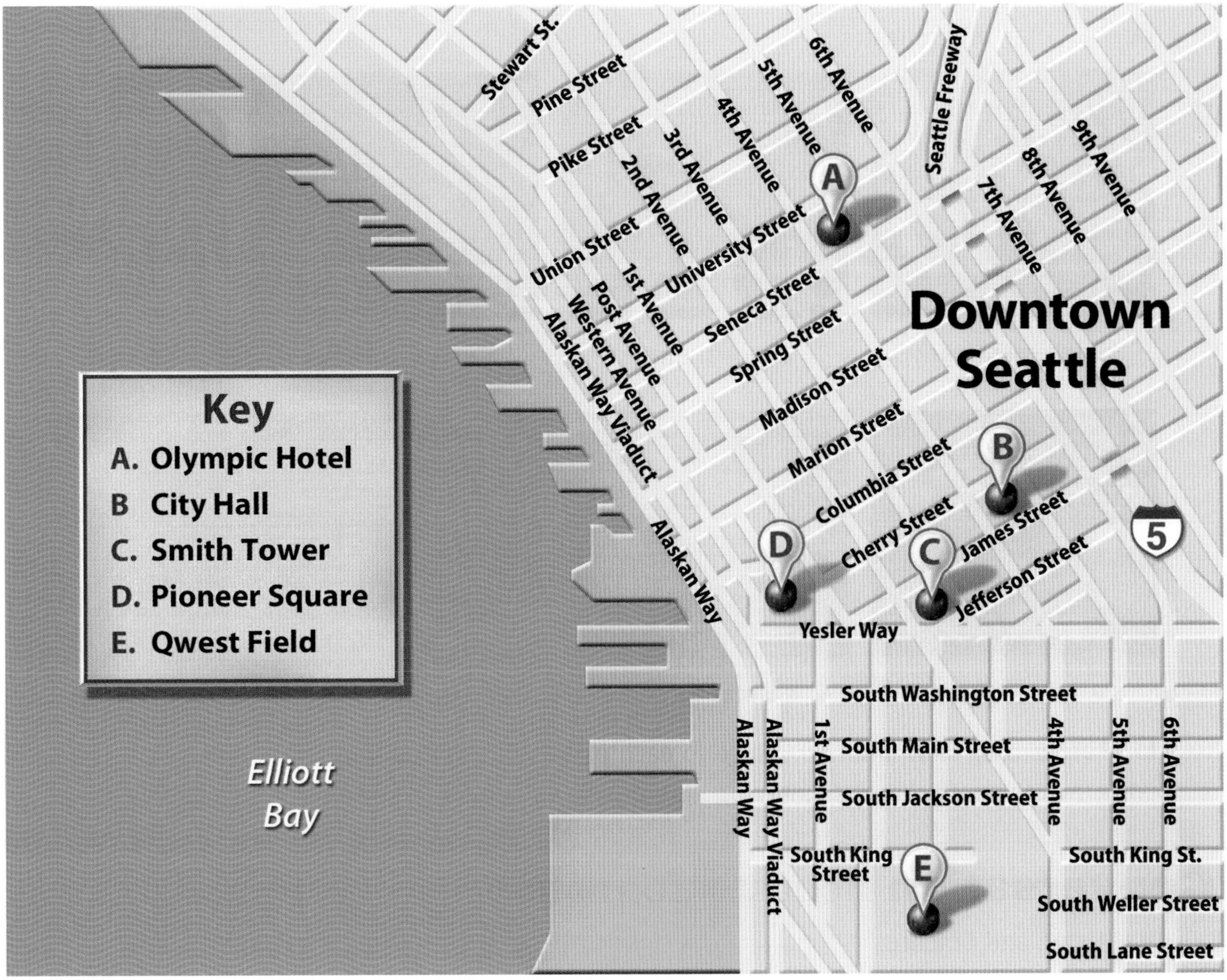

B 🔊 Listen to Carl and Alice go from the library to Pike Place Market. Follow their route. Then mark a ✓ at the market.

C Pair work Give directions from Pioneer Square to other places on the map. Your partner follows them. Take turns.

4 Speaking How do I get to . . . ?

A Pair work Draw a simple map of the neighborhood around your school. Label different places and street names.

B Pair work Role-play the situation. Then change roles.

Student A: You are a tourist in town. Ask for directions to places in the neighborhood.
Student B: You meet a tourist in your town. Give him or her directions to places in your neighborhood. Start at your school.

A: *How do I get to the train station?*
B: *Walk down Main Street . . .*

I can ask for and give directions. ✓

C Fun in the city

1 Vocabulary Places to visit

A Listen and repeat.

amusement park

aquarium

movie theater

museum

science center

swimming pool

water park

zoo

B Pair work How often do you go to each place? Tell your partner.

"Our town has a swimming pool, but I hardly ever go there."

2 Conversation Tourist information

Listen and practice.

Larry: Hello. Can I help you?
Maggie: Yes. Is there a museum near here?
Larry: Let's see. . . . Yes. There's a museum across from the park.
Maggie: And is there an aquarium in this city?
Larry: Yes, there is. It's near the museum. It's a very nice aquarium.
Maggie: Great. I have one more question. Are there any amusement parks?
Larry: There aren't any amusement parks, but there's a nice water park.

3 Grammar — *There is, there are*

There's a museum.	**There are** two swimming pools.
There isn't an amusement park.	**There aren't** any good zoos in this city.
Is there an aquarium in this city?	**Are there** any swimming pools near here?
Yes, **there is**. No, **there isn't**.	Yes, **there are**. No, **there aren't**.

Contraction There's = There is

A Complete the questions about the city with *Is there a / an . . . ?* or *Are there any . . . ?* Then compare with a partner.

1. *Is there a* ____________ zoo?
2. ____________ water parks?
3. ____________ aquarium?
4. ____________ museums?
5. ____________ amusement park?
6. ____________ movie theaters?

B Pair work Ask and answer the questions in Part A. Use the map on the right.

A: *Is there a zoo?*
B: *Yes, there is. There's one zoo.*

4 Speaking Is there . . . ? Are there . . . ?

A Pair work Add two items to the chart. Then interview your partner. Check (✓) the places that are in his or her neighborhood, and ask for more information.

	Places	Locations	Extra information
☐	movie theaters		
☐	museums		
☐	science center		
☐	swimming pool		
☐			
☐			

A: *Are there any movie theaters in your neighborhood?*
B: *Yes, there's one. It's on University Avenue.*
A: *How often do you go there?*

B Class activity Tell the class about two interesting places in your partner's neighborhood.

5 Keep talking!

Go to page 143 for more practice.

I can talk about interesting places in my town. ☐

D A great place to visit

1 Reading

A Is there an aquarium in your town or city? If yes, do you like it? If no, do you want one?

B Read the poster. Where is the Monterey Bay Aquarium?

MONTEREY BAY AQUARIUM

California's Monterey Bay Aquarium is a great place for people of all ages.

More than 35,000 different ocean animals live in the aquarium, including sharks, rays, and penguins.

There are 200 different exhibits and over 600 kinds of plants and animals in the aquarium.

Almost 2,000,000 people visit the aquarium every year! Visitors usually spend from two to three hours at the aquarium.

The water in the aquarium comes from Monterey Bay. It has food for many animals in the aquarium.

There aren't any whales or dolphins in the aquarium because you can see them in the bay!

Visitor information cards in Spanish, French, Chinese, Japanese, and other languages are at the information desk.

The aquarium is on the corner of David Avenue and Cannery Row in Monterey, California.

Can't visit? Go to the E-quarium on our website. See live webcasts and download videos and podcasts.

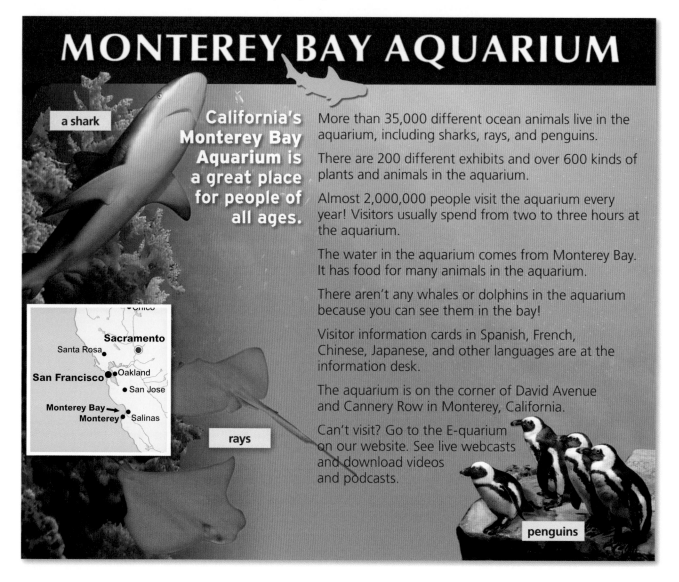

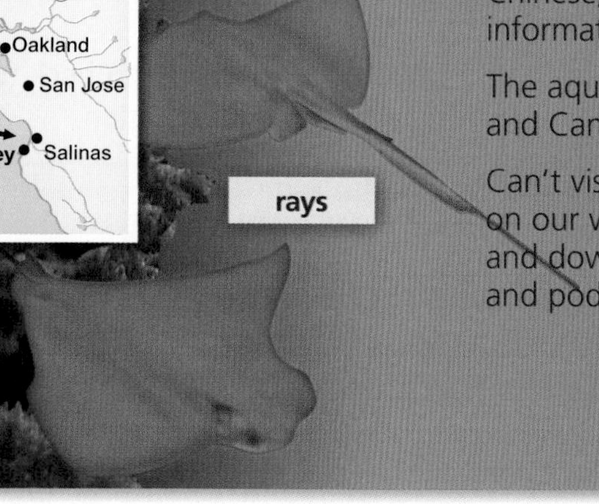

C Read the poster again. Answer the questions.

1. What animals live in the aquarium? *Sharks, rays, and penguins live in the aquarium.*
2. Where does the aquarium's water come from? ______
3. Are there any whales or dolphins in the aquarium? ______
4. Where are the visitor information cards? ______
5. What is on their website? ______

D Pair work What is your favorite place to visit in your town or city? Why? Tell your partner.

"I like the modern art museum because it has cool paintings. I go to the museum once a month."

2 **Listening** City information

A 🔊 Listen to three tourists ask for information about two places in the city. Write the places in the chart.

	Place 1	Place 2
1.	(movie theater)	
2.		
3.		

B 🔊 Listen again. Which places are in the city? Circle the correct answers.

3 **Writing and speaking** Group poster presentation

A Group work Choose an interesting place in your city. What do you know about it? Make a list.

B Group work Create and design a poster about the place. Use your list from Part A.

COME TO THE IMAGINE SCIENCE CENTER!
Great for kids, teens, and adults.

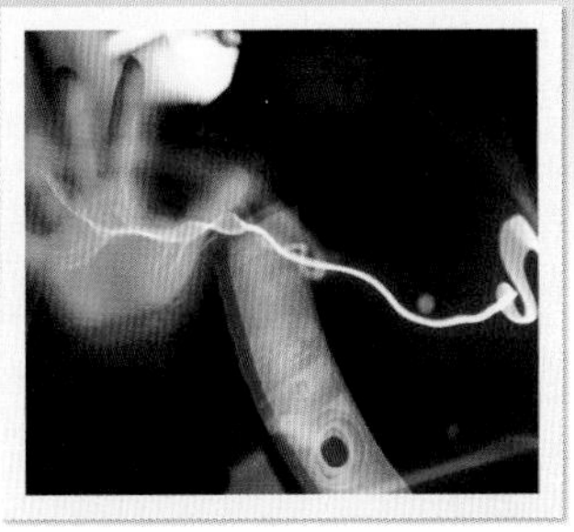

- *We're open every day from 9:00 to 6:00.*
- *There's a free audio tour in ten languages.*
- *There's an excellent café in the museum.*
- *Try our science experiments.*
- *Learn about plant life.*
- *There are over 10,000 books in the bookstore.*

C Class activity Present your posters. Ask and answer questions for more information.

A: *The Imagine Science Center is a great place to visit.*
B: *It's open every day from 9:00 to 6:00.*
C: *There's a free audio tour. You can listen to the tour in ten languages.*
D: *Where is the Imagine Science Center?*
C: *It's at 367 First Avenue, near the park.*

I can give a presentation on a city attraction. ☑

Wrap-up

1 Quick pair review

Lesson A Brainstorm! Make a list of places in a neighborhood. How many do you know? You have one minute.

Lesson B Do you remember? Circle the correct answers. You have two minutes.

A: Excuse me. **Where** / **How** do I get to the library from here?
B: Walk up Third Avenue and **turn** / **take** left on Elm Street.
A: Is the library on Elm Street?
B: No, it's not. **Go** / **Turn** two blocks on Elm Street. Then **take** / **walk** a right on Main Street. The library is **on** / **in** the right.
A: Thanks!

Lesson C Find out! What are two kinds of places both you and your partner like to visit in your city or other cities? What are two kinds of places you don't like to visit? You have two minutes.

A: *I like museums. Do you?*
B: *Not really. How about water parks? I love those!*
A: *I do, too!*

Lesson D Guess! Describe a place to visit in your area, but don't say its name! Can your partner guess the name? Take turns. You have two minutes.

A: *I go there with my friends on weekends.*
B: *Is it Mall Marina?*
A: *No. There are rides and games there.*
B: *Is it the amusement park, Fantasy Land?*
A: *Yes!*

2 In the real world

What zoos do you know? Go online and find information in English about a zoo. Then write about it.

- What is the name of the zoo? Where is it?
- What animals and exhibits are there?
- Can you watch videos or take a tour on the website?

The San Diego Zoo
The San Diego Zoo is a famous zoo in California. You can see pandas there. You can also . . .

What are you doing?

LESSON A
- Actions and prepositions
- Present continuous statements

LESSON B
- Asking if someone can talk now
- Explaining that you can't talk now

LESSON C
- Activities
- Present continuous questions

LESSON D
- Reading: "Status Updates"
- Writing: My status update

Warm-up

A Look at the picture. Make eight sentences about it.

B Do you ever do these things on a subway, train, or bus?

A I'm looking for you.

1 Vocabulary Actions and prepositions

A Listen and repeat.

start

hold

look for

wave

sit

stand

run

end

B Listen and repeat.

behind

in

in front of

on

under

C Pair work Tell your partner to sit and stand in different places in the classroom. Use the prepositions. Take turns.

"Stand in front of the door."

2 Language in context Meeting a friend

A Listen to Amy and Claudio meet at a soccer game. Where is Amy? Where is Claudio?

Amy: Hi, Claudio. It's Amy. I'm standing under the scoreboard. Where are you?

Claudio: I'm sitting in front of the big clock. Do you see me?

Amy: No, I don't.

Claudio: Well, I'm wearing a red shirt.

Amy: But, Claudio, everyone is wearing a red shirt!

B What about you? Where do you usually meet your friends at big games or other events?

3 Grammar ◄)) Present continuous statements

I'm **standing** under the scoreboard.	I'm **not sitting**.	*Spelling*
You're **running**.	You're **not walking**.	run → run**ning**
He's **sitting** in front of the big clock.	He's **not standing**.	sit → sit**ting**
It's **starting**.	It's **not ending**.	wave → wav**ing**
We're **holding** scarves.	We're **not waving**.	
They're **playing** soccer.	They're **not playing** tennis.	

A Complete Claudio's text messages with the present continuous forms of the verbs.
Then compare with a partner.

1.

Where are you, Tim?
I **'m looking** _____
(look) for you. The game

(start), but my favorite
player _____
(not / play) right now. Please
text me.

2.

Amy and
I _____
(watch) the game. But
where are you, Tim?
We _____
(sit) in row 56. Wait!
I _____
(get) a message. Is it you?

3.

Amy and I

(hold) signs.
We _____
(wave) in front of the TV
cameras. Can you see us?

B Pair work Make ten sentences about people in your class with the present
continuous. Tell your partner.

"I'm sitting behind Eva. Lily and Mei are wearing sweaters."

4 Listening Someone is . . .

◄)) Listen to the sound effects. What is happening? Circle the correct answers.

1. Someone is (watching a game) / watching a movie.
2. Someone is **getting up** / **going to bed**.
3. Someone is **walking** / **running**.

4. Some people are **playing tennis** /
 playing soccer.
5. The game is **starting** / **ending**.

5 Speaking Guess the action.

Group work Perform an action. Your group guesses it. Take turns.

cook	run	stand
play tennis	sit	watch TV
play the guitar	sleep	wave

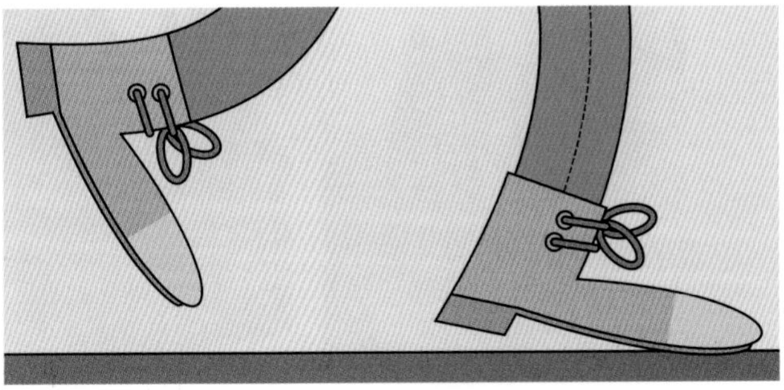

A: *You're dancing.*
B: *No, I'm not.*
A: *You're playing soccer.*
B: *Yes, that's right.*

6 Keep talking!

Go to page 144 for more practice.

 I can describe what people are doing right now. ☑

B I can't talk right now.

1 Interactions Can you talk?

A Look at the pictures. What is Amanda doing?

B Listen and practice.

Amanda: Hello?
Justin: Hi, Amanda. It's Justin. Is this a good time to talk?

Amanda: Oh, sorry. I can't talk right now. I'm cooking dinner. Can I call you back?
Justin: OK, sure. Talk to you later.
Amanda: Thanks. Bye.

C Listen to the expressions. Then practice the conversation again with the new expressions.

Asking if someone can talk now

Is this a good time to talk?
Can you talk right now?
Do you have a minute?

Explaining that you can't talk now

I can't talk right now.
I'm busy right now.
This isn't a good time.

D Pair work Practice the conversation again with the reasons below.

clean

do my homework

play volleyball

wait for the doctor

2 Listening Do you have a minute?

A 🔊 Listen to four phone conversations. Number the questions you hear from 1 to 4.

_____ Can you talk right now? _____ Is this a good time to talk?

_____ Is this a good time? _1_ Do you have a minute?

B 🔊 Listen again. Why can't each person talk right now? Write the reason.

1. Eric _is having dinner_ . 3. Ji-won _____ .
2. Renee _____ . 4. Carmen _____ .

3 Speaking Role play

A Complete the sentences with reasons why you can't talk on the phone.

I'm watching _____ . I'm eating _____ .

I'm playing _____ . I'm _____ .

B Pair work Role-play the situations. Then change roles.

Student A: Answer the phone. Explain that you can't talk now and say why. Use the reasons from Part A.

Student B: Call Student A. Identify yourself and ask if he or she can talk right now.

| I can ask if someone can talk now. | ☑ |
| I can explain why I can't talk on the telephone. | ☑ |

C These days

1 Vocabulary Activities

A Listen and repeat.

create a website

learn to drive

look for a job

study for an exam

study Italian

take a dance class

take tennis lessons

tutor a student

B Pair work Which activities are fun? Which are not fun? Compare answers with a partner.

2 Conversation Old friends

Listen and practice.

Jill: Long time no see, Wendy!
Wendy: Oh, hi, Jill.
Jill: What are you doing these days?
Wendy: I'm learning to drive. I'm also tutoring a student. Oh, and I'm taking a dance class.
Jill: You sound really busy.
Wendy: I am. How about you, Jill? Are *you* doing anything special these days?
Jill: Yes, I am. I'm studying Italian.
Wendy: Really? Why are you studying Italian?
Jill: Because . . . Oh, my phone is ringing. Hello? Sorry, Wendy. It's my new friend, Luigi.
Wendy: Oh.
Jill: *Ciao, Luigi! Come stai?*

3 Grammar Present continuous questions

What **are** you **doing** these days?	**Are** you **doing** anything special these days?
I**'m learning** to drive.	Yes, I **am**. No, I**'m not**.
What class **is** Wendy **taking**?	**Is** she **tutoring** a student?
She**'s taking** a dance class.	Yes, she **is**. No, she**'s not**.
Where **are** they **studying**?	**Are** they **taking** tennis lessons?
They**'re studying** online.	Yes, they **are**. No, they**'re not**.

A Complete the questions with the present continuous forms of the verbs. Then compare with a partner.

1. ___*Are*___ you ___*taking*___ (take) music lessons these days?
2. What classes ____________ you ____________ (take)?
3. ____________ you and your friends ____________ (buy) CDs these days?
4. What ____________ your classmates ____________ (learn) in this class?
5. What languages ____________ you ____________ (study)?
6. ____________ you ____________ (learn) to drive?

B Pair work Ask and answer the questions in Part A. Answer with your own information.

4 Pronunciation Intonation in questions

Listen and repeat. Notice the intonation of *yes / no* and *Wh-* questions.

Are you watching a lot of TV? What TV shows are you watching?

5 Speaking Busy lives

Class activity Add two activities to the chart. Then find classmates who are doing each thing these days. Write their names, and ask questions for more information.

Are you . . . these days?	Name	Extra information
studying another language		
reading a good book		
watching a lot of TV		
taking any fun classes		
downloading a lot of music		

6 Keep talking!

Go to page 145 for more practice.

I can describe what people are doing these days.

D What's new?

1 Reading

A What are you and your classmates doing right now?

B Read the status updates. Which two people are waiting for other people?

SIGN UP | SIGN IN | SEARCH

Status Updates

What are you doing?

Donna Bristol I'm standing under the JB Cola sign on Main Street. I'm waiting for my friend Hank. But Hank is never late! Hank?
Apr 19 8:33 p.m.

Hank Jones I'm standing in line. Donna, please wait!! I'm in a store on First Avenue. The line isn't moving.
Apr 19 8:50 p.m.

Fernando Sanchez I'm studying English. I'm doing grammar exercises on my DVD-ROM. I'm getting them all correct. Yay!
Apr 19 9:05 p.m.

Zack Parker I'm enjoying Singapore!! I love vacations! How are my friends in Chicago doing?
Apr 19 9:17 p.m.

Hee-jin Park I'm having a great evening. I'm at my favorite restaurant with my two friends Alex and Eddie. We're waiting for dessert.
Apr 19 9:28 p.m.

Jessica King I'm looking for a good French dictionary. I'm taking a French class and need help with my vocabulary.
Apr 19 9:44 p.m.

Arthur Henderson I'm waiting for my daughter to come home. It's almost 10:00 p.m. Where are you, Lisa? You know the rules!
Apr 19 9:58 p.m.

Lisa Henderson I'm at a basketball game. Sorry, Dad. My favorite player is playing. 15 more minutes??
Apr 19 10:02 p.m.

C Read the updates again. Complete the sentences with first names.

1. *Zack* is on vacation.
2. ______ is having dinner.
3. ______ is standing in line.
4. ______ is watching a basketball game.
5. ______ and ______ are students.
6. ______ is studying English.

D Pair work How often do you write messages like the ones above? What do you write about? Tell your partner.

"I love status updates. I write them twice a day. I usually write about the new music I find online."

2 Writing My status update

A Write a status update about what you're doing right now or these days.

josie9: I'm studying Italian on the weekends.

B Group work Pass your paper to the classmate on your right. Read and respond to your classmate's update. Continue to pass, read, and respond to each update three times.

josie9: I'm studying Italian on the weekends.

93arren: I'm not studying Italian, but I'm learning to drive.

3 Speaking Makoto's Desk

Group work Look at Makoto's desk. What do you think he's doing these days?

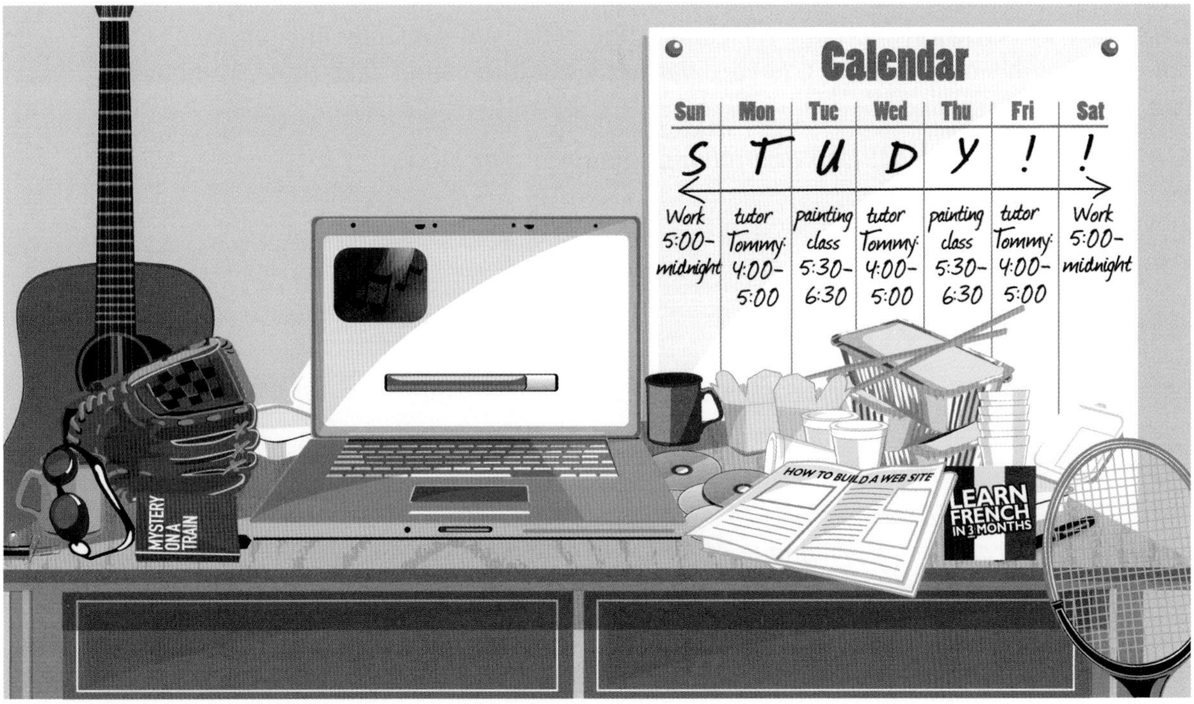

A: *I think he's studying French.*
B: *Right. And he's taking a painting class.*
C: *Do you think he's drinking a lot of coffee?*

I can discuss what people are doing.

Wrap-up

1 Quick pair review

Lesson A Do you remember? Complete the sentences with the correct prepositions. You have one minute.

1. The ball is ____________ the bench.
2. The ball is ____________ the bench.
3. The ball is ____________ the bench.
4. The ball is ____________ the bench.

Lesson B Brainstorm! Make a list of phone expressions. How many do you know? You have two minutes.

Lesson C Find out! What are two things both you and your partner are doing these days? You have one minute.

A: *What are you doing these days?*
B: *I'm taking tango lessons. Are you?*
A: *No, I'm not.*

Lesson D Guess! Describe the clothes and actions of someone in your class, but don't say his or her name! Can your partner guess the name? Take turns. You have two minutes.

A: *He's wearing a baseball cap and talking to Angela right now.*
B: *Is it Sebastian?*
A: *Yes, it is.*

2 In the real world

Go to a mall or park. What are people doing? Write about them.

People in the Park

I am in the park. Two women are walking. One woman is wearing a red T-shirt. A man is sitting next to me. He is eating his lunch. He is also . . .

Past experiences

LESSON A	LESSON B	LESSON C	LESSON D
• Weekend activities • Simple past regular verbs	• Showing that you're listening • Expressing surprise	• Things to do • Simple past irregular verbs; *yes / no* questions	• Reading: "Matt's Movie Reviews" • Writing: A blog post

Warm-up

A Look at the pictures. Make three sentences about each one.

B How are *you* different now?

A Last weekend

1 Vocabulary Weekend activities

A Listen and repeat.

listen to music

play basketball

play in a band

shop for new clothes

stay home

stay out late

visit relatives

watch an old movie

B Pair work Do you do any of the activities in Part A? When do you do them? Tell your partner.

"My friends and I usually play basketball on Saturday mornings."

2 Language in context Carmen's weekend

A Listen to Carmen talk about last weekend. Number the pictures from 1 to 3.

1. Last Saturday morning, my brother Pedro called me. We talked for hours. I uploaded some photos, and I listened to music.
2. I stayed out late on Saturday night. Pedro and I watched an old movie. We laughed a lot. We loved it!
3. On Sunday afternoon, I stayed home. I watched another movie. I didn't like the ending at all. I cried.

B What about you? What do you usually do on weekends?

3 Grammar — Simple past regular verbs

I **listened** to music last Saturday.	I **didn't watch** a movie.	*Spelling*
You **stayed** home.	You **didn't stay** out late.	stay → stay**ed**
He **called** me on Saturday.	He **didn't call** me on Sunday.	love → love**d**
We **laughed**.	We **didn't cry**.	cry → cr**ied**
They **stayed** out late.	They **didn't stay** at home.	shop → shop**ped**

A Write sentences about the things Pedro did and didn't do last weekend.

Things to Do

- ✓ *call Carmen*
- ✗ *listen to music*
- ✓ *watch a movie*
- ✓ *upload photos*
- ✗ *play basketball*
- ✗ *shop for new clothes*

1. *Pedro called Carmen.*
2. ______
3. ______
4. ______
5. ______
6. ______

B Pair work Make true sentences about your weekend with the past forms of the verbs in Part A. Tell your partner.

4 Pronunciation Simple past *-ed* endings

A Listen and repeat. Notice that some verbs have an extra syllable in the simple past tense.

Same syllable (most verbs)		Extra syllable (verbs ending in *t* and *d*)	
call / called		chat / chat·ted	
listen / listened		start / start·ed	
play / played		upload / upload·ed	

B Listen. Complete the chart with the correct verbs.

download / downloaded   shop / shopped   visit / visited
post / posted   stay / stayed   watch / watched

5 Speaking A fun weekend

A Complete the phrases with your own ideas.

chat with ______   exercise ______   study ______   visit ______
cook ______   look for ______   talk to ______   walk to ______

B Pair work Tell your partner about the things you did and didn't do last weekend. Use the phrases from Part A to help you.

A: *I chatted online with my friends last weekend. How about you?*
B: *I didn't chat online with my friends, but I called them.*

6 Keep talking!

Go to page 146 for more practice.

I can say what I did last weekend. ☐

B You're kidding!

1 Interactions — Expressing surprise

A Look at the pictures. What do you think Ted and Valerie are talking about?

B Listen and practice.

Ted: I checked our phone bill this morning.
Valerie: Uh-huh.
Ted: It's usually $59 a month, but this month it's $590.

Valerie: Really? That's not right!
Ted: I know. I didn't pay it. I called the phone company, and they fixed it.
Valerie: Oh, that's good.

C Listen to the expressions. Then practice the conversation again with the new expressions.

Showing that you're listening	*Expressing surprise*
Uh-huh.	Really?
Oh?	What?
Oh, yeah?	You're kidding!

D Check (✓) the best responses. Then practice with a partner.

1. I watched a movie last night. ☑ Uh-huh. ☐ Really?
2. I downloaded 500 songs yesterday. ☐ You're kidding! ☐ Oh?
3. I didn't study for the big test. ☐ Oh, yeah? ☐ What?
4. I played tennis with my friends on Sunday. ☐ You're kidding! ☐ Oh, yeah?

2 Listening What a week!

A Listen to Diana tell her friend about the past week. Number the pictures from 1 to 4.

B Listen again. What surprises Diana's friend? Complete the sentences.

1. Diana didn't ___*answer*___ three ___*questions*___ .
2. Diana's ________ boyfriend ________ her.
3. Julie didn't ________ the ________ .
4. Diana ________ home on ________ .

3 Speaking Really?

A Match the sentences. Then compare with a partner.

1. Last night, I studied for my English test for five hours. _*b*_
2. I just checked my email. ____
3. Last week, I downloaded two movies. ____
4. On Thursday, I started a new class. ____

a. I watched them with my dad.
b. But I didn't get a good score.
c. I'm learning Chinese.
d. I have 100 new messages.

B Pair work Role-play the situations in Part A. Then change roles.

Student A: Say the lines from Part A.
Student B: Show interest or express surprise.

A: *Last night, I studied for my English test for five hours, but I didn't get a good score.*
B: *You're kidding! Why not?*

C Pair work Role-play new situations. Use your own ideas.

I can show that I'm listening.
I can express surprise.

C Did you make dinner last night?

1 Vocabulary Things to do

A Listen and repeat.

do laundry

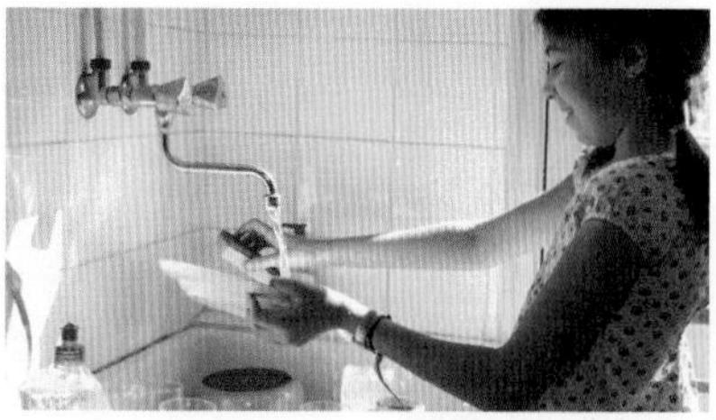

do the dishes

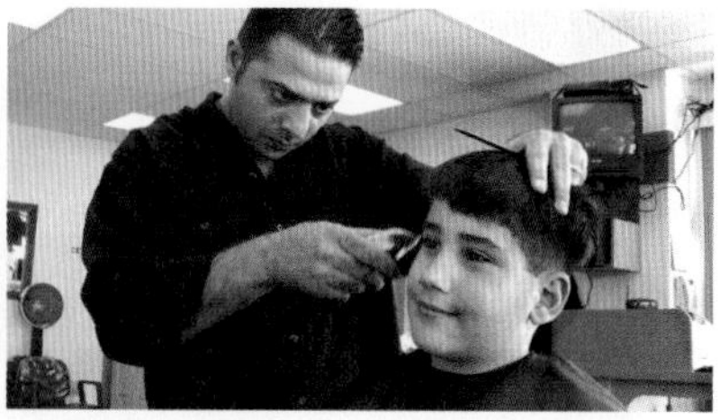

get a haircut

go grocery shopping

have a party

make dinner

see a play

see friends

sleep

B Pair work How often do you do the things in Part A? Tell your partner.

"I do laundry once a week. I do the dishes every day. . . ."

2 Conversation Last night

Listen and practice.

Mindy: Hi, Pete. Did you see Jennifer last night?
Pete: Yes, I did. But the day didn't go so well.
Mindy: Really? What happened?
Pete: Well, I did my laundry yesterday morning, but my favorite white shirt turned pink.
Mindy: You're kidding!
Pete: Then I got a haircut, but I really didn't like it.
Mindy: Oh, yeah? Did you make dinner for Jennifer?
Pete: Well, I slept for a while, so I didn't go grocery shopping.
Mindy: Oh. Did you eat anything?
Pete: Yeah, we did. Jennifer bought a pizza for us.
Mindy: Really?

3 Grammar 🔊 Simple past irregular verbs; yes / no questions

I **saw** Jennifer last night.
She **bought** a pizza.
They **ate** a pizza.

I **didn't see** Jennifer last week.
She **didn't buy** soup.
They **didn't eat** salad.

Did you **see** Jennifer last night?
 Yes, I **did.** No, I **didn't.**
Did she **buy** dinner?
 Yes, she **did.** No, she **didn't.**
Did they **eat** dinner?
 Yes, they **did.** No, they **didn't.**

A Complete the conversation with the simple past tense forms of the verbs. Then practice with a partner.

 A: Hey, Pablo. _Did_ you _do_ (do) today's homework?
 B: No, I _didn't_ . I _____ (not / have) time.
 A: Really? Why not?
 B: I _____ (see) some friends yesterday. We _____ (eat) lunch, and then we _____ (go) to the mall.
 A: Oh, yeah? _____ you _____ (buy) any clothes?
 B: I _____ (not / buy) anything! So, _____ you _____ (do) your homework?
 A: Yes, I did. And no, you can't see it!

🔊 **Common irregular verbs**

buy → **bought**	have → **had**
do → **did**	make → **made**
drink → **drank**	meet → **met**
drive → **drove**	read → **read**
eat → **ate**	see → **saw**
fall → **fell**	sleep → **slept**
get → **got**	take → **took**
go → **went**	write → **wrote**

Go to page 152 for a list of more irregular verbs.

B Put the words in order to make questions. Then compare with a partner.

1. last night / you / see / did / your friends _Did you see your friends last night?_
2. go / last weekend / you / did / grocery shopping _____
3. watch / you / a movie / did / last night _____
4. yesterday / stay home / you / did _____
5. make dinner / did / on Thursday / you _____
6. you / did / last Saturday / have a party _____

C Pair work Ask and answer the questions in Part B. Answer with your own information.

 A: *Did you see your friends last night?*
 B: *Yes, I did. I saw two friends. We ate out at a restaurant.*

4 Speaking Did you?

A Pair work Add two past time expressions to the list. Then ask and answer *Did you . . . ?* questions with each time expression. Take notes.

 A: *Did you make dinner last night?*
 B: *Yes, I did. Did you do laundry last night?*
 A: *No, I didn't.*

Past time expressions	
last night	last week
yesterday	last weekend

B Group work Tell your group about your partner's answers. Did anyone do anything interesting?

5 Keep talking!

Go to page 147 for more practice.

I can talk about routine events in the past. ✓

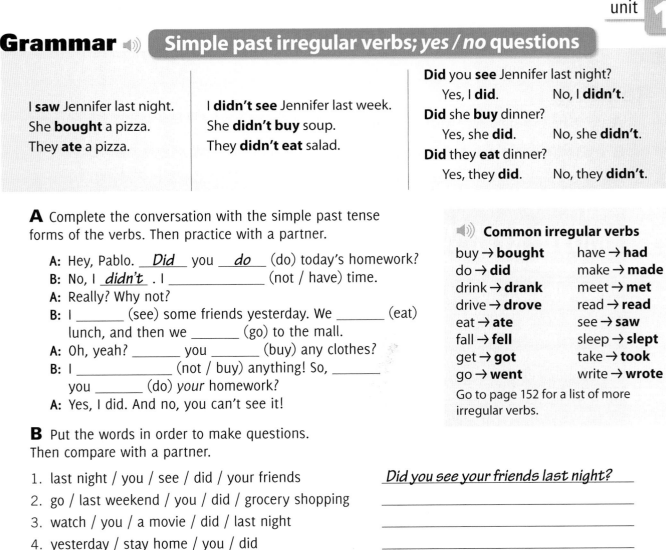

D I saw a great movie.

1 Reading

A Do you ever read blogs? What kinds of blogs do you read?

B Read Matt's blog. Who liked the movie?

MATT'S
MOVIE REVIEWS

Home | Reviews | Contact Me

Too Young to Love

On Friday, my friend Naomi and I hung out together. We had a very good time. We saw a great old movie at the Cineplex. They are showing old movies all month. Did anyone see "Too Young to Love"? I loved it! It's a story about two young people who are in love. Their parents think they are too young, so they can't get married. It's not a sad movie. It's really funny! We laughed a lot. Monday, 11:00 a.m.

cgirl: I saw "Too Young to Love." I also saw the play. Both are good. See the movie and the play!
Monday, 11:26 a.m.

Oscar: "Too Young to Love"?! You're kidding! I hated the movie, but I liked the music. The sound track had some really good old songs.
Monday, 1:00 p.m.

Tomas: My friend and I saw it. She laughed. I cried because I paid for the tickets, and I didn't like it at all.
Tuesday, 7:00 a.m.

Joe C: I liked "Too Young to Love." I saw three old movies at the Cineplex last month, and I really liked all of them.
Tuesday, 12:45 p.m.

Maria: What?! "Too Young to Love"?! I hated the movie, but I loved the book.
Tuesday, 1:15 p.m.

C Read the blog again. Correct the false sentences.

1. Matt saw the movie on ~~Saturday~~. *Matt saw the movie on Friday.*
2. Oscar hated the music. ______
3. Tomas liked *Too Young to Love*. ______
4. Joe C didn't see any movies at the Cineplex last month. ______
5. Maria hated the book *Too Young to Love*. ______

D Pair work Do you or your friends ever post your everyday activities on a blog? What do you post? Tell your partner.

"My friend Rosa has a blog. She posts news about her neighborhood once a week."

2 Writing A blog post

A Choose one day last week. Complete the chart with information about the things you did that day.

Day	Activities	Places	Other information

B Write a blog post about that day. Use the model and your answers in Part A to help you.

C Pair work Share your post. Ask and answer questions for more information.

"Did you have a good time? Did you eat out?"

Friday
After class, I met my friend Terry. We went shopping at the mall. I bought a new watch. I didn't pay much for it, but I really like it. I went home at 8:00 p.m.

3 Listening A busy week

A Listen to Matt talk about last week. What activities did he do? Check (✓) the correct answers.

- ☐ did laundry
- ☑ got up early
- ☐ got up late
- ☐ made dinner
- ☐ played soccer
- ☐ played the guitar
- ☐ read books
- ☐ stayed out late
- ☐ worked

B Listen again. What activities did Matt enjoy? Circle the activities above.

4 Speaking I played in a band last year.

A Class activity Add two past activities to the chart. Then find classmates who did each thing. Write their names, and ask questions for more information.

Find someone who . . .	Name	Extra information
bought a cell phone last year		
got a haircut last week		
saw a friend yesterday		
made dinner last night		
watched a game on TV last weekend		
wrote a blog post yesterday		

A: *Did you buy a cell phone last year, Alex?*
B: *Yes, I did.*

B Share your information.

"Alex bought a cell phone last year."

I can talk about past activities.

Wrap-up

1 Quick pair review

Lesson A Find out! What are three things both you and your partner did after class yesterday? What are three things you didn't do? You have two minutes.

A: *I walked home after class yesterday. Did you?*
B: *Yes, I did. I watched TV at home. Did you?*
A: *No, I didn't. I listened to music.*

Lesson B Do you remember? Circle the correct answers. You have two minutes.

1. **A:** I listened to all of Taylor Swift's songs today.
   B: **Oh? / You're kidding!** *All* of them? She has a lot!
2. **A:** Janet uploaded photos from the party.
   B: **Uh-huh. / Really?** I know. I looked at them this morning.
3. **A:** Charlie's band played at The Red Room downtown on Saturday night!
   B: **What? / Oh?** No way! That's so cool! I didn't know that.
4. **A:** I visited my grandmother last weekend.
   B: **You're kidding! / Oh, yeah?** How is she doing?

Lesson C Test your partner! Say eight irregular verbs in the simple present. Can your partner write the simple past forms of the verbs correctly? Check his or her answers. You have two minutes.

1. ____________ 3. ____________ 5. ____________ 7. ____________
2. ____________ 4. ____________ 6. ____________ 8. ____________

Lesson D Guess! Make two true sentences and one false sentence about your activities last week. Can your partner guess the false sentence? Take turns. You have two minutes.

A: *I watched 20 movies last week. I played basketball in the park. I saw a play.*
B: *You didn't watch 20 movies.*
A: *You're right. I only watched 12.*

2 In the real world

Did anyone else do the same things as you yesterday? Go online and find three English-speaking bloggers who did the same activities as you yesterday. Then write about them.

- What activities did both you and the bloggers do yesterday?
- What are the bloggers' names?
- Where are they from?

Bloggers and Me

I played basketball yesterday. Three bloggers also played basketball yesterday. Diego is from California. He played basketball with his brother.

Getting away

LESSON A	LESSON B	LESSON C	LESSON D
• Adjectives • Past of *be*	• Reacting to good news • Reacting to bad news	• Vacation activities • Simple past *Wh-* questions	• Reading: "Travel Tales" • Writing: A postcard

Warm-up

A Do you know any of these places? Which ones?

B What are some popular places to visit in your country? in your city?

A Where were you?

1 Vocabulary Adjectives

A Listen and repeat.

exciting / fun / great

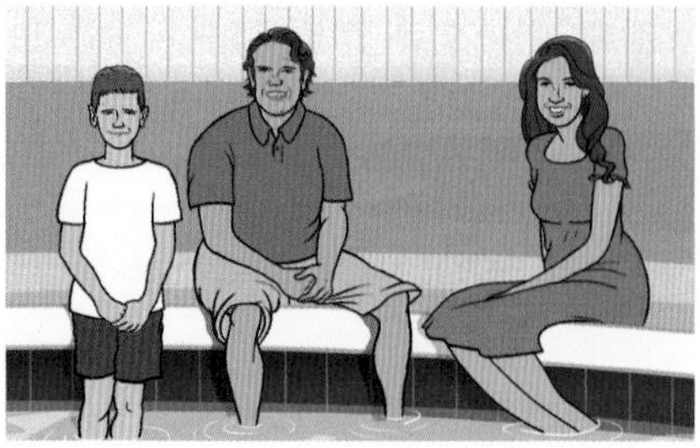
all right / OK / so-so

awful / terrible

boring

interesting

noisy

quiet

B **Pair work** Think of things that each adjective describes. Discuss your ideas.

A: *Sports are exciting.*
B: *Basketball is exciting, but I think soccer is boring.*

2 Language in context Quick getaways

A Listen to four people talk about recent trips. Number the pictures from 1 to 4.

1. We went on a school trip last week. We went to a theater and saw an exciting play. The actors were great.

   – Olivia

2. We just had a three-day weekend. I went away with my family. It was a fun trip, but our hotel wasn't very nice. In fact, it was terrible.

   – Ichiro

3. I was at my brother's apartment last weekend. He doesn't have a TV or a computer. It was quiet and kind of boring.

   – Brian

4. My friend and I went on a day trip last week. We took a local bus to an old town. The bus was awful and noisy, but the trip was interesting. Look what I bought!

   – Eleanor

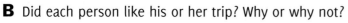

B Did each person like his or her trip? Why or why not?

3 **Grammar** 🔊 | Past of *be*

Where were you last weekend?	**Was** your trip interesting?	
I **was** at my brother's apartment.	Yes, it **was**.	No, it **wasn't**.
How was your weekend?	**Were** the people nice?	
It **was** quiet and kind of boring.	Yes, they **were**.	No, they **weren't**.

I / he / she / it	*you / we / they*	*Contractions*	
was	**were**	wasn't = was not	weren't = were not

A Complete the guest comment card with *was, were, wasn't,* or *weren't*. Then compare with a partner.

> ❧ *Guest comments* ❧
>
> My wife, son, and I _____**were**_____ guests at your hotel last week. Unfortunately, we _____ happy with our room. The room _____ clean, and the beds _____ awful. And the room _____ near the street. The noise _____ terrible in the early morning. But the people at the hotel _____ great, so that _____ good!

B Read the answers. Write the questions. Then practice with a partner.

1. *How was your weekend?* It was great.
2. _____ Yes, my weekend was interesting.
3. _____ I was on a trip.
4. _____ No, I wasn't at the theater on Friday.
5. _____ Yes, I was at home on Sunday afternoon.
6. _____ My parents were in Tahiti.

C Pair work Ask and answer the questions in Part B. Answer with your own information.

4 **Speaking** Where were you last Friday night?

A Pair work Interview your partner. Take notes.

Where were you . . . ?	Location	Extra information
at this time yesterday		
on your birthday		
on New Year's Eve		
last Friday night		

B Group work Tell your group about your partner's answers. Who was in an interesting place? Who did interesting things?

5 **Keep talking!**

Go to page **148** for more practice.

> *I can describe where I was in the past.* ☑

B That's great!

1 Good news, bad news

A Listen and repeat.

I got a promotion. I lost my wallet. I missed my flight. I was sick. I won a contest.

B Pair work Which things are good news? Which are bad news? Can you think of other examples? Discuss your ideas.

2 Interactions Reacting to news

A Listen and practice.

Meg: Did you have a good weekend?
Joe: Yes! I won a trip in a contest, so I went away last weekend.
Meg: Really? That's great!

Joe: And how was your weekend?
Meg: It wasn't so good. I lost my wallet.
Joe: Oh, no! What happened?

B Listen to the expressions. Then practice the conversation again with the new expressions.

Reacting to good news

That's great!
That's excellent!
That's awesome!

Reacting to bad news

Oh, no!
That's too bad.
That's terrible!

C Pair work Practice the conversation again with the examples from Exercise 1. React to the news.

A: *Did you have a good weekend?*
B: *Yes! I got a promotion, so I went shopping.*

3 Listening A short trip

A Listen to Sam tell a friend about a short trip. Number the pictures from 1 to 6.

☐

☐

1

☐

☐

☐

B Listen again. Was Sam's trip great, good, bad, or awful?

4 Speaking That's . . . !

A Write three good things and three bad things that happened to you last week.

	Good things that happened	Bad things that happened
1.		
2.		
3.		

B **Class activity** Ask your classmates about their week. React to the news.

A: *Did you do anything interesting last week?*
B: *Well, I started a new job.*
A: *That's excellent!*
B: *Yeah. But I lost my cell phone.*
A: *That's terrible!*

I can react to news. ☐

C My vacation

1 Vocabulary Vacation activities

A Listen and repeat.

buy souvenirs

go sightseeing

go to a festival

go to the beach

relax

shop in markets

take a tour

take pictures

B Pair work Did you do any of the activities in Part A on your last vacation? Tell your partner.

"On my last vacation, I bought souvenirs and took pictures. I didn't go to the beach."

2 Conversation Back from vacation

Listen and practice.

Dave: How was your vacation, Kate?
Kate: Oh, it was exciting. We had a great time.
Dave: Where did you go?
Kate: I went to Veracruz, Mexico.
Dave: That's great. Who did you travel with?
Kate: My sister.
Dave: When did you get back?
Kate: Last night. I got home at midnight.
Dave: Really? That's late! So, what did you do there?
Kate: Well, we went to a festival called *Carnaval*. We also shopped in local markets and took lots of pictures. Look, I bought you a souvenir.
Dave: Thanks! I love it!

3 Grammar ◄)) | Simple past *Wh-* questions

Where did you **go** on vacation?	**What did** you **do** there?
I went to Veracruz, Mexico.	We went to a festival and shopped.
When did you **get** back?	**Why did** you **go** to Veracruz?
Last night.	Because the festival is famous.
Who did you **travel** with?	**How did** you **get** to Veracruz?
My sister.	By plane.

Match the questions and the answers. Then practice with a partner.

1. Where did you go on vacation? __*f*__ a. We got back last week.
2. Who did you go with? _____ b. We took the bus and the train.
3. When did you get back? _____ c. We relaxed and took pictures.
4. What did you do on vacation? _____ d. Because I have friends there.
5. Why did you go to Vietnam? _____ e. I went with my brother.
6. How did you travel in Vietnam? _____ f. I went to Vietnam.

4 Pronunciation Reduction of *did you*

A ◄)) Listen and repeat. Notice how *did you* is pronounced /dɪdʒə/ after *Wh-* question words.

Where **did you** go? What **did you** do? When **did you** get back?

B Pair work Practice the questions in the grammar chart. Reduce *did you* to /dɪdʒə/ after *Wh-* question words.

5 Speaking What a vacation!

A Answer the questions.

- Where did you go on your last vacation? _____
- Who did you go with? _____
- When did you go? _____
- What did you do there? _____
- How did you travel? _____
- Did you buy anything? _____
- What did you like about the vacation? _____
- What didn't you like about the vacation? _____

B Group work Tell your group about your last vacation. Ask and answer questions for more information.

fly → flew

6 Keep talking!
Go to page 149 for more practice.

take a boat → took a boat

I can talk about my last vacation. ☑

D Travel experiences

1 Reading

A How often do you go on vacation? Where do you go?

B Read the travel blog posts. What country is each person visiting?

travel tales

I'm here in Chiang Mai, Thailand. Yesterday, I went on a short elephant ride. There was a man on the elephant in front of me. His name was Alan Johnson. My name is Alan Johnson, too! ______

Alan Johnson Posted on October 12,10:30 a.m.

My sister and I are in Paris, France. It's our first trip overseas. We went to an outdoor café the other day, and Johnny Depp was at the next table. How exciting! ______

Mary O'Connor Posted on October 14, 6:48 p.m.

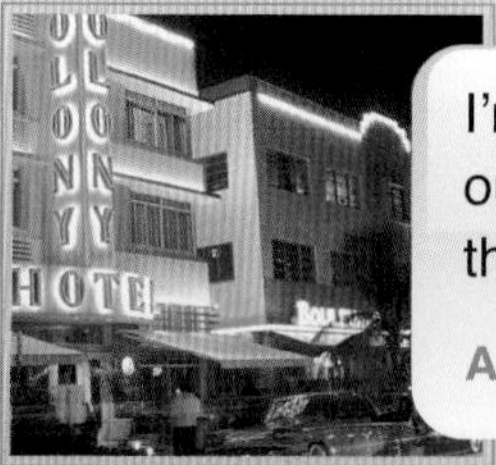

I'm here with my parents at a hotel in Miami, Florida. We came to visit our relatives. We all went to bed last night at about midnight. At 3:00 in the morning, we heard a fire alarm. ______

Anita Gonzalez Posted on October 15, 8:06 a.m.

I'm in Granada, Nicaragua. I came here to help build houses. It's a great country. We finished our first house yesterday. We're not staying in a hotel. We're staying in a school. __1__

Diane Nicholson Posted on October 21, 9:12 p.m.

C Read the blog posts again. What is the last sentence of each post? Number the posts from 1 to 4.

1. Last night, we all slept in one big room!
2. He was nice to us, and I have a cool photo now.
3. I can't believe that we have the same name!
4. We ran down to the street and were fine.

D Pair work What adjectives describe each travel experience? Discuss your ideas.

A: *I think Alan Johnson's trip was very exciting!*
B: *Me, too. I love elephants, and Thailand is an interesting country.*

2 Listening Three different trips

A Listen to three people talk about their vacations. How do they describe them? Check (✓) the correct answers.

	How were their vacations?		What was one thing they liked?
1.	☐ awful ☐ boring	☑ great ☐ so-so	*shopping*
2.	☐ fun ☐ interesting	☐ OK ☐ terrible	
3.	☐ awful ☐ boring	☐ exciting ☐ great	

B Listen again. What did they like about their trips? Write one thing for each person in the chart.

3 Writing and speaking A postcard

A Read Sofia's postcard to Jack about her vacation.

Dear Jack,

Linda and I are having a great time here in Morocco. We took a train from Casablanca to Marrakech yesterday. Last night, we went to a big "souk," or market. We walked around the market for hours! I bought a nice souvenir for you!

See you soon!
Sofia

B Write a postcard to a friend or family member about an experience you had on vacation. Use the model in Part A to help you.

C Class activity Post your postcards around the room. Read your classmates' postcards. Then write questions about five postcards that interest you.

1. Eddie – What did you buy for your sister?

2. Jung-woo – Who did you travel with?

3. Marcus – When did you take this vacation?

D Class activity Find the classmates who wrote the five postcards. Ask them your questions.

A: *Eddie, what did you buy your sister?*
B: *I bought a scarf.*
A: *I see, thanks. Excuse me, Jung-woo, who did you travel with?*

I can describe a vacation. ☐

Wrap-up

1 Quick pair review

Lesson A Brainstorm! Make a list of adjectives. How many do you know? You have one minute.

Lesson B Do you remember? Check (✓) the correct answers. You have one minute.

1. I won a free ticket to Jamaica.	☑ That's great!	☐ Oh, no!
2. I lost my cell phone.	☐ That's terrible!	☐ That's excellent!
3. My sister missed her flight.	☐ That's awesome.	☐ That's too bad.
4. Charlie met Leonardo DiCaprio.	☐ Oh, no!	☐ That's great!

Lesson C Find out! What are two things both you and your partner did on your last vacation? You have two minutes.

A: *Did you go sightseeing on your last vacation?*
B: *Yes, I did. How about you?*
A: *Yes, I went sightseeing, too.*

Lesson D Test your partner! Describe a vacation. Can your partner draw a postcard of your vacation? Check his or her drawing. You have two minutes.

"Last year, my sister and I went to Madrid, Spain. We shopped in El Rastro Market and went to art museums."

2 In the real world

Do you ever read travel blogs? Go online and find a travel blog in English. Then write about it.

- Where did the blogger go?
- When did he or she go there?
- What did he or she do there?

Kelly's Travel Blog

Kelly is a blogger from Canada. Last week, she went on vacation to Scotland. She went sightseeing in Glasgow. She went to . . .

Time to celebrate

LESSON A
- Months and dates
- *Be going to*; *yes / no* questions

LESSON B
- Declining an invitation
- Accepting an invitation

LESSON C
- Party checklist
- *Wh-* questions with *be going to*; object pronouns

LESSON D
- Reading: "Birthday Traditions"
- Writing: A thank-you note

Warm-up

graduation

____

____

____

A Label the pictures with the correct words.

birthday	✓graduation	holiday	wedding

B What special events do you celebrate?

A I'm going to get married.

1 Vocabulary Months and dates

A Listen and repeat.

January	February	March	April	May	June
July	August	September	October	November	December

1st	first	**9th**	ninth	**17th**	seventeenth	**25th**	twenty-fifth
2nd	second	**10th**	tenth	**18th**	eighteenth	**26th**	twenty-sixth
3rd	third	**11th**	eleventh	**19th**	nineteenth	**27th**	twenty-seventh
4th	fourth	**12th**	twelfth	**20th**	twentieth	**28th**	twenty-eighth
5th	fifth	**13th**	thirteenth	**21st**	twenty-first	**29th**	twenty-ninth
6th	sixth	**14th**	fourteenth	**22nd**	twenty-second	**30th**	thirtieth
7th	seventh	**15th**	fifteenth	**23rd**	twenty-third	**31st**	thirty-first
8th	eighth	**16th**	sixteenth	**24th**	twenty-fourth		

B Class activity When is your birthday? Stand in the order of your birthdays, from the first to the last in the year.

A: *My birthday is July twenty-eighth.*
B: *Mine is July twentieth. You're next to me.*

2 Language in context Special days

A Listen to three people talk about special days. What are the dates of the special days?

I'm going to graduate from high school on June 8th. I'm going to start college in September.

– Sarah

My eightieth birthday is on August 21st. I'm going to go skydiving for the first time. I can't wait!

– Walter

My boyfriend, Kenta, and I are going to get married on October 16th. We're going to have a big wedding.

– Mari

B What about you? What days of the year are special to you? Why?

3 Grammar Be going to; yes / no questions

I'**m going to graduate** on June 8th. I'**m not going to start** college in July.	**Are** you **going to start** college? Yes, I am. No, I'm not.
Walter'**s going to go** skydiving. He'**s not going to play** basketball.	**Is** Walter **going to go** skydiving? Yes, he is. No, he isn't.
Mari and Kenta **are going to get** married. They'**re not going to have** a small wedding.	**Are** they **going to have** a big wedding? Yes, they are. No, they aren't.

A Complete the conversation with the correct forms of *be going to*. Then practice with a partner.

A: *Are* you *going to graduate* (graduate) from college this year?
B: Yeah, on May 30th. My parents ________ (have) a big party for me.
A: Great! ______ the party ________ (be) at their house?
B: No, it ________ (not / be) at the house. They ________ (have) it at a restaurant.
A: ______ you ________ (get) a job right away?
B: No, I'm not. First, I ________ (travel). Then I ________ (look) for a job.

B Pair work Ask and answer three *Are you going to . . . ?* questions. Answer with your own information.

4 Pronunciation Reduction of *going to* before verbs

A Listen and repeat. Notice how *going to* is reduced to /gənə/ in informal spoken English.

Are you **going to** do anything special? Yes. I'm **going to** go skydiving.

B Pair work Practice the sentences in the grammar chart. Reduce *going to* to /gənə/.

5 Speaking Three special days

A Write the dates and your plans for three special days or holidays next year.

	Special day: ________	Special day: ________	Special day: ________
Dates			
Plans			

B Pair work Tell your partner about your special days. Ask and answer questions for more information.

6 Keep talking!

Go to page 150 for more practice.

I can talk about my plans for specific dates.

B Sure. I'd love to.

1 Interactions Invitations

A How often do you go to the movies with your friends?

B Listen and practice.

Bill: Hello?
Brandon: Hey, Bill. It's Brandon. Listen, do you want to see a movie tonight?
Bill: Tonight? I'm sorry. I can't.
Brandon: Oh, OK. Well, maybe some other time.

Melissa: Hello?
Brandon: Hi, Melissa. This is Brandon. Do you want to see a movie tonight?
Melissa: A movie? Sure. I'd love to.
Brandon: Great.

C Listen to the expressions. Then practice the conversation again with the new expressions.

Declining an invitation

I'm sorry. I can't.
I'm afraid I can't.
I'm really sorry, but I can't.

Accepting an invitation

Sure. I'd love to.
Sounds good.
Yeah. That sounds great.

D Pair work Practice the conversations again with the activities below.

get some ice cream	hang out	play video games	watch a DVD

A: *Hello?*
B: *Hey, Bill. It's Brandon. Listen, do you want to get some ice cream tonight?*

2 Listening I'd love to, but . . .

A Listen to four people invite their friends to do things tonight. Number the pictures from 1 to 4.

B Listen again. Do the friends accept or decline the invitations? Check (✓) the correct answers.

1. ☑ accept ☐ decline
2. ☐ accept ☐ decline
3. ☐ accept ☐ decline
4. ☐ accept ☐ decline

3 Speaking Do you want to hang out?

Class activity "Call" your classmates and invite them to do something with you right now. Your classmates accept the invitations or decline them with excuses. Use the ideas below or your own ideas.

Possible things to do	Possible excuses	Responses to excuses
go out for coffee	I'm cooking dinner.	Oh, that's OK.
go to a party	I'm not feeling well.	Maybe next time.
see a movie	I'm eating lunch.	I'm sorry you can't make it.
go to the mall	I'm studying for an exam.	OK, I understand.
hang out	I'm doing my homework.	That's all right.
go shopping	I'm working late tonight.	No problem.

A: *Hello?*
B: *Hi, it's me. Do you want to go to the mall?*
A: *I'm really sorry, but I can't. I'm not feeling well.*
B: *OK, I understand. Maybe next time.*

I can accept or decline an invitation.

C Planning a party

1 Vocabulary Party checklist

A Match the things on the checklist and the pictures. Then listen and check your answers.

THINGS TO DO

1. [g] *bake a cake*
2. [ ] *buy a gift*
3. [ ] *choose the music*
4. [ ] *decorate the room*
5. [ ] *make a guest list*
6. [ ] *plan the menu*
7. [ ] *prepare the food*
8. [ ] *send invitations*

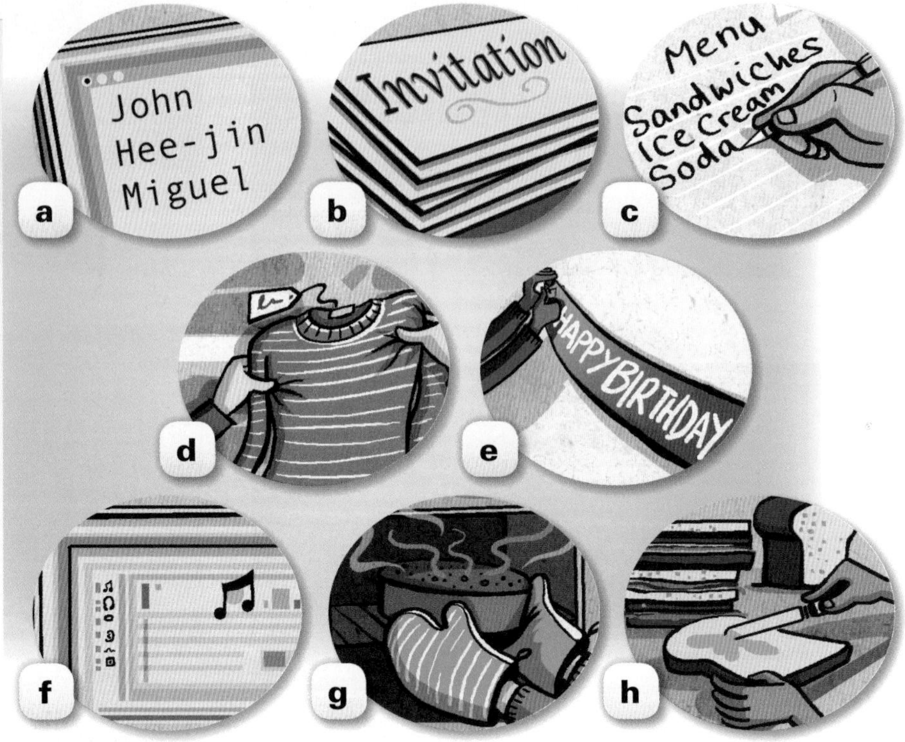

B Pair work When is a good time to do each thing in Part A? Discuss your ideas.

2 weeks before the party	2–3 days before the party	the morning of the party
1 week before the party	the day before the party	1 hour before the party

"A good time to make a guest list is two weeks before the party."

2 Conversation I can bake!

Listen and practice.

Andrea: We have a lot of things to do for Eric's birthday party. Look, I made a checklist.
Mark: Good idea. Who's going to help us?
Andrea: Rosario. She's going to send the invitations.
Mark: How is she going to send them?
Andrea: By email.
Mark: Good. That's easy. What are we going to buy for Eric?
Andrea: Let's get him a sweater.
Mark: Great. Who's going to bake the cake?
Andrea: I'm going to bake it.
Mark: Um, do you think that's a good idea?
Andrea: Hey, I can bake!
Mark: OK.

3 **Grammar** 🔊 | *Wh-* questions with *be going to*; object pronouns

What are we going to buy **Eric**?	Let's get **him** a sweater.
Who's going to bake **the cake**?	Andrea's going to bake **it**.
How is she going to send **the invitations**?	She's going to send **them** by email.

Subject	I	you	he	she	it	we	they
Object	me	you	him	her	it	us	them

A Complete the conversation with the correct forms of *be going to*. Then practice with a partner.

A: What time ___*are*___ you ___*going to go*___ (go) to Eric's birthday party?
B: I _____ (go) to the party at 6:45.
A: How _____ you _____ (get) there?
B: My friend Jason _____ (drive). Do you want a ride?
A: Um, sure, thanks! What _____ you _____ (do) after the party?
B: Jason and I _____ (go) out. I think we _____ (see) a movie.

B Rewrite the sentences. Use object pronouns. Then compare with a partner.

1. He's not going to invite Mary. *He's not going to invite her.* _____
2. Let's call Bill and Ami again. _____
3. I'm going to see Eric tomorrow. _____
4. He's going to help Debbie and me. _____
5. We're going to buy the present tomorrow. _____
6. Call Rosario at 5:00. _____

C Class activity Ask your classmates what they're going to do tonight. Answer with your own information.

4 **Speaking** Let's decide together.

A Pair work Discuss the situations.

Your classmate Masao is in the hospital. He has nothing to do. What are you going to bring him?	You're planning your friend's birthday party. Where is it going to be? What are you going to eat and drink?	You want music for your teacher's birthday party. What songs are you going to play? How are you going to listen to them?

A: *What are we going to bring to Masao?*
B: *Let's bring him a new video game.*
A: *That's a great idea. How about . . . ?*

B Group work Share your ideas with another pair. Ask and answer questions for more information.

5 **Keep talking!**

Go to page 151 for more practice.

I can discuss and agree on plans. ✓

D Birthdays

1 Reading

A What was the last party you went to? What did you do at the party?

B Read the article. Which birthdays are special in each country?

Birthday Traditions
around the world

Nigeria

In Nigeria, the first, fifth, tenth, and fifteenth birthdays are very special. To celebrate these birthdays, people have big parties and invite up to 100 people. They eat "jollof rice." This is rice with tomatoes, red peppers, onions, and cassava, a kind of potato.

Japan

The third, fifth, and seventh birthdays are very important in Japan. Every year on November 15th, children of these ages celebrate the *Shichi-go-san* (Seven-five-three) Festival. They usually wear traditional clothes and eat "thousand-year candy" for a long life.

Ecuador

In Ecuador, a family has a big party when a girl turns 15 years old. The birthday girl wears a dress, and her father puts her first pair of high-heeled shoes on her. Then he dances with her. Fourteen other girls dance with fourteen other boys at the same time.

South Korea

Parents in South Korea sometimes try to guess a child's future on his or her first birthday. They put the child in front of some objects, such as a book and a coin. They wait to see which object the child takes. For example, a book means the child is going to be a teacher. A coin means the child is going to have a lot of money.

C Read the article again. Answer the questions.

1. On special birthdays, what do Nigerian children eat? *They eat "jollof rice."*
2. Who celebrates *Shichi-go-san?* ______
3 Who dances with a 15-year-old Ecuadorian girl at her birthday party? ______
4. How do South Korean parents guess a child's future? ______

D Pair work How did you celebrate your last birthday? Tell your partner.

"I celebrated my last birthday with my friends. We ate out at a nice restaurant."

2 Listening Sweet 16

A Listen to Amanda, a 16-year-old American girl, describe her "Sweet 16" birthday party. Check (✓) the true sentences.

1. ☑ Amanda's birthday is July 14th.
2. ☐ ~~Her parents~~ She made a guest list.
3. ☐ She sent the invitations.
4. ☐ She and her father decorated the room.
5. ☐ She had pizza, ice cream, and cake.
6. ☐ Forty of her friends came.
7. ☐ She got a gift from her parents.
8. ☐ She's going to have a party on her 18th birthday.

B Listen again. Correct the false sentences.

3 Writing A thank-you note

A Think of a birthday gift (or any gift) you received. Answer the questions.

- What is the gift? ______________________
- Who is it from? ______________________
- Why did you get it? ______________________
- What do you like about it? ______________________

Dear Liz,

Thanks a lot for the birthday gift. I love the sweater. Blue and green are my favorite colors. Thank you for coming to my party!

Thanks again,
Sun-hee

B Write a thank-you note for the gift. Use the model and your answers in Part A to help you.

C Group work Share your thank-you notes. Did any of you write about similar gifts?

4 Speaking How we celebrate

A Group work Discuss the ways people celebrate birthdays in your culture. Use the questions below and your own ideas.

- Which birthdays are very special?
- Do people celebrate with family, friends, or both?
- What do people eat and drink?
- What do people do?
- Do they give gifts? What kinds of gifts?
- How do you usually celebrate birthdays?

B Group work Tell your group how you are going to celebrate your next birthday. Are you going to do any of the things you discussed in Part A?

a birthday party in Mexico

I can describe birthday traditions in my culture. ☐

Wrap-up

1 Quick pair review

Lesson A Guess! Say three dates when you are going to do something special. Can your partner guess what you are going to do? Take turns. You have three minutes.

A: *I'm going to do something special on June 17th.*
B: *Are you going to graduate?*
A: *Yes, I am!*

Lesson B Do you remember? Read the sentences. Write A (accepting an invitation), D (declining an invitation), or E (making an excuse). You have one minute.

1. I'd love to. ____
2. I'm studying for an exam. ____
3. That sounds great. ____
4. I'm really sorry, but I can't. ____
5. I'm working late tonight. ____
6. I'm afraid I can't. ____

Lesson C Brainstorm! Make a list of things you do to plan a party. How many do you know? You have two minutes.

Lesson D Find out! What are three activities both you and your partner do on your birthdays? You have two minutes.

A: *I eat cake on my birthday. Do you?*
B: *Yes, I eat cake, too.*

2 In the real world

When is your birthday? Go online and find information in English about two important events that happened that day. Then write about them.

- Where did the events happen?
- Who participated in the events?
- Why were the events important?

My Birthday

My birthday is December 17th. On this day in 1903, the Wright brothers flew an airplane for 12 seconds. This was important because . . .

Name circle

A Group work Stand in a circle. Go around the circle and say your first names. Repeat your classmates' names before you say your own name.

My name is Eduardo.
His name is Eduardo. My name is Ming-mei.
His name is Eduardo. Her name is Ming-mei. My name is Adam.
His name is Eduardo. Her name is Ming-mei. His name is Adam. My name . . .

B Group work Go around the circle again. Repeat your classmates' full names.

A: *My name is Eduardo Sanchez.*
B: *His name is Eduardo Sanchez. My name is Ming-mei Lee.*
C: *His name is Eduardo Sanchez. Her name is Ming-mei Lee. My name . . .*

Entertainment awards

Student A

Pair work You and your partner have pictures of the same people, but some of the jobs and cities are different. Ask questions to find the differences. Circle them.

A: *Is Antonio Loren a model in your picture?*
B: *Yes, he is.*
A: *OK. That's the same. Is he from Rome?*
B: *No, he's from Milan. That's different.*

Around the world

A Create a "new" identity. Write your new name and the country and city you are from.

Name:
Country:
City:

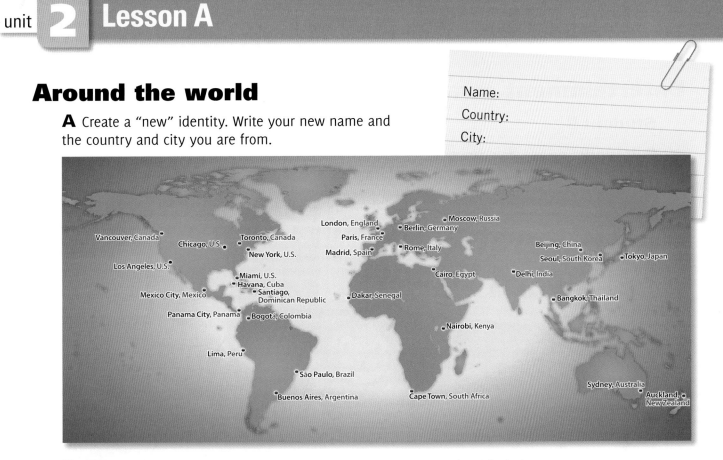

B Group work Interview four classmates. Complete the cards with their "new" identities.

Name:
Country:
City:

Name:
Country:
City:

Name:
Country:
City:

Name:
Country:
City:

A: *Hi. What's your name?*
B: *Hi. My name is Sophie Manet.*
A: *Where are you from, Sophie?*
B: *I'm from France.*
A: *Oh, you're French. What city are you from?*
B: *I'm from Paris.*

Entertainment awards

Student B

Pair work You and your partner have pictures of the same people, but some of the jobs and cities are different. Ask questions to find the differences. Circle them.

A: *Is Antonio Loren a model in your picture?*
B: *Yes, he is.*
A: *OK. That's the same. Is he from Rome?*
B: *No, he's from Milan. That's different.*

Family tree

A Draw your family tree. Include your family members, their names, and their ages.

My Family Tree

B Pair work Tell your partner about your family tree, but don't show it! Your partner draws it on another sheet of paper. Take turns.

A: *My grandfather is George. He's 72 years old. My grandmother is Anna.*
B: *How do you spell "Anna"?*
A: *A-N-N-A.*
B: *OK, thanks.*
A: *She's 68. Their kids are . . .*

C Pair work Compare your drawing with your partner's family tree. Are they the same?

Cleaning the closet

Pair work Look at Dean and Lucy's closet. What things are in their closet?

A: *What's that?*
B: *It's a dictionary. What's that?*
A: *It's a cell phone. Hey, what are these?*

What color?

Student A

A Pair work You and your partner have pictures of the same people, but some of their clothes are different colors. Describe the clothing to find the differences. Circle them.

A: *In my picture, Alice's coat is blue and white.*
B: *That's the same in mine. And her pants are gray.*
A: *In my picture, her pants are green. That's different.*

B Pair work Cover the picture. What is the same? Answer with the information you remember.

A: *Alice's coat is blue and white.*
B: *Yes. And Ben's pants are . . .*

What color?

Student B

A Pair work You and your partner have pictures of the same people, but some of their clothes are different colors. Describe the clothing to find the differences. Circle them.

A: *In my picture, Alice's coat is blue and white.*
B: *That's the same in mine. And her pants are gray.*
A: *In my picture, her pants are green. That's different.*

B Pair work Cover the picture. What is the same? Answer with the information you remember.

A: *Alice's coat is blue and white.*
B: *Yes. And Ben's pants are . . .*

Car, train, bus, or bicycle?

A Look at the ways people get to work in Los Angeles.

How people in Los Angeles get to work

65%	drive alone
15%	drive with others
10%	take the bus
4%	walk
1%	ride a bicycle
5%	other

Source: www.fhwa.dot.gov/ctpp/jtw/jtw4.htm

Note: % = percent

B Pair work Guess the ways people get to work in New York City. Complete the chart with the numbers. Then check your answers on the bottom of page 134.

1%	6%	6%	8%	8%	14%	25%	32%

How people in New York City get to work

______ %	drive alone
______ %	drive with others
______ %	take the bus
______ %	walk
______ %	take the subway
______ %	take the train
______ %	take a taxi
______ %	other

Source: www.fhwa.dot.gov/ctpp/jtw/jtw4.htm

C Group work Guess the ways people get to work where *you* live. Rank them from 1 to 8.

______ drive alone ______ ride a bicycle ______ take the bus ______ walk
______ drive with others ______ take a taxi ______ take the train or subway ______ other

A: *I think number 1 is "take the train or subway."*
B: *I agree. I think number 2 is "drive alone."*

Routines

A Class activity Find classmates who do each thing. Write their names.

Find someone who . . .	Name	Find someone who . . .	Name
gets up before 6:00		sleeps a lot on weekends	
studies in the morning		walks to class	
takes a shower at night		has a red cell phone	
has coffee at home		studies on the bus	
reads every day		takes a bath in the morning	
goes to bed early		drives a sports car	
watches TV after midnight		doesn't have a dictionary	

take a shower

take a bath

drive a sports car

A: *Do you get up before 6:00, Donna?*
B: *No, I don't. I get up at 6:30.*
A: *How about you, Michael? Do you get up before 6:00?*
C: *Yes, I do.*

B Share your information.

A: *Michael gets up before 6:00.*
B: *And Angela gets up before 6:00. David studies in the morning.*

Answers to Keep talking! Unit 4 Lesson A, Part B (page 133): 25% drive alone, 6% drive with others, 14% take the bus, 8% walk, 32% take the subway, 8% take the train, 1% take a taxi, 6% other

On the computer

A Add two more questions about online activities to the chart.

Do you ever . . . ?	Name: ______________
read people's blogs	
buy books online	
use online dictionaries	
search the Internet in English	
check the weather online	
get directions online	
check movie times online	

check the weather

get directions

check movie times

B Pair work Interview your partner. Complete the chart with his or her answers. Use adverbs of frequency.

A: *Naoko, do you ever read people's blogs?*
B: *Oh, yes. I often do. Do you?*
A: *I hardly ever do.*
B: *Do you ever . . . ?*

C Pair work Tell another classmate about your partner's answers.

A: *Naoko often reads people's blogs.*
B: *Sasha never does.*

Follow-up questions

A Add two follow-up questions about each topic to the charts.

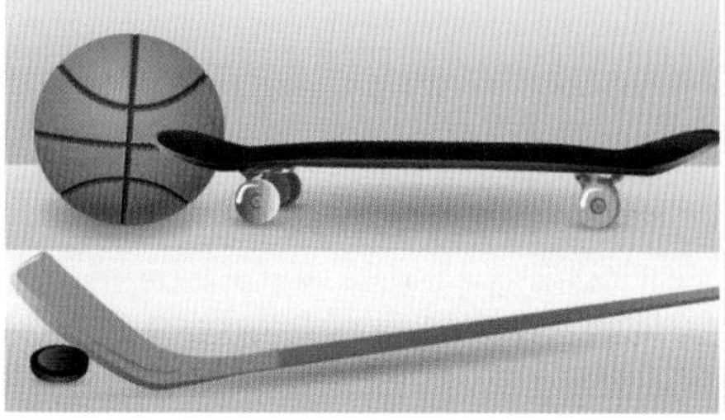

Sports and games	Questions	Name: ________
	Do you ever play sports?	
	What do you play?	
	Who do you play with?	

Shopping	Questions	Name: ________
	Do you ever go shopping?	
	Where do you shop?	
	What do you buy there?	

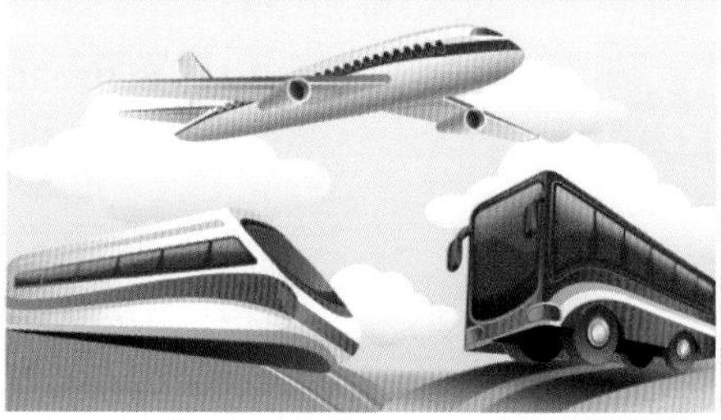

Getting around	Questions	Name: ________
	Do you ever take the bus?	
	Why do you take the bus?	
	When do you take it?	

B Class activity Find a classmate who does each activity. Then ask the follow-up questions. Take notes.

A: *Do you ever play sports, Samantha.*
B: *Yes, I sometimes do.*
A: *What do you play?*
B: *I play tennis.*

C Share your information. What answers are popular in your class?

Job details

A Look at the picture for two minutes. Try to remember the people's names, jobs, and other information.

B Pair work Cover the picture. Ask the questions and answer with the information you remember.

- What does Pam do?
- Where does she work?
- Who does she work with?
- What does Paul do?
- How does Jane get to work?
- What does Tommy do?
- Where does Mei-li work?
- What does she do?
- What company does Mitch work for?
- What does Carla do?

A: *What does Pam do?*
B: *I think she's a waitress.*
A: *Yes, I think so, too. Where does she work?*

C Pair work Ask and answer two more questions about the picture.

Start to finish

Group work Play the game. Put a small object on *Start*. Toss a coin.

 Move 1 space.
Heads

 Move 2 spaces.
Tails

Read the question. Can you do what it says? Take turns.

Yes. → Move ahead. No. ← Move back.

START	Can you spell your first name backward? *Carlos: S-O-L-R-A-C.* ← 1 space 2 spaces →	Can you whistle?  ← 2 spaces 1 space →	Can you name the days of the week in English? *Monday, . . .* ← 2 spaces 1 space →
Can you answer this question? What time is it? ← 2 spaces 1 space →	Can you read music?  ← 1 space 3 spaces →	Can you name eight nationalities? ← 1 space 1 space →	Can you name nine colors?  ← 3 spaces 1 space →
Can you shoot a basketball?  ← 1 space 2 space →	What can you do online? Name two things. ← 2 spaces 1 space →	Can you sing karaoke in English?  ← 2 spaces 2 spaces →	Can you name eight countries in alphabetical order? *Australia, Brazil, Canada . . .* ← 2 spaces 1 space →
Can you count from 1 to 20 in English? ← 2 spaces 1 space →	Can you text with two thumbs?  ← 2 spaces 1 space →	Can you answer this question? What's your morning routine? ← 2 spaces 2 spaces →	Can you talk about your family for one minute?  ← 3 spaces 1 space →
Can you name six things in the classroom? 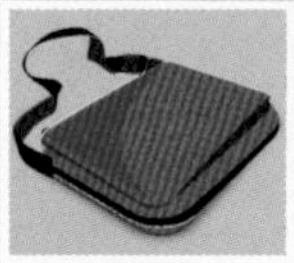 ← 3 spaces 3 spaces →	Can you answer this question? What do you usually do on Saturday night? ← 1 spaces 2 spaces →	Can you name seven ways of getting around?  ← 1 spaces 2 spaces →	FINISH

What's in your shopping basket?

A Choose seven items to put into your shopping basket. Circle them.

B Pair work Find out what is in your partner's basket. Can you make the dishes below with the food in your baskets?

Stew
beef
carrots
noodles

Fruit smoothie
apples
bananas
milk

Spaghetti and meatballs
beef
cheese
pasta
tomatoes

A: *I have beef and noodles. Do you have any carrots?*
B: *Yes, I do. We can make stew!*

C Pair work What else can you make with the food in your baskets?

How often do you eat standing up?

Group work Add two eating habits to the list. Then discuss how often you do each thing.

drink coffee in the morning

drink tea

eat alone

eat candy in class

eat fast food for breakfast

eat on the street

eat standing up

____
(your own idea)

____
(your own idea)

A: *Do you ever drink coffee in the morning?*
B: *Yes, I do.*
C: *How often do you drink coffee in the morning?*
B: *I drink coffee in the morning three times a week. How about you?*

What's missing?

Student A

A Pair work You and your partner have pictures of the same neighborhood, but different places are missing. Ask questions to get the names. Write them.

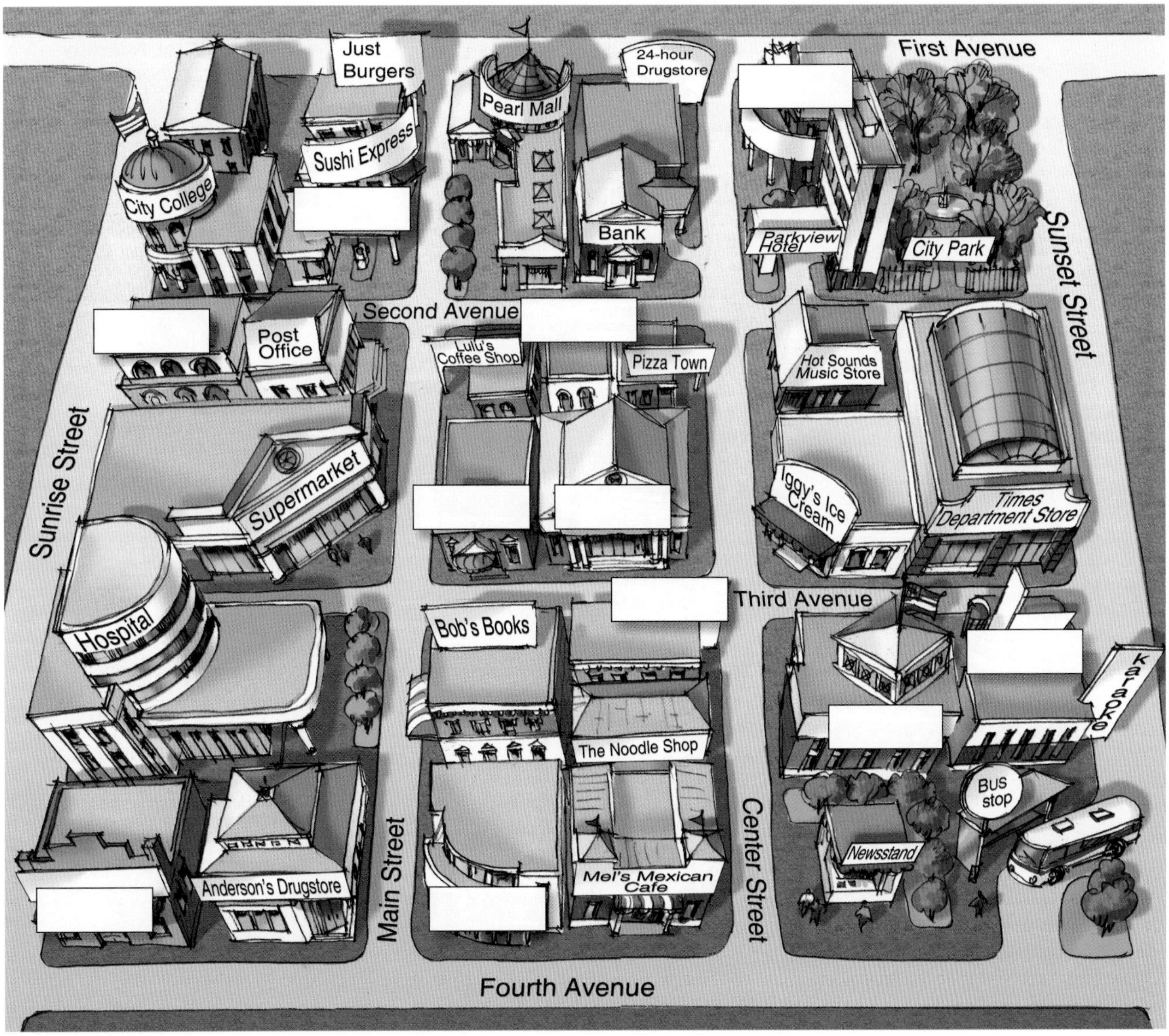

A: *What's across from the post office?*
B: *The gas station.*

B Pair work Cover the picture. Tell your partner six things you remember.

A: *The gas station is across from the post office.*
B: *That's right.*

What's missing?

Student B

A Pair work You and your partner have pictures of the same neighborhood, but different places are missing. Ask questions to get the names. Write them.

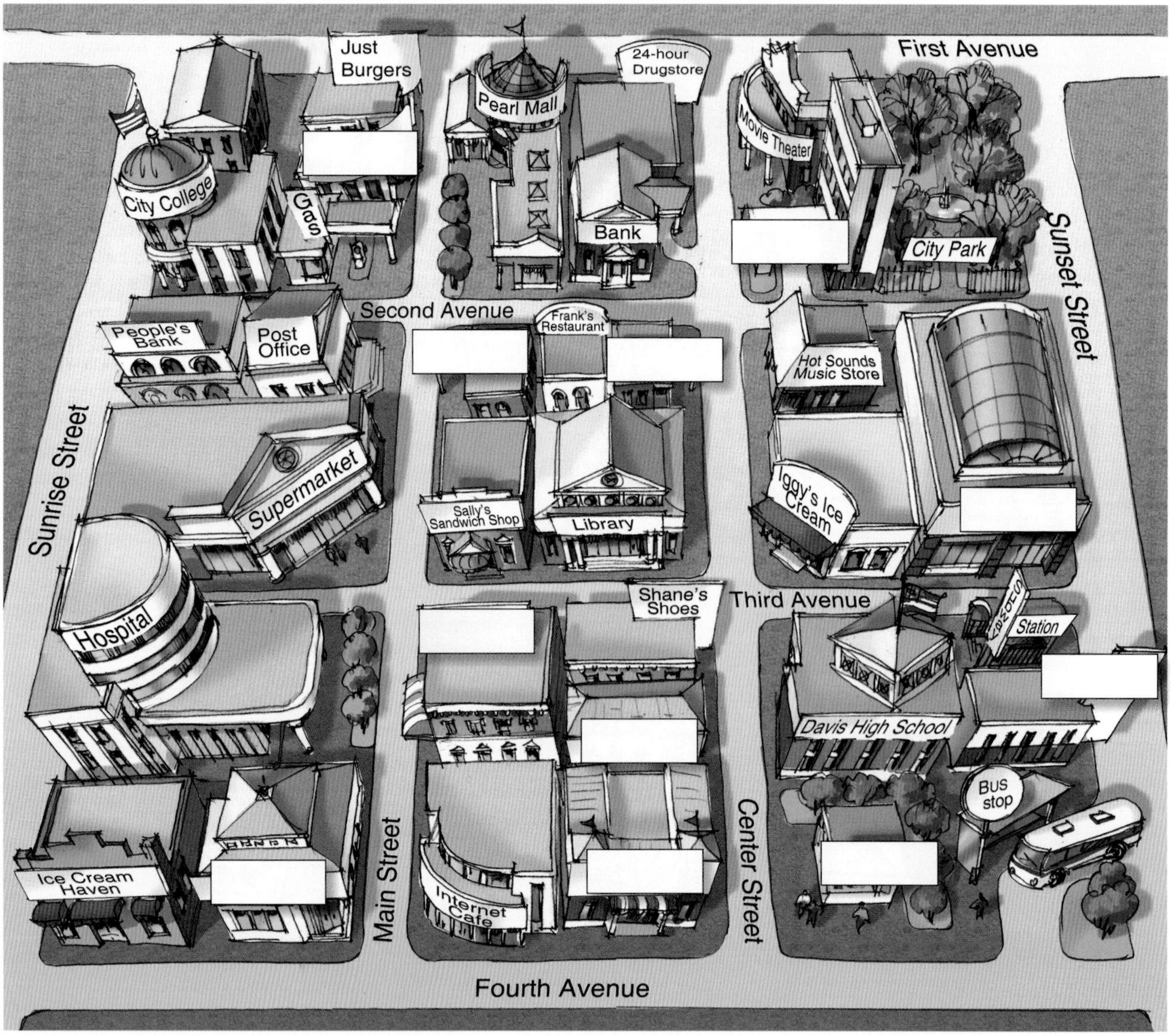

A: *What's next to the movie theater?*
B: *Parkview Hotel.*

B Pair work Cover the picture. Tell your partner six things you remember.

A: *Parkview Hotel is next to the movie theater.*
B: *That's right.*

An unusual zoo

Pair work What's wrong at this zoo? Make ten sentences about the people, animals, and other things in the zoo. Use *There is . . .*, *There are . . .*, and prepositions of location.

"There's a bear in the car."

Neighbors

A Pair work Look through the windows. What are the people doing? Discuss your ideas.

A: *I think the man is doing his homework. What do you think?*
B: *I think he's writing a letter. He's sitting, too.*

B Pair work What are the people actually doing? Go to page 153 to check your answers.

Who is it?

A Write three sentences about what you're doing these days on three pieces of paper. Don't write your name!

I'm tutoring a student.	*I'm taking tennis lessons.*	*I'm not studying every night!*

B Group work Put your papers on the table. Take one paper and read the sentences. Your group guesses the name. Take turns.

A: *This person is tutoring a student.*
B: *Is it Juliana?*
C: *No, it's not me!*
D: *Is it Kate?*

C Group work Discuss the activities you're doing these days. Ask and answer questions for more information.

A: *Who are you tutoring these days, Ken?*
B: *I'm tutoring a friend of mine. His name is Luke.*
C: *Are you tutoring him in English?*
B: *No, I'm not. I'm tutoring him in Japanese.*

Picture story

A Pair work Look at the pictures of John and Alice Gordon. What did they do last weekend? Use the verbs to discuss your ideas.

clean	fix	play	stay out	watch
dance	paint	shop for	study	

A: *John and Alice cleaned the house.*
B: *Alice fixed her bike.*

B Pair work Cover the pictures. What did John and Alice do last weekend? Answer with the information you remember.

Memories

Group work Make five true sentences about your past activities with the phrases below. Your group asks three questions about each sentence for more information. Take turns.

Yesterday	Last night	Last weekend	Last month	Last year
I drank . . .	I ate . . .	I saw . . .	I bought . . .	I went . . .
I got up . . .	I went to bed . . .	I had . . .	I read . . .	I met . . .
I did . . .	I slept . . .	I drove . . .	I made . . .	I took . . .

A: *Last night, I ate soup for dinner.*
B: *Did you eat in a restaurant?*
A: *No, I didn't. I ate at home.*
C: *Did you make the soup?*
A: *No, I didn't. My son made it.*
D: *Did you . . . ?*

School trips

A Pair work Add three more questions about school or work trips to the list. Then interview your partner. Take notes.

1. What was your favorite school or work trip?
   ___
2. How old were you?
   ___
3. How was the trip?
   ___
4. Was there anything bad about the trip?
   ___
5. Did you take a bus there?
   ___
6. Were you there all day?
   ___
7. Did you buy anything?
   ___
8. ___
   ___
9. ___
   ___
10. ___
    ___

B Pair work Tell another classmate about your partner's answers.

"Michi's favorite school trip was to a cookie factory. She was ten years old. The trip was . . ."

What a vacation!

A Look at the items from Maggie's vacation. Write five questions and answers about her vacation.

1. *Where did Maggie go on vacation?*
   New York City.
2. *What kind of music did she hear?*
   Jazz music.

B Group work Cover the picture. Ask your questions. How many correct answers did your group get?

This weekend

A Make eight true sentences about your plans with the phrases below.

My plans		
	dress up	
	eat out	
	go to a concert	tonight
	go to bed late	this evening
I'm going to	go to the mall	tomorrow
I'm not going to	go window-shopping	this weekend
	hang out	next Monday
	study	next Friday
	watch a movie	
	work	

dress up go to a concert go window-shopping

B Pair work Tell your partner about your plans. Ask and answer questions for more information.

A: *I'm going to go to bed late tonight.*
B: *Are you going to watch a movie tonight?*
A: *No, I'm not. I'm going to study.*

Party planners

A Group work Plan an end-of-class party. Take notes.

Date of party	Time of party	Place of party

Food and drink	Decorations	Music

A: *When are we going to have our party?*
B: *Let's have it after class on Friday at 8:00.*
C: *OK. Now, where are we going to have it?*
D: *Let's have it here at the school.*

B Class activity Share your ideas. Ask and answer questions for more information.

A: *We're going to have our party on Friday at 8:00.*
B: *It's going to be here at our school.*
C: *Which room is the party going to be in?*

C Class activity Vote for your favorite plan.

Irregular verbs

Base form	Simple past
be	was, were
become	became
build	built
buy	bought
can	could
choose	chose
come	came
do	did
draw	drew
drink	drank
drive	drove
eat	ate
fall	fell
feel	felt
fly	flew
get	got
give	gave
go	went
hang	hung
have	had
hear	heard
hold	held
know	knew
leave	left

Base form	Simple past
lose	lost
make	made
meet	met
pay	paid
read	read
ride	rode
run	ran
say	said
see	saw
sell	sold
send	sent
sing	sang
sit	sat
sleep	slept
speak	spoke
spend	spent
stand	stood
swim	swam
take	took
teach	taught
think	thought
wear	wore
win	won
write	wrote

Answer key

Unit 9 Lesson A (page 144)

Keep talking! Neighbors

Credits

Illustration credits

Peter Ellis: 7, 16, 26, 106, 144, 153; Tom Garrett: 25, 31, 35, 55, 65, 89, 130; John Goodwin: 4, 20, 93, 95, 129, 138 *(icons)*; Kim Johnson: 2, 3, 6, 10, 30, 40 *(bottom)*, 50, 59, 67, 70, 90, 99, 110, 131, 132, 146, 151; Dean MacAdam: 41, 47, 60, 69, 80, 85, 100, 120 *(bottom)*, 126, 127, 137, 143, 147; Michael Mantel: 39, 56, 109 Garry Parsons: 36, 46 *(bottom)*, 53, 86, 96, 116, 120 *(top)*, 125, 134, 145; Maria Rabinky: 15, 75, 76 *(top)*, 81, 141, 142; Cristina Sampaio: 40 *(top)*, 57, 87 *(bottom)*, 108, 140; Rob Schuster: 5, 27 *(bottom)*, 29, 46 *(top)*, 52, 78, 79, 119, 138 *(board)*, 149; Otto Steinenger: 27 *(top)*, 33

Photography credits

8 ©Media Bakery; 9 ©Media Bakery; 10 *(clockwise from top left)* ©Everett Collection; ©Everett Collection; ©Petite Poupee/Flickr; ©Frederick M. Brown/Getty Images; ©Kris Connor/Getty Images; ©Jeff Christensen/AP Wide World Photo; 12 *(clockwise from top left)* ©Elisabetta Villa/Getty Images; ©Everett Collection; ©Scott Gries/Getty Images; ©Kevin Mazur/Getty Images; ©Jamie McDonald/Getty Images; ©GV Cruz/Getty Images; 13 *(top to bottom)* ©Allstar Picture Library/Alamy; ©Allstar Picture Library/Alamy; ©Jon Kopaloff/Getty Images; ©Jon Kopaloff/Getty Images; 17 ©Photo Library; 18 ©Alamy; 22 *(clockwise from top left)* ©Media Bakery; ©Photo Library; ©Alamy; ©Derek Trask/Alamy; 23 *(top row, left to right)* ©Jenny Acheson/Getty Images; ©Media Bakery; ©Golden Pixels/Alamy; ©Michael Newman/Photo Edit; *(bottom)* ©Media Bakery; 26 *(top row, left to right)* ©Istock; ©Istock; ©Shutterstock; ©Adventure House; *(middle row, left to right)* ©Shutterstock; ©Media Bakery; ©Istock; ©Istock; *(bottom row, left to right)* ©Istock; ©Istock; ©Shutterstock; ©Dorling Kindersley/Getty Images; 28 *(top row, left to right)* ©Shutterstock; ©Dorling Kindersley/Getty Images; ©Shutterstock; ©David Young-Wolff/Photo Edit; ©Shutterstock; *(bottom)* ©Frank Veronsky; 32 *(clockwise from top left)* ©Alamy; ©Lenscap/Alamy; ©Shutterstock; ©Shutterstock; ©Media Bakery; ©Urikiri-Shashin-Kan/Alamy; 33 *(clockwise from top left)* ©Dorling Kindersley/Getty Images; ©Istock; ©Istock; ©Shutterstock; ©Getty Images; ©Shutterstock; ©Shutterstock; ©Alamy; 34 *(clockwise from top left)* ©Shutterstock; ©Shutterstock; ©Helene Rogers/Alamy; ©Shutterstock; ©Shutterstock; ©Istock; 36 *(clockwise from top left)* ©Getty Images; ©Liu Xiaoyang/Alamy; ©Patrick Eden/Alamy; ©Tony Anderson/Getty Images; ©Alamy; ©Media Bakery; ©David Gee/Alamy; ©Alamy; 38 *(top two rows)* ©Shutterstock; *(bottom row)* ©Frank Veronsky; 39 ©Shutterstock; 42 *(top to bottom)* ©Shutterstock; ©Media Bakery; ©Istock; ©Media Bakery; ©Istock; ©Shutterstock; 44 *(all)* ©Shutterstock; 45 *(clockwise from top left)* ©Media Bakery; ©Media Bakery; ©Alex Segre/Alamy; ©Media Bakery; 46 *(middle row, left to right)* ©Camille Tokerud/Getty Images; ©Dreamstime; ©Media Bakery; 48 *(background store images)* ©Alamy; *(foreground people images)* ©Frank Veronsky; 49 *(all)* ©Shutterstock; 50 *(top row, left to right)* ©Photo Stock Israel/Alamy; ©Ryan McVay/Getty Images; ©Media Bakery; *(middle row, left to right)* ©Media Bakery; ©Alamy; ©Alamy; *(bottom row, left to right)* ©Robert Clayton/Alamy; ©David Sanger/Alamy; ©Perry Mastrovito/Getty Images; ©Alamy; ©Getty Images; 52 *(clockwise from top left)* ©Dreamstime; ©Norma Zuniga/Getty Images; ©David White/Alamy; ©Shutterstock; ©Alex Segre/Alamy; 53 *(left to right)* ©Kevin Foy/Alamy; ©Stephen Dunn/Getty Images; ©Alamy; ©Daniel Dempster/Alamy; 56 *(both)* ©Media Bakery; 58 *(top row)* ©Frank Veronsky; *(bottom row, left to right)* ©Golden Pixels/Alamy; ©Workbook Stock/Getty Images; ©Getty Images; ©Media Bakery; 60 *(clockwise from top left)* ©Media Bakery; ©Alamy; ©Alamy; ©Media Bakery; ©Media Bakery; ©Marmaduke St. John/Alamy; ©Media Bakery; ©Media Bakery; 62 *(top to bottom)* ©Media Bakery; ©Media Bakery; ©Getty Images; 63 *(left to right)* ©Media Bakery; ©China Photos/Getty Images; ©Media Bakery 66 *(bananas)* ©Veer; *(beans)* ©Bon Appetit/Alamy; *(pasta)* ©Inmagine; *(all other food)* ©Shutterstock; *(bottom row, left to right)* ©Chris Rout/Alamy; ©Getty Images; ©Alamy; 67 *(all)* ©Shutterstock; 68 ©Frank Veronsky; 70 *(sushi)* ©Veer; *(all other food)* ©Shutterstock; 72 *(clockwise from top left)* ©Veer; ©Shutterstock; ©Alamy; ©Judd Pilossof/Getty Images; 73 *(globe, food)* ©Shutterstock; *(man)* ©Adventure House; 77 *(left to right)* ©Media Bakery; ©Jeff Greenberg/Alamy; ©Cris Haigh/Alamy; ©Ian Dagnall/Alamy; 78 ©Frank Veronsky; 80 *(clockwise from top left)* ©Joe McBride/Getty Images; ©Alamy; ©Erik Dreyer/Getty Images; ©Tomas Abad/Alamy; ©Alex Segre/Alamy; ©Wolfgang Kaehler/Alamy; ©Alamy; ©Frans Lemmens/Alamy; 82 *(all)* ©Stephen Saks/Alamy; 83 *(left to right)* ©Rob Walls/Alamy; ©Javier Larera/Photo Library; ©Ian Shaw/Photo Library; 88 *(clockwise from top left)* ©Alamy; ©Media Bakery; ©Getty Images; ©Alamy; ©Bruce Laurance/Getty Images; ©Alamy; 90 *(clockwise from top left)* ©Alamy; ©Alamy; ©Leander Baerenz/Getty Images; ©Alamy; ©Media Bakery; ©Alamy; ©Hans Neleman/Getty Images; ©Andrea Matone/Alamy; 91 ©Alamy; 92 *(top to bottom)* ©Media Bakery; ©Shutterstock; ©Alamy; ©Kaz Chiba/Getty Images; ©Media Bakery; ©Paul Williams/Alamy; ©Ron Chapple/Getty Images; ©Shutterstock; 96 *(clockwise from top left)* ©Alamy; ©Media Bakery; ©Neil Beckerman/Getty Images; ©Charles Gullung/Getty Images; ©Inmagine; ©Getty Images; ©Alamy; ©Alamy; 98 ©Frank Veronsky; 100 *(top row, left to right)* ©Media Bakery; ©Media Bakery; ©Jim West/Alamy; *(middle row, left to right)* ©Getty Images; ©Getty Images; ©Alexey Stiop/Alamy; *(bottom row, left to right)* ©Vehbi Koca/Alamy; ©Media Bakery; ©Media Bakery; 102 ©Media Bakery; 105 *(Costa Rica beach)* ©Franck Guiziou/Getty Images; *(Golden Gate Bridge)* ©Getty Images; *(trolley)* ©Mitchell Funk/Getty Images; *(all others)* ©Shutterstock; 106 *(left to right)* ©Gavin Hellier/Alamy; ©Alamy; ©Lebrecht Music and Arts Photo Library/Alamy; ©Red Cover/Alamy; 108 ©Frank Veronsky; 110 *(clockwise from top left)* ©Otto Stadler/Getty Images; ©Andrew Watson/Getty Images; ©Alamy; ©Alamy; ©Bill Bachmann/Alamy; ©Alamy; ©Yadid Levy/Alamy; ©JL Images/Alamy; 111 *(both)* ©Shutterstock; 112 *(top to bottom)* ©Corbis; ©Jeffrey Mayer/Getty Images; ©Media Bakery; ©Jeff Greenberg/Alamy; 113 ©Rohan/Getty Images; 115 *(clockwise from top left)* ©Media Bakery; ©Peter Titmuss/Alamy; ©Media Bakery; ©Hiroko Masuike/Getty Images; 117 ©Media Bakery; 118 ©Frank Veronsky; 122 *(clockwise from top left)* ©Flickr; ©Jon Arnold Images Ltd./Alamy; ©Amanda Ahn/Alamy; ©Adam Eastland/Alamy; 123 ©ML Pearson/Alamy; 133 *(top to bottom)* ©Media Bakery; ©David Grossman/Alamy; 139 *(fish)* ©Holdger Burmeister/Alamy; *(noodles)* ©Dreamstime; *(rice)* ©David Lee/Alamy; *(cheese)* ©Media Bakery; *(beans)* ©Alistair Heap/Alamy; *(milk, spaghetti, cereal)* ©Alamy; *(all other food, top group)* ©Shutterstock; *(bottom row, left to right)* ©Valerie Janssen/Getty Images; ©Media Blitz Images Limited/Alamy; ©Alamy; 148 *(left to right)* ©Alibi Productions/Alamy; ©Media Bakery; 149 *(clockwise from top left)* ©Alamy; ©Sandra Baker/Alamy; ©Edward Simons/Alamy; 150 *(left to right)* ©Media Bakery; ©Alamy; ©Neil Beckerman/Getty Images

Four Corners

Jack C. Richards · David Bohlke

1

Video Activity Sheets

CAMBRIDGE UNIVERSITY PRESS

unit 1

Famous names

Before you watch

Match the words and the pictures. Then compare with a partner.

a. a park	b. a reporter	c. an interview

1. ☐

2. ☐

3. ☐

While you watch

A Label the pictures with the correct names.

Amanda	Bo	Emi	Irma

1. ________________

2. ________________

3. ________________

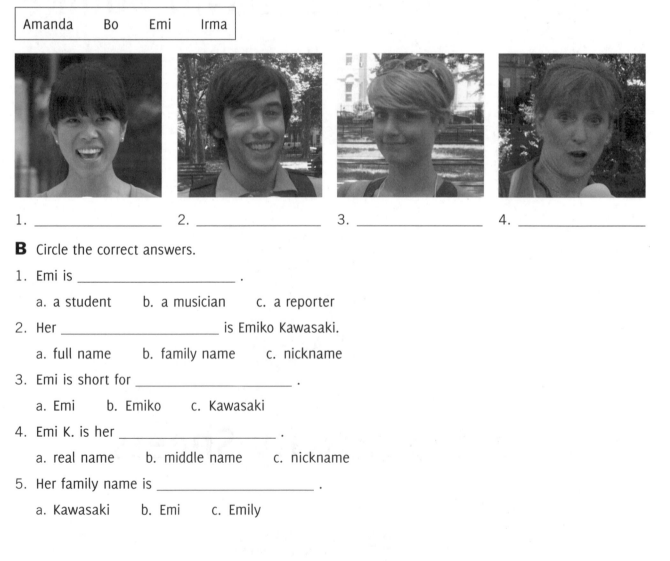

4. ________________

B Circle the correct answers.

1. Emi is ____________________ .
   a. a student b. a musician c. a reporter
2. Her ____________________ is Emiko Kawasaki.
   a. full name b. family name c. nickname
3. Emi is short for ____________________ .
   a. Emi b. Emiko c. Kawasaki
4. Emi K. is her ____________________ .
   a. real name b. middle name c. nickname
5. Her family name is ____________________ .
   a. Kawasaki b. Emi c. Emily

C Write T (true) or F (false).

1. Paul Hewson is a singer from Ireland. ______
2. Jennifer Anastassakis is a celebrity. ______
3. Sean Combs is a jazz singer. ______
4. Irma is not a hip-hop fan. ______

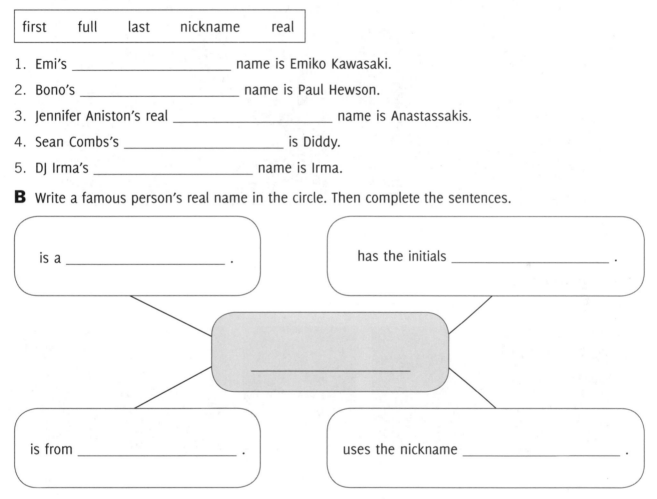

After you watch

A Complete the sentences with the correct words.

first	full	last	nickname	real

1. Emi's ____________________ name is Emiko Kawasaki.
2. Bono's ____________________ name is Paul Hewson.
3. Jennifer Aniston's real ____________________ name is Anastassakis.
4. Sean Combs's ____________________ is Diddy.
5. DJ Irma's ____________________ name is Irma.

B Write a famous person's real name in the circle. Then complete the sentences.

____

is a ____________________ .

has the initials ____________________ .

is from ____________________ .

uses the nickname ____________________ .

C **Pair work** Tell your partner about the person in Part B.

Surprise!

Before you watch

A Label the picture with the correct words. Then compare with a partner.

✓Danielle	mother	boyfriend	father	grandmother

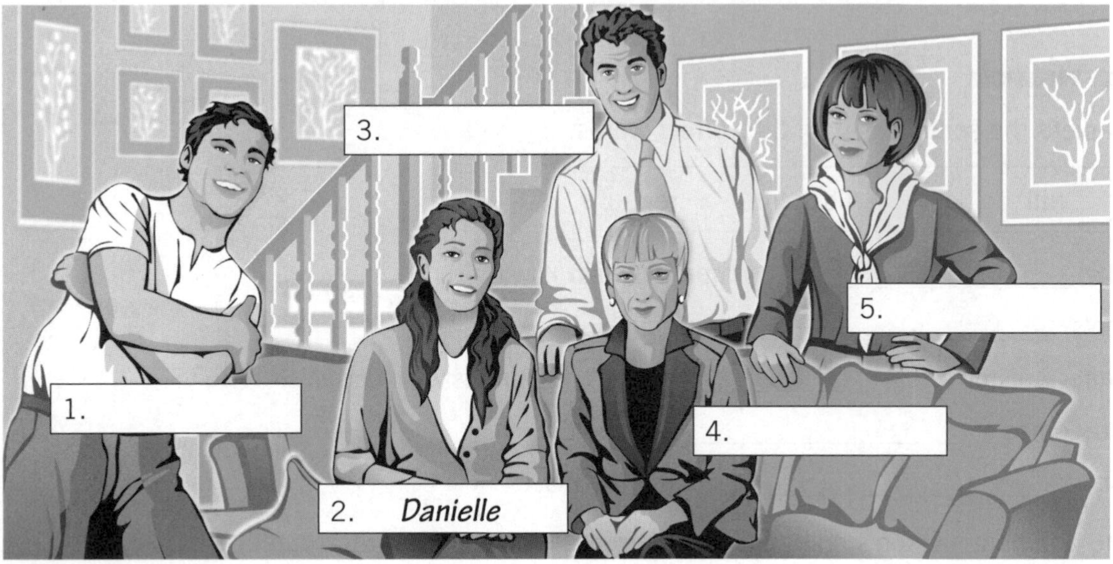

B Which person in Part A is *not* a member of the family?

While you watch

A Write D (Danielle), I (Irma), M (Max), P (Peter), or W (Wendy).

Danielle

Irma

Max

Peter

Wendy

1. _______ is Peter's mother.
2. _______ is Danielle's brother.
3. _______ is Peter's wife.
4. _______ is Peter and Wendy's daughter.
5. _______ is Irma's son.
6. _______ is Wendy's husband.
7. _______ is Max's sister.
8. _______ is Danielle and Max's mother.

B Circle the correct answers.

1. Danielle is home from ________________ .

   a. college b. vacation c. work

2. ________________ nickname is Chef Dad.

   a. Max's b. Paul's c. Peter's

3. Danielle's mother is ________________ years old.

   a. 44 b. 47 c. 67

4. Max is ________________ .

   a. at home b. in film school c. in Toronto

5. Paul is Danielle's ________________ .

   a. brother b. boyfriend c. teacher

C Write Y (yes) or N (no).

1. Is Danielle a student? ______
2. Is Wendy a grandmother? ______
3. Is Irma 67 years old? ______
4. Is Max in the house? ______
5. Is Paul a member of Danielle's family? ______

After you watch

A What are the two surprises in the video? Check (✓) the correct answers.

☐ Danielle is home from college.

☐ Max is in Toronto.

☐ Paul is Danielle's new boyfriend.

B Pair work Who is in your family? What are their names and ages? Which family members live in your home? Tell your partner.

unit **3**

My favorite things

Before you watch

Circle your guesses. Then compare with the class.

1. What is a roommate?

   a. a student in your class b. a member of your family c. a friend who lives with you

2. What is a teddy bear?

a.  b.  c. 

3. What is a robe?

a.  b.  c. 

While you watch

A What are Nick's favorite things? Check (✓) the correct answers.

- ☐ his baseball
- ☐ his cap
- ☐ his cell phone
- ☐ his laptop
- ☐ his picture
- ☐ his robe
- ☐ his T-shirt
- ☐ his teddy bear
- ☐ his video camera

B Write T (true) or F (false).

1. The video is for Ben's parents. _______
2. Nick is from New Hampshire. _______
3. The robe is from Japan. _______
4. The picture is of New York. _______
5. The teddy bear is from Nick's friend. _______

C Circle the correct answers.

1. Nick and Ben are ______________________ .

   a. roommates b. teachers c. artists

2. A *yukata* is a ______________________ .

   a. shirt b. robe c. jacket

3. Nick's cap is from his high school ______________________ team.

   a. tennis b. golf c. baseball

4. ______________________ is the artist of the picture.

   a. Ben b. Nick's grandmother c. Nick

5. Nick's ______________________ are from Vermont.

   a. parents b. grandparents c. friends

6. Nick's teddy bear is ______________________ years old.

   a. 9 b. 19 c. 20

After you watch

A Which of Nick's things is *your* favorite? Why?

B **Group work** Tell your group about your favorite things.

- What are they?
- Where are they from?
- How old are they?

unit 4

My busy Monday

Before you watch

Match the words and the pictures. Then compare with a partner.

a. drink coffee	c. go to school	e. ride a bike
b. get up	d. make a video	f. text with friends

1. ☐

2. ☐

3. ☐

4. ☐

5. ☐

6. ☐

While you watch

A What does Ben do on Mondays? Number the sentences from 1 to 7.

_____ He has class.
_____ He goes to bed very late.
_____ He drinks coffee.
_____ He texts with his friends.
_____ He exercises.
__1__ He gets up.
_____ He rides his bike.

Ben

B Circle the correct answers.

1. Nick ____________________ for Ben.

   a. makes a video b. cooks dinner c. drives a car

2. The video is for ____________________ .

   a. Ben's friends b. Ben's class c. Ben's family

3. Ben's favorite class is at ____________________ .

   a. 7:30 b. 9:00 c. 4:30

4. Lila is Ben's ____________________ .

   a. teacher b. classmate c. student

5. Ben exercises ____________________ .

   a. at school b. at home c. at the park

C Write T (true) or F (false).

1. Ben has orange juice, tea, cereal, and milk for breakfast. ______
2. Ben's favorite class is English. ______
3. Ben is early for class. ______
4. Ben exercises at the park at 3:30. ______
5. Lila rides a bike to school and runs in the park. ______
6. Ben texts with his friends in the afternoon. ______

After you watch

A Make a list of your routine activities at different times of the day.

Morning	Afternoon	Evening	Night
get up			

B **Group work** How is your daily routine the same as Ben's? How is it different?

"I get up late every morning. I don't have cereal for breakfast like Ben. I don't have time to eat!"

unit **5**

What do you do for fun?

Before you watch

A Label the groups of pictures. Which pictures show New Jersey, U.S.A.? Which show Seoul, South Korea?

1. ______________________________ 2. ______________________________

B Soon-mi lives in Seoul, South Korea. Danielle lives in a small town in New Jersey, U.S.A. Make a list of things you think they do for fun.

While you watch

A Check (✓) the correct answers. (More than one answer is possible.)

	Soon-mi	Danielle
1. Who often goes dancing?	☐	☐
2. Who hangs out at home?	☐	☐
3. Who cooks dinner for friends?	☐	☐
4. Who watches DVDs?	☐	☐
5. Who plays video games?	☐	☐
6. Who goes to a karaoke club?	☐	☐
7. Who sings songs in English?	☐	☐

B Circle the correct answers.

1. In the video, it's ____________________ in Seoul.

   a. 8:30 a.m. b. 4:30 p.m. c. 8:30 p.m.

2. In New Jersey, it's ____________________ .

   a. early morning b. early afternoon c. early evening

3. Soon-mi and her sister always ____________________ on her sister's birthday.

   a. eat out b. go dancing c. eat out and go dancing

4. Danielle usually ____________________ around town.

   a. drives b. takes the bus c. walks

5. Sometimes Danielle ____________________ .

   a. takes the train b. walks c. takes the subway

C Write T (true) or F (false).

1. Soon-mi teaches English to Danielle. ______
2. Danielle plays video games at an arcade. ______
3. Soon-mi often goes dancing at a club. ______
4. Soon-mi goes to an arcade near the bus station. ______
5. They have a dance club in Danielle's town. ______
6. Soon-mi knows a lot of songs in English. ______

After you watch

A Pair work Do you ever do the same activities as Danielle and Soon-mi? What other activities do you do? Tell your partner.

A: *Danielle studies Korean with Soon-mi. I never do that. I study English.*

B: *Soon-mi eats out on her sister's birthday. I sometimes eat out on my sister's birthday, too.*

B Group work Sing a song – or part of a song – that you know in English! Your group guesses the name of the song. Take turns.

unit **6**

Hidden talent

Before you watch

A Match the words and the pictures. Then compare with a partner.

a. mime	b. play the harmonica	c. play the guitar	d. play the kazoo

1.  2.  3.  4. 

B What is a hidden talent? Check (✓) your guess. Then compare with the class.

☐ Something you can do well, and people know about it

☐ Something you can do well, but people don't know about it

☐ Something you can't do well, and people know about it

While you watch

A Who does each thing in the video? Check (✓) the correct answers. (More than one answer is possible.)

	Emi	Alicia	Christine	Joey
1. Who dances?	☐	☐	☐	☐
2. Who plays the harmonica?	☐	☐	☐	☐
3. Who plays the kazoo?	☐	☐	☐	☐
4. Who mimes?	☐	☐	☐	☐
5. Who sings?	☐	☐	☐	☐
6. Who speaks French?	☐	☐	☐	☐

B Circle the correct answers.

1. Emi *does not* speak ____________________ in the video.

   a. French b. English c. Chinese

2. Alicia *cannot* play ____________________ .

   a. the guitar b. the harmonica c. the kazoo

3. Christine *is not* ____________________ .

   a. a model b. a waitress c. an actress

4. Joey *does not* work on ____________________ .

   a. Saturdays b. Thursdays c. Tuesdays

C Write T (true) or F (false).

1. Emi is a reporter for *Street Talk*. _______
2. Alicia can dance very well. _______
3. Christine doesn't have a hidden talent. _______
4. Joey is a taxi driver. _______

After you watch

A Pair work Do you have any of the same hidden talents as Emi, Alicia, Christine, or Joey? Who do you know with the same hidden talents? Tell your partner.

"Emi speaks French. I can't speak French, but my mother can."

B Group work Interview your group. What are their hidden talents?

Name	Hidden talent

C Class activity Share interesting hidden talents from your group.

"Jen can fix computers. Carlos can . . ."

unit 7

My favorite meal

Before you watch

A Check (✓) the food you like. Then compare with a partner.

☐ honey ☐ nuts ☐ oats ☐ raisins ☐ yogurt

B In the video, Ben makes a meal with the food in Part A. What meal do you think he makes? Check (✓) your guess. Then compare with the class.

☐ breakfast ☐ lunch ☐ dinner

C Write *a, an,* or *some*. Then compare with a partner.

1. ______ apple	5. ______ honey	9. ______ raisins
2. ______ banana	6. ______ milk	10. ______ tea
3. ______ egg	7. ______ nuts	11. ______ tomato
4. ______ granola	8. ______ oats	12. ______ yogurt

While you watch

A What does Ben do? Number the pictures from 1 to 5.

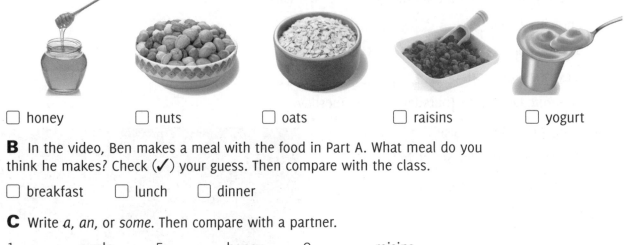

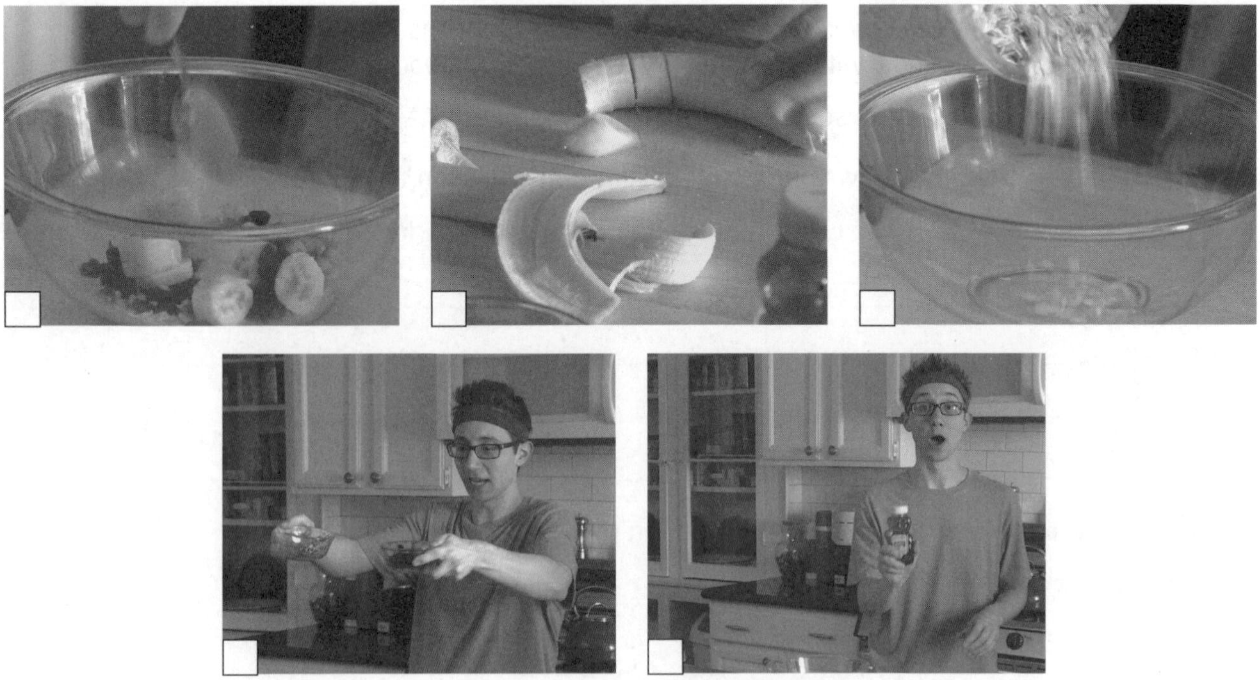

B Circle the correct answers.

1. Ben is ______________________ .

   a. at school b. at work c. at home

2. Ben's favorite meal is ______________________ .

   a. breakfast b. lunch c. dinner

3. He loves granola. Granola is a kind of ______________________ .

   a. pasta b. cereal c. coffee

4. Ben likes to ______________________ in the morning.

   a. exercise b. drink tea c. play soccer

After you watch

A How does Ben make granola? Complete the sentences with the correct words.

banana	honey	nuts	oats	raisins	yogurt

First, I put some ______________________ in a bowl. I add some ______________________ and ______________________ . Then I add the ______________________ . I usually like ______________________ on my granola. And I always have some ______________________ on it.

B What do you usually have for breakfast? Make a list of the food.

____

____

C **Pair work** Tell your partner about your breakfast. Do you eat the same food?

unit **8**

Kim's Coffee Shop!

Before you watch

A Look at the picture. Circle the correct answers. Then compare with a partner.

1. The picture is from a commercial. What is a commercial?

   a. an advertisement on TV b. a magazine review c. a newspaper article

2. Where are the people?

   a. in a club b. in a coffee shop c. in an office

B What kind of information about the place do you think is in the commercial? Make a list. Then compare with a partner.

Information
the name of the place
____
____
____
____
____
____

While you watch

A What do people do in the commercial? Check (✓) the correct answers.

☐ dance	☐ eat a snack	☐ play the guitar	☐ study English
☐ drink coffee	☐ eat pasta	☐ read the newspaper	☐ use the Internet
☐ drink tea	☐ listen to music	☐ sing	☐ write a letter

B Who talks about each thing? Draw a line from each thing to Marco or Danielle.

Marco

the coffee

the Internet

the woman's laptop

the snacks

the music

Danielle

C Write T (true) or F (false).

1. The cookie costs 85 cents. ______
2. Kim's Coffee Shop is on the corner of First Avenue and Elm Street. ______
3. It is open six days a week. ______
4. Kim's Coffee Shop opens at 7:00 a.m. ______
5. It closes at midnight. ______

After you watch

A Answer the questions.

1. What is your favorite coffee shop?

____

2. Where is it?

____

3. What do you like about it?

____

4. Who do you usually go there with?

____

5. What do you usually do there?

____

B Group work Tell your group about your favorite coffee shop. Ask and answer questions for more information.

"My favorite coffee shop is A Cup of Joe. It's on . . ."

What are you doing these days?

Before you watch

Complete the sentences with the present continuous forms of the verbs.

answer	hold	interview	stand	wear

1. Emi ______*is interviewing*______ Bo.
2. Emi ____________________ in front of him.
3. She ____________________ a microphone.
4. Bo ____________________ a T-shirt.
5. He ____________________ Emi's question.

While you watch

A Who is doing each thing these days? Check (✓) the correct answers. (More than one answer is possible.)

	Emi	Bo	Soon-mi	Alicia
1. Who is eating in good restaurants?	☐	☐	☐	☐
2. Who is exercising a lot?	☐	☐	☐	☐
3. Who is learning to drive?	☐	☐	☐	☐
4. Who is reading a book?	☐	☐	☐	☐
5. Who is shopping?	☐	☐	☐	☐
6. Who is studying a language?	☐	☐	☐	☐
7. Who is taking a dance class?	☐	☐	☐	☐

B Write Y (yes) or N (no).

1. Does Emi know how to drive? _______
2. Can Bo speak French well? _______
3. Does Soon-mi like Italian food? _______
4. Is Alicia getting ready for a trip to Portugal? _______

C Circle the correct answers.

1. Emi is *not* taking ______________________ lessons these days.
   a. dance   b. piano   c. tennis
2. Bo does *not* say anything in ______________________ in the video.
   a. English   b. French   c. Japanese
3. Soon-mi does *not* have ______________________ in her bag.
   a. clothes   b. food   c. gifts
4. Alicia is *not* ______________________ these days.
   a. playing soccer   b. riding her bike   c. swimming

After you watch

A Pair work Are you doing any of the same things as Emi, Bo, Soon-mi, or Alicia these days? What other things are you doing these days? Ask and answer questions.

A: *Are you reading a good book these days?*
B: *Yes, I am. I'm reading . . .*

B Pair work Tell another classmate about the things your partner is doing these days.

"Dana is reading a good book these days. She's reading . . ."

unit **10**

I had a party last night.

Before you watch

Look at the pictures. Complete the sentences with the simple past forms of the verbs. Then compare with a partner.

dance	drink	eat	✓have	invite	play

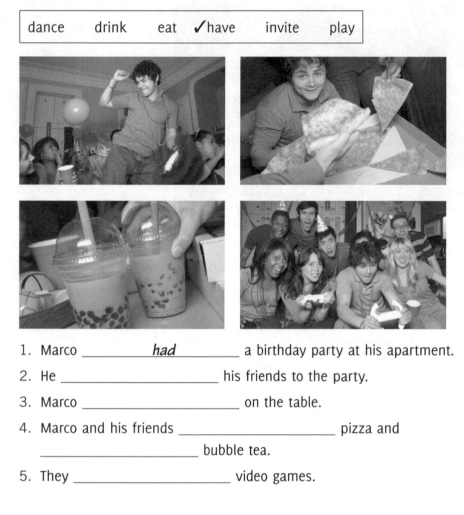

1. Marco ____*had*____ a birthday party at his apartment.
2. He ____________ his friends to the party.
3. Marco ____________ on the table.
4. Marco and his friends ____________ pizza and ____________ bubble tea.
5. They ____________ video games.

While you watch

A What happened? Number the events from 1 to 10.

_______ Marco had a birthday party.
___*1*___ Marco saw Nick and Ben at the library.
_______ Marco saw Alicia and Bo.
_______ Marco went to class.
_______ Marco invited Alicia and Bo to dinner.
_______ Marco's classmates had text messages about his birthday.
_______ They saw all the food in Marco's shopping cart.
_______ Marco invited Nick and Ben to dinner.
_______ Marco went grocery shopping and bought a lot of food.
_______ Marco invited his classmates to his apartment.

B Circle the correct answers.

1. Marco's birthday party was on ____________________ .

   a. Friday b. Saturday c. Sunday

2. Marco had a ____________________ party.

   a. small, quiet b. big, noisy c. surprise

3. Marco wanted ____________________ on his birthday.

   a. a lot of gifts b. a big, noisy party c. a nice, quiet evening

4. Marco *didn't* invite his ____________________ to his party.

   a. friends b. classmates c. parents

5. Nick and Ben gave Marco ____________________ .

   a. a video game b. a book c. a party

C Write T (true) or F (false).

1. Marco liked his party. _______
2. Marco and his friends ate some food. _______
3. They drank coffee. _______
4. They played soccer. _______
5. They danced. _______

After you watch

A Answer the questions about the last party you had or went to.

1. Who had the party and why?

   ____

2. Where did you go for the party?

   ____

3. Who went to the party?

   ____

4. What did you eat and drink?

   ____

5. What did you do at the party?

   ____

B **Group work** Tell your group about the last party you had or went to. Ask and answer questions for more information.

"I went to a party at my school. My classmates were there. We ate . . ."

unit 11

Danielle Down Under!

Before you watch

A Complete the sentences with the correct words. Then compare with a partner.

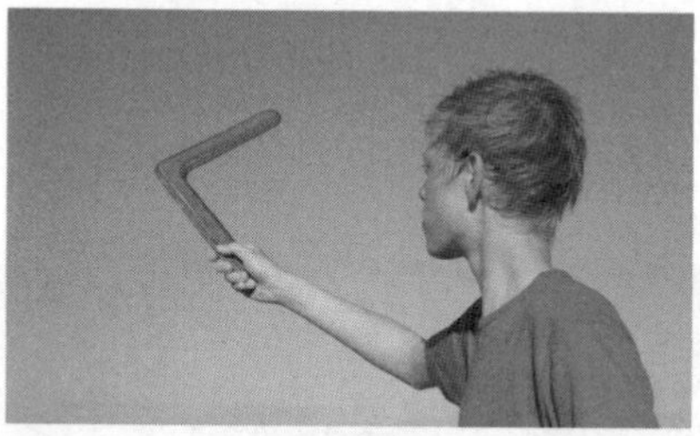

a boomerang

a kangaroo

a koala bear

a national park

an opera house

a tour guide

1. ____________________ and ____________________ are animals.
2. ____________________ is a place where actors and actresses sing.
3. ____________________ is a person who tells tourists about special places.
4. ____________________ is a place in a country with special land.
5. ____________________ is an example of a souvenir.

B Where do you think the pictures in Part A are from? Check (✓) your guess.

☐ Africa ☐ Asia ☐ Australia

While you watch

A Where did Danielle go on her trip? Check (✓) the places she visited. Mark an ✗ on the places she *didn't* visit.

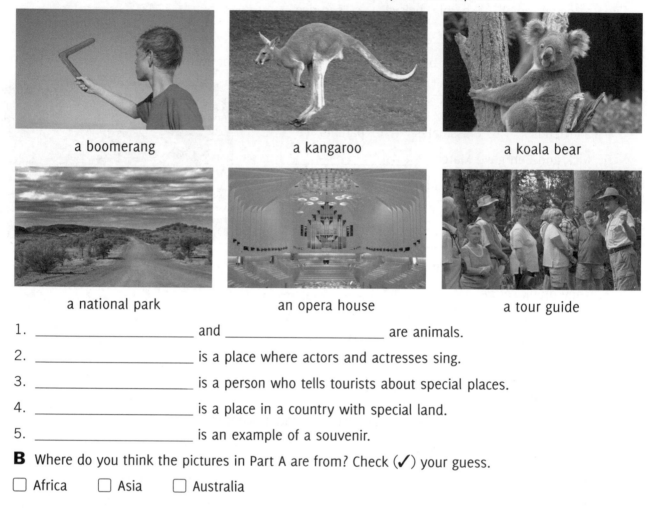

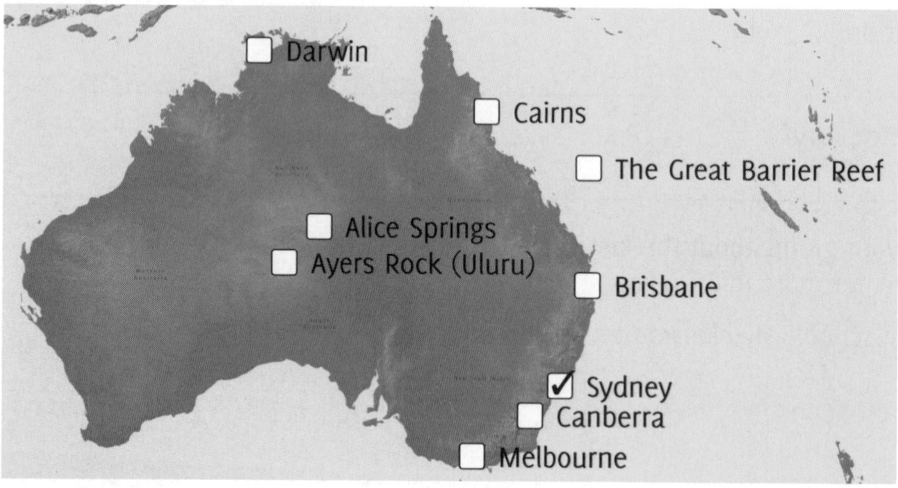

B Complete the sentences with the correct places from Part A.

1. Danielle visited the famous opera house in ___*Sydney*___ .
2. She and Amy flew from Sydney to ______________ .
3. They rented a car and drove to ______________ .
4. They took a tour at ______________ .
5. Danielle and Amy flew from Alice Springs to ______________ .
6. They saw some beautiful fish at ______________ .
7. Danielle and Amy missed their flight to ______________ .

C How does Danielle describe each thing? Match the phrases.

1. Australia is really _______ .
2. The Sydney Opera House was _______ .
3. Sleeping on Amy's floor was _______ .
4. The drive to Uluru was _______ .
5. Their tour in Uluru was _______ .
6. The tour guide was _______ .
7. The Great Barrier Reef was _______ .

a. very cute
b. free, but not comfortable
c. excellent
d. hot, but quiet and relaxing
e. a little boring
f. amazing
g. fun, but tiring

After you watch

A Pair work What do you think was interesting, fun, or boring about Danielle's vacation? Tell your partner.

B Pair work Interview your partner about a trip he or she took. Complete the chart with his or her answers.

Questions	Name: ______________
1. Where did you go?	
2. How did you travel?	
3. Who did you go with?	
4. What did you do there?	
5. What did you buy?	

C Group work Tell another pair about your partner's trip.

"David went to Veracruz with his family. He ate delicious seafood."

unit 12

A graduation party

Before you watch

A Label the pictures with the correct words. Then compare with a partner.

class	graduation	job	summer

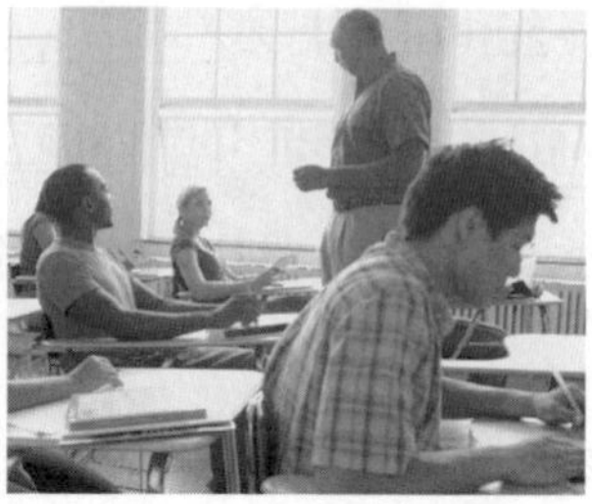

1. ________________ 2. ________________ 3. ________________ 4. ________________

B Answer the questions. Then compare with a partner.

1. What months of the year do students go to class in your school?
____
2. When do students graduate from your school?
____
3. What do you usually do in the summer?
____
4. When do most people in your country look for their first job?
____

While you watch

A What do Bo's parents think Bo is going to do? Circle the correct answers.

1. They think Bo is going to get ________________ this summer.
   a. a job b. a cat c. an award
2. They think he's going to ________________ this summer.
   a. relax b. travel c. take classes
3. They think he's going to be a ________________ someday.
   a. teacher b. doctor c. pilot
4. They think he's going to go to ________________ .
   a. Toronto b. the beach c. medical school
5. They think he's going to take ________________ classes.
   a. science b. English c. art

B Match the sentences and the people who say them.

1. He's going to get married. _______
2. I'm going to sleep and watch TV. _______
3. He's going to travel. _______
4. We're going to go to Toronto in August. _______
5. What is Bo going to do this summer? _______
6. He's going to take some science classes. _______

a. Alicia
b. Bo
c. Bo's dad
d. Bo's mom
e. Marco
f. Nick

C Write T (true) or F (false).

1. Alicia is making the video as a graduation gift for Bo. _______
2. Bo's mother says he's going to become an accountant. _______
3. Nick is going to travel with Marco this summer. _______
4. They're going to fly to Toronto in August. _______
5. Before their trip, they're going to look for a job. _______

After you watch

A Pair work What do you think Bo is going to do this summer? Why? Discuss your ideas.

"I think Bo is going to get a job because he doesn't have any money."

B Pair work Write three things you think your partner is going to do next year. Then check your guesses.

1. ______________________________
2. ______________________________
3. ______________________________

A: *I think you are going to get married next year.*
B: *No, I don't think so. I don't have a girlfriend! I think you are going to go skydiving.*
A: *That's right!*

C Pair work Tell your partner three real plans you have for next year.

"I'm going to go to Puerto Rico next summer."

Credits

Photography credits

T-173, T-175, T-176, T-178, T-179, T-180, T-181 *(bottom)*, T-182, T-183, T-184, T-185 *(bottom)*, T-186, T-187, T-188, T-189, T-190, T-191, T-192, T-194, T-196
Video screen grabs courtesy of Steadman Productions, Boston, MA

Four Corners

Jack C. Richards · David Bohlke
with Kathryn O'Dell

1

Workbook

CAMBRIDGE
UNIVERSITY PRESS

Contents

New friends

A What's your name?

1 **What are their names? Read the clues and complete the chart with ✓ (yes) or ✗ (no). There is one answer for each person.**

- Rick is a married man.
- Wendy is a married woman.
- Vera is a single woman.
- Margie's family name is Lee.

Teachers at LCC				
	Miss Garcia	Mr. Jones	Mrs. Wilson	Ms. Lee
1. Rick	✗	✓	✗	✗
2. Wendy		✗		
3. Vera		✗		
4. Margie		✗		

2 **Answer the questions. Use the information in Exercise 1.**

1. Rick: What's his full name? *Rick Jones*
2. Wendy: What's her last name? ____________
3. Vera: What's her full name? ____________
4. Margie: What's her last name? ____________

3 **Circle the correct words to complete the conversation.**

A: Hello, everyone. I'm your teacher, (**Mr.**) / **Ms.**[1] Johnson.
My **first** / **family**[2] name is Carl. What are your **name** / **names**[3]?

B: I'm Jon. My **family** / **full**[4] name is Lincoln.

C: I'm Sue. My **full** / **middle**[5] name is Sue Anne Harris.

4 Match the two parts of each sentence.

1. My name __d__ a. is a student.
2. What's __e__ b. their names?
3. Our names __c__ c. are Tom and John.
4. Melissa __a__ d. is Diana.
5. Mr. Tan and Ms. Bedford __f__ e. his name?
6. What are __b__ f. are teachers.

5 Complete the webpage with the correct form of *be*.

Meet me and my friends!

1. Hi! My name ___*is*___ Liz Nelson.

2. Mr. Chang ____________ my English teacher.

3. Danny and Hannah ____________ my classmates.

4. Jack and Penny ____________ my friends.

5. Alicia and Leyla ____________ my new friends.

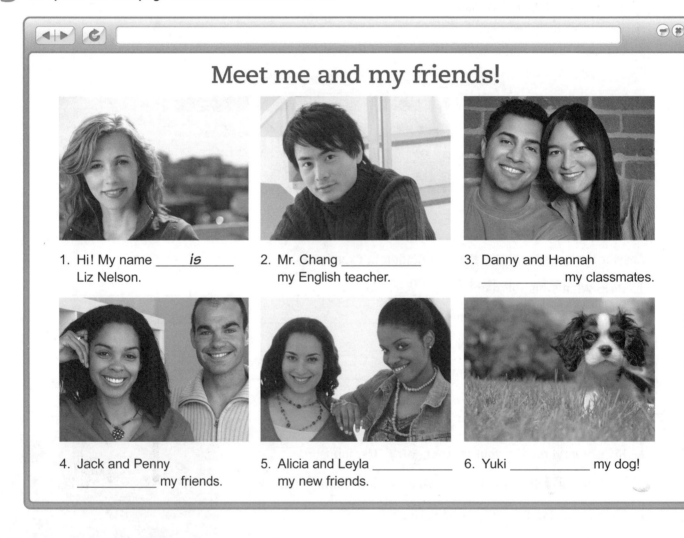

6. Yuki ____________ my dog!

6 Read the answers. Then write the questions. Use possessive adjectives. Use the example as a model.

1. ___*What are their names*___? Their names are Jack and Penny.
2. ______________________________? Her name is Liz.
3. ______________________________? His name is Mr. Chang.
4. ______________________________? Their names are Danny and Hannah.

7 **Complete the messages with the correct possessive adjectives from the box. Use each adjective only once.**

her	her	his	✓my	their

Flor07	Hi, Charlie. How are you?
CharlieD	Pretty good, thanks. And you?
Flor07	I'm fine. ___*My*___ (1) English class is good. Two of my classmates are friends. ___________ (2) names are Judy and Mark.
CharlieD	Cool! What is your teacher's name?
Flor07	___________ (3) name is Mrs. Richards.
CharlieD	What's ___________ (4) first name?
Flor07	Anna. What's your teacher's name?
CharlieD	___________ (5) name is Mr. Lawrence.

8 **Look at the example. Complete the chart with information about you and your English teacher.**

	Title	First name	Middle name	Family name
Example:	*Ms.*	*Kendra*	*Lily*	*Johnson*
you				
your teacher				

9 **Write sentences about you and your teacher. Use the model and your answers in the chart in Exercise 8 to help you.**

Example: Hi. My first name is Kendra. My family name is Johnson.
My full name is Kendra Lily Johnson. My teacher is Ms. Henderson.
Her first name is Laura.

____

____

____

____

____

B How do you spell . . . ?

1 Complete the sequences with the correct letters.

1. B D *F* H J
2. M P S V ______
3. ______ C E G I
4. V ______ X Y Z
5. L ______ P R T
6. I M Q ______ Y

2 Complete the conversation with the correct questions.

Clerk: Hello. *What's your name* ____________ ? (1)

Terrance: My name is Terrance Nichols.

Clerk: ______________________________ , (2) Mr. Nichols?

Terrance: N-I-C-H-O-L-S.

Clerk: OK. ______________________________ ? (3)

Terrance: T-E-R-R-A-N-C-E.

Clerk: Thank you.

3 Write a conversation about Ms. Michelle Griffin's name. Use the conversation in Exercise 2 as a model.

Clerk: *Hello.* ______________________________

Michelle: ______________________________

Clerk: ______________________________

Michelle: ______________________________

Clerk: ______________________________

Michelle: ______________________________

Clerk: ______________________________

C Are you a student?

1 Write the jobs under the correct pictures.

actor	actress	artist	✓model	musician	singer

1. Eddie Tucker
   England
   model

2. Piao GuangXie
   China
   ____

3. Benjamin Bratt
   the United States
   ____

4. Maria Rita
   Brazil
   ____

5. Sandra Oh
   Canada
   ____

6. Galo Ochoa
   Mexico
   ____

2 Write two sentences about each person in Exercise 1. Write the countries they are from and their jobs.

1. *Eddie Tucker is from England. He's a model.*
2. ____________
3. ____________
4. ____________
5. ____________
6. ____________

3 Put the words in the correct order to make sentences.

1. is / Canada / He / from / . *He is from Canada.*
2. from / I / Vancouver / am / . ______________________
3. actor / am / an / I / . ______________________
4. is / She / singer / a / . ______________________

4 Complete the conversation with the sentences from Exercise 3. Rewrite the sentences with contractions.

Becky: Hi, Mia. This is my friend Nick.

Mia: Hi, Nick. Are you a student?

Nick: No, I'm not. *I'm an actor* (1) .

Mia: Oh. Are you from the United States?

Nick: No, I'm not.

Becky: ______________________ (2) .

Mia: Oh. Are you from Toronto?

Nick: No, I'm not. ______________________ (3) .
Are you a student, Mia?

Mia: Yes, I am.

Becky: ______________________ (4) , too!

5 Answer the questions about the people in Exercise 4.

1. Is Nick an actor? *Yes, he is.*
2. Is Nick from Toronto? ______________________
3. Is Mia a teacher? ______________________
4. Is Mia a singer? ______________________

6 Answer the questions with your own information.

1. Is your teacher from the United States? ______________________
2. Are you a student? ______________________
3. Are you a singer? ______________________
4. Are you an artist? ______________________

7 Look at the pictures. Read the answers. Then write the *yes* / *no* questions.

1. *Is she from Canada* ?
   No, she isn't.

2. ______________________ ?
   Yes, he is.

3. ______________________ ?
   Yes, I am.

4. ______________________ ?
   No, it isn't.

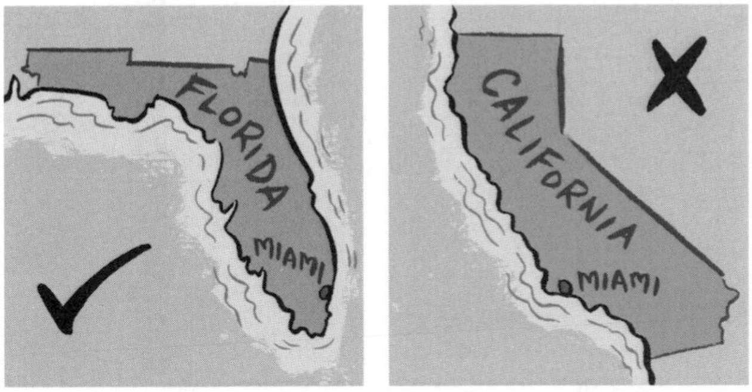

5. ______________________ ?
   Yes, it is.

6. ______________________ ?
   No, she isn't.

8 Write two sentences about each picture in Exercise 7.

1. *She isn't from Canada. She's from the United States.*
2. ______________________
3. ______________________
4. ______________________
5. ______________________
6. ______________________

D Names and jobs

1 Read the text. Write the first names of the people.

1. *Marina* 2. ________ 3. ________ 4. ________ 5. ________

TALENT FAIR

Saturday, 2:00 – 8:00 p.m.

See our talented students and classmates at the community fair.

Marina Soares and Tiago Arantes are from Brazil. Marina is a singer and Tiago is a musician in the band Beach Rock.

Listen to their music in Room B.

Meet the artist J.P. from Canada. (Information for his fans: his full name is Jacob Paul Larson.)

See his paintings in Room D.

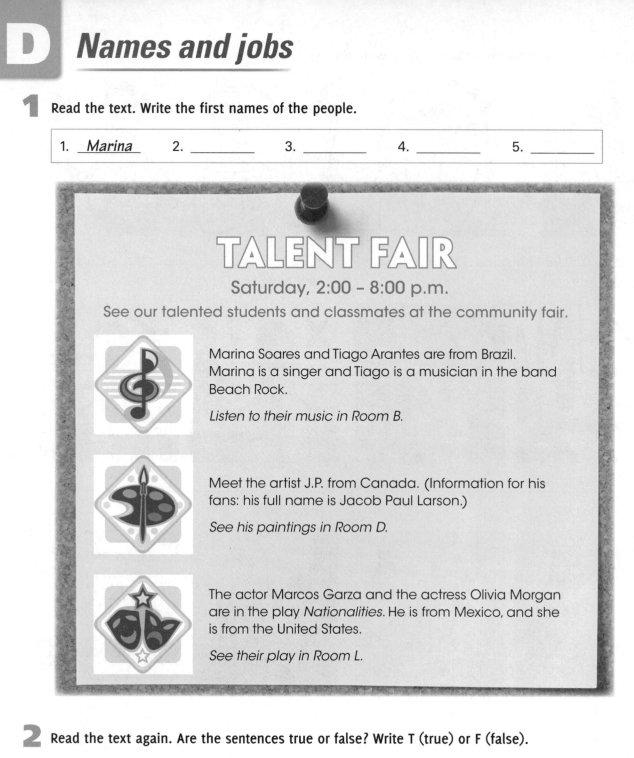

The actor Marcos Garza and the actress Olivia Morgan are in the play *Nationalities.* He is from Mexico, and she is from the United States.

See their play in Room L.

2 Read the text again. Are the sentences true or false? Write T (true) or F (false).

1. Marina is from Brazil. *T*
2. Tiago is a singer. ______
3. J.P.'s last name is Paul. ______
4. J.P. isn't from the United States. ______
5. Mr. Garza is an actor. ______
6. Olivia is from Mexico. ______

People and places

A Where are you from?

1 Cross out the word that doesn't belong in each list.

1. Australia	Greece	~~Ecuadorian~~	Chile
2. Chilean	Spain	Thai	Colombian
3. Ecuador	Peru	Greek	Saudi Arabia
4. Thai	Australian	Saudi	Colombia
5. Saudi	Thailand	Chilean	Ecuadorian

2 Complete the chart with the correct nationalities for the countries.

Brazil	Canada	Japan	South Korea	Turkey
Britain	China	Mexico	Spain	the United States

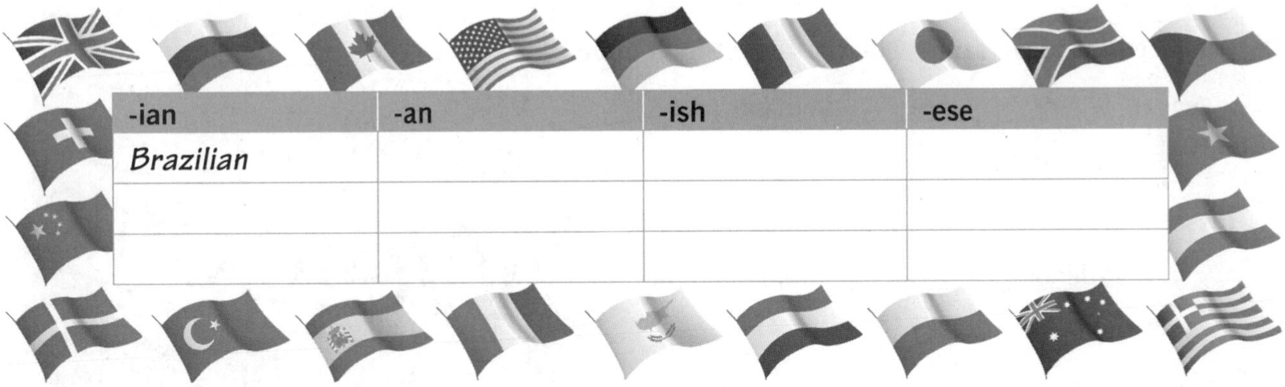

-ian	-an	-ish	-ese
Brazilian			

3 Rewrite the sentences. Use a subject pronoun and a nationality.

1. Kanya is from Thailand. *She's Thai.*
2. Joe is from Britain. ______
3. George is from Greece. ______
4. Mrs. Karim is from Saudi Arabia. ______
5. Emma is from the United States. ______
6. Mr. Morioka is from Japan. ______

4 Write sentences with the information in parentheses and the correct form of *be*.

1. (Carla and Rafael / be / from Peru.) *Carla and Rafael are from Peru.*
2. (Be / Josh and Ann / Canadian?) ____________________
3. (Jon and I / not / be / from China.) ____________________
4. (Be / Kyle and Tim / American?) ____________________

5 Complete the conversations with the sentences from Exercise 4. Use subject pronouns and contractions when possible.

1. **A:** Where are Carla and Rafael from?
   B: *They're from Peru* .
2. **A:** ____________________ ?
   B: Yes, they are.
3. **A:** Are you from China?
   B: No, ____________________ .
4. **A:** ____________________ ?
   B: No, they're not.

6 Complete the conversation with the correct form of *be*.

Eva: Hi! Where *are* (1) you and your friends from?

Tessa: I ________ (2) from the United States, but my friends ________ (3) from different countries.

Eva: Oh. Where ________ (4) they from?

Tessa: Well, Kaan ________ (5) from Turkey, and Mari ________ (6) from Japan. Roberto and Mateo ________ (7) from Mexico.

Eva: Oh. ________ (8) Roberto and Mateo from Mexico City?

Tessa: No, they ________ (9) . Roberto ________ (10) from Monterrey, and Mateo ________ (11) from Puebla.

Eva: Really? I ________ (12) from Puebla, too!

7 Circle the correct words to complete each sentence.

1. **Are** / **Where are** you and Denise from?
2. **What** / **Where** city is Ahmed from?
3. **Are** / **Is** you Japanese?
4. **Are** / **What** country are they from?
5. **What** / **Where** are they from?
6. **Are** / **Is** they Turkish?

8 Read the information in the guest book. Answer the questions.

Welcome to our

CULTURAL CENTER

PLEASE TELL US YOUR NAME AND ORIGIN

GUESTS

Name	City	Country
Mr. Kwan Moon	Pusan	South Korea
Mrs. Emily Hanson	Dallas	the United States
Leo Gonzales	Lima	Peru
Mr. Evren Mutlu	Istanbul	Turkey
Mike Peters	Toronto	Canada
Daniel Reynolds	Memphis	the United States
Isabel Ramirez	Guayaquil	Ecuador
Ms. Aya Sato	Tokyo	Japan
Mr. Todd Sutton	Vancouver	Canada

1. Are Leo and Isabel American? *No, they aren't.*
2. What city is Emily from? *She's from Dallas.*
3. Is Kwan from Pusan? ______
4. Where are Todd and Mike from? ______
5. What city is Daniel from? ______
6. Where is Evren from? ______
7. Is Mr. Reynolds from Toronto? ______
8. Are Aya and Leo from Turkey? ______

B What's your email address?

1 **Write the phone numbers.**

1. 903-2521: *nine-zero-three, two-five-two-one*
2. 588-6713: ______________________
3. 402-1359: ______________________
4. 266-5012: ______________________

2 **Complete the conversation with the correct questions from the box.**

How do you spell your last name?	✓What's your last name?
What city are you from in Thailand?	What's your phone number?
What's your email address?	

Alice: Hey, Dao. *What's your last name?* (1)

Dao: It's Kanok.

Alice: ______________________ (2)

Dao: K-A-N-O-K.

Alice: OK. ______________________ (3)

Dao: It's 296-754-9078.

Alice: Thanks. ______________________ (4)

Dao: It's daothai@cup.org.

Alice: Thai? ______________________ (5)

Dao: Bangkok.

3 **Look at the information in Alice's phone. Complete the conversation.**
Use Exercise 2 as a model.

Alice: Hey, Victor. How do you spell your last name?

Victor: ______________________ .

Alice: OK. ______________________ ?

Victor: ______________________ .

Alice: Thanks. ______________________ ?

Victor: ______________________ .

Alice: Thanks.

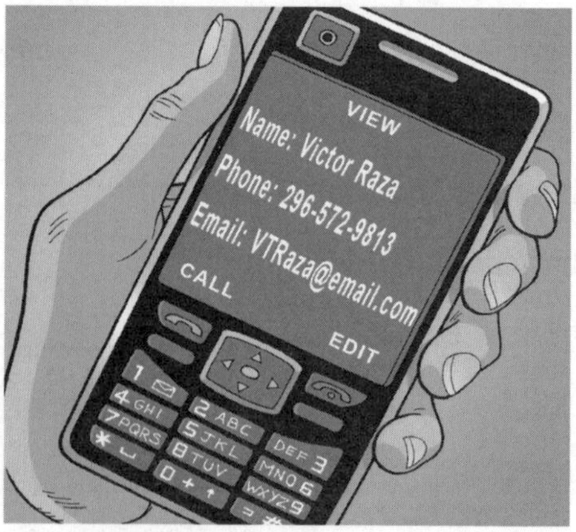

C Family

1 Look at Victoria's family tree. Label each of her family members with the correct word from the box.

brother	father	✓grandmother	mother	son
daughter	grandfather	husband	sister	

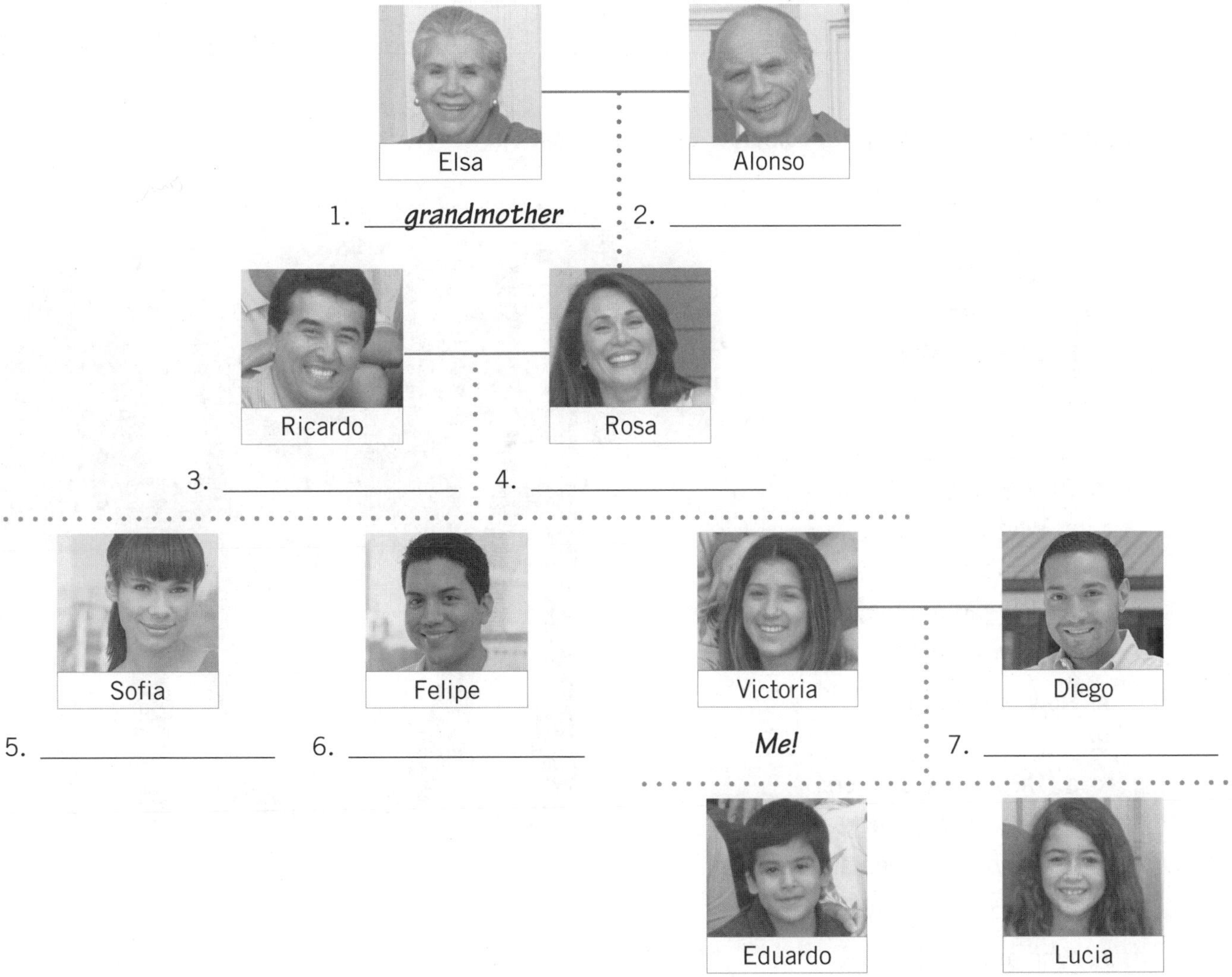

1. *grandmother*
2. ______________
3. ______________
4. ______________
5. ______________
6. ______________

Me! (Victoria)

7. ______________
8. ______________
9. ______________

2 Look at the family tree in Exercise 1. Rewrite the sentences to correct the underlined mistakes.

1. Diego: "Victoria is my grandmother." *Victoria is my wife.*
2. Eduardo: "Lucia is my brother." ______________
3. Lucia: "Ricardo is my father." ______________
4. Rosa: "Alonso is my son." ______________
5. Sofia: "Felipe is my grandfather." ______________
6. Ricardo: "Sofia is my sister." ______________

3 Put the numbers in order. Then write the words.

16	93	✓102	67	38	41
29	✓12	85	54	15	76

12 *twelve* ______ ______ ______ ______

______ ______ ______ ______ ______ ______

______ ______ ______ ______ ______ ______

______ ______ ______ ______ *102* *one hundred and two*

4 Circle the correct sentence to complete each conversation.

1. **A:** ______________________
   B: That's my mother.
   a. How old is she?
   (b.) Who's that?
   c. Where is she from?
   d. How old is that?

2. **A:** ______________________
   B: They're Greg and Ted.
   a. Who are they?
   b. Who's that?
   c. How old are they?
   d. How old is he?

3. **A:** How old are they?
   B: ______________________
   a. They're my brothers.
   b. He's twenty-five.
   c. They're nineteen and fourteen.
   d. She's my daughter.

4. **A:** Who are they?
   B: ______________________
   a. They're twenty and thirty.
   b. They're my parents.
   c. That's my father.
   d. She's fifty-four.

5. **A:** ______________________
   B: She's twelve.
   a. How old is your sister?
   b. Who's that?
   c. Who are they?
   d. How old is your father?

5 Complete the questions with *How old* and the correct form of *be*. Then answer the questions. Use pronouns and write the numbers in parentheses as words.

1. *How old is* Mr. Haik? *He's thirty-nine*. (39)
2. ______ Paula? ______. (45)
3. ______ Mr. and Mrs. Ryu? ______. (72 / 68)
4. ______ Jake? ______. (11)
5. ______ Cora and Steven? ______. (13 / 20)

6 Look at Lucy's information. Complete the conversation.

Last name: Nelson	**First name:** Lucy	**Middle name:** Amy
Age: 27	**Phone:** 212-555-1783	**Email:** lucyluc@cup.org

Emergency Contacts:

Name	Relation	Age	Phone
Brice Nelson	husband	28	212-555-1783
Kelly Bourne	mother	52	212-555-8604
John Bourne	father	56	212-555-8604

Clerk: Hello, Lucy. *What's your last name* (1)?
Lucy: Nelson.
Clerk: OK. And how old are you?
Lucy: ______ (2).
Clerk: And your emergency contacts – ______ (3)?
Lucy: They're Brice Nelson, Kelly Bourne, and John Bourne.
Clerk: Who's Brice Nelson?
Lucy: ______ (4).
Clerk: OK. ______ (5).
Lucy: He's 28.
Clerk: OK. And who are Kelly and John Bourne?
Lucy: They're my parents.
Clerk: ______ (6)?
Lucy: She's 52 and he's 56.

D Family and friends

1 **Read the webpage. Answer the questions.**

1. How old is Arzu? ______________________
2. How old is Yasemin? ______________________

The Baran Family

WHERE ARE YOU?

Hi! I'm Adem Baran. I'm American, but my parents and my grandparents are from Turkey. We're all in the United States now, but where is the rest of our family? If you are a Baran, write to me.

Hello, Adem. My name is Leyla. Your grandfather and my father are brothers. I'm in Turkey with my husband and my daughter, but my sons are in the United States. My mother, Arzu, is here, too. She's 92!

Hey, Adem. I'm Faruk. Leyla is my mother. I'm a teacher at a college in Boston. I'm here with my wife, Sibel, and my daughter, Yasemin. She's 6. My brother is in the United States, too. His name is Ismail, and he's an artist. He's in Chicago. He's single. What city in the United States are you in?

2 **Read the webpage again. Answer the questions.**

1. What's Adem's family name? *His family name is Baran.*
2. Where is Adem from? ______________________
3. Are Leyla and Arzu American? ______________________
4. Are Faruk and Ismail brothers? ______________________
5. Is Ismail in the United States? ______________________
6. Is Ismail a teacher? ______________________

What's that?

A Is this your notebook?

1 Find and circle nine more everyday items in the wordsquare.

t	d	i	c	t	i	o	n	a	r	y	d
n	p	h	e	k	b	o	s	u	l	m	u
o	a	c	l	y	b	a	g	m	s	z	e
t	w	a	l	t	c	i	h	b	f	p	r
e	l	a	p	t	o	p	z	r	y	d	a
b	d	b	h	h	v	e	t	e	e	r	s
o	n	n	o	g	l	n	o	l	e	o	e
o	w	h	n	c	q	y	r	l	l	x	r
k	b	w	e	s	u	j	w	a	t	c	h
a	c	t	n	a	i	s	s	u	m	r	l
l	g	s	u	n	g	l	a	s	s	e	s

2 Label each everyday item in the picture. Use the words from Exercise 1 and *a* or *an*.

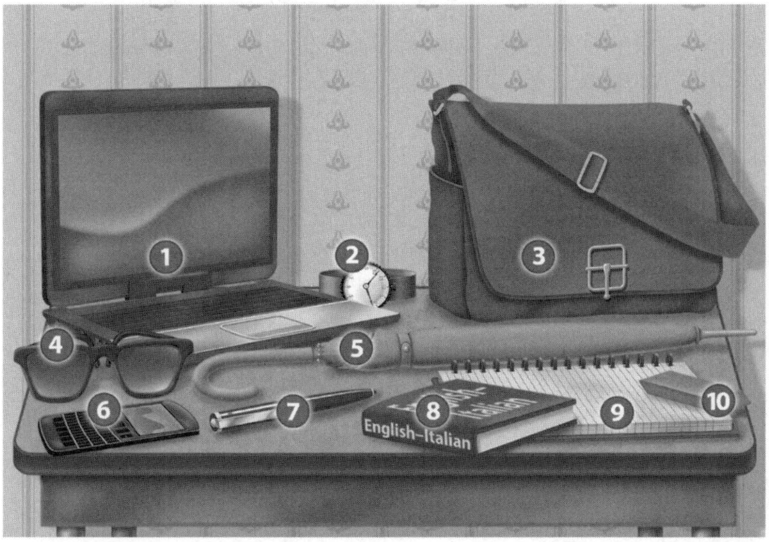

1. *a laptop*
2. ______
3. ______
4. ______
5. ______
6. ______
7. ______
8. ______
9. ______
10. ______

3 Write the plural form of the words.

1. umbrella _umbrellas_
2. book ______________
3. address ______________
4. laptop ______________
5. watch ______________
6. actress ______________
7. dictionary ______________
8. key ______________
9. eraser ______________
10. cell phone ______________

4 Circle the correct words to complete the conversations.

1. **A:** What's that?
   B: It's **a cell phone** / **two cell phones**.
2. **A:** What are those?
   B: **It's** / **They're** my books.
3. **A:** **What's that** / **What are those**?
   B: It's an umbrella.
4. **A:** **Are these** / **Is this** your laptop?
   B: No, it's not.
5. **A:** Is this my bag?
   B: Yes, **it is** / **they are**.
6. **A:** What are these?
   B: They're **a key** / **keys**.
7. **A:** **What's that** / **What are these**?
   B: They're your pens.
8. **A:** **Are those** / **Is this** your dictionary?
   B: No, it isn't.

5 Write the correct questions and answers under each picture.

✓Is that your bag?	What's that?	It's my dictionary.	No, it's not.
Is this your bag?	What's this?	It's my key.	Yes, it is.

1. A: *Is that your bag?*
   B: ______

2. A: ______
   B: ______

3. A: ______
   B: ______

4. A: ______
   B: ______

6 Rewrite the conversations in Exercise 5 in the plural form.

1. A: *Are those your bags?*
   B: ______
2. A: ______
   B: ______
3. A: ______
   B: ______
4. A: ______
   B: ______

B What's this called in English?

1 **Look at the pictures. Complete the conversations with the correct words from the box.**

an alarm clock	a coin	a hairbrush	say this	✓this called	the word

A. **Beth:** Excuse me. What's *this called* (1) in English?
Jim: It's ______________ (2).
Beth: Thanks.

B. **Al:** Excuse me. How do you ______________ (1) in English?
Lin: It's ______________ (2).
Al: Thank you.

C. **Mel:** Excuse me. What's ______________ (1) for this in English?
Jay: It's ______________ (2).
Mel: Oh! Thanks.

2 **Look at the pictures. Write conversations. Use Exercise 1 as a model.**

A. **Fran:** Excuse me. What's this called in English?
Pat: ______________________________
Fran: ______________________________

B. **Gabe:** ______________________________
Tim: ______________________________
Gabe: ______________________________

C. **Jill:** ______________________________
Yuka: ______________________________
Jill: ______________________________

C Clothing

1 **Put the letters in the correct order to make color words.**

1. r d e	*red*	7. h i t w e	________
2. w l o y l e	________	8. c a b k l	________
3. y a r g	________	9. l p p u r e	________
4. l u b e	________	10. k i p n	________
5. e g o r n a	________	11. n o r w b	________
6. n g e r e	________		

2 **You are a clothing designer. Choose one picture. Choose colors and label the clothes. Use the examples to help you.**

Example: *The jacket is red and black.* or *The jacket is blue.*

1. ____________________
____
2. ____________________
____
3. ____________________
____
4. ____________________
____
5. ____________________
____
6. ____________________
____
7. ____________________
____

3 **Look at the pictures. Complete the questions with *whose*. Then check (✓) all of the possible answers.**

Sam

1. *Whose sweater is* ________ this?

- [x] It's Sam's.
- [x] It's his.
- [ ] They're his.
- [x] It's his sweater.
- [ ] It's hers.
- [ ] It's our sweater.

Jenny

2. ________ those?

- [ ] They're theirs.
- [ ] It's hers.
- [ ] They're hers.
- [ ] It's her.
- [ ] They're yours.
- [ ] They're Jenny's.

Bill and Meg

3. ________ these?

- [ ] They're ours.
- [ ] They're our bags.
- [ ] They're theirs.
- [ ] They're their bags.
- [ ] They're Bill and Meg's bags.
- [ ] They're Bill and Meg's.

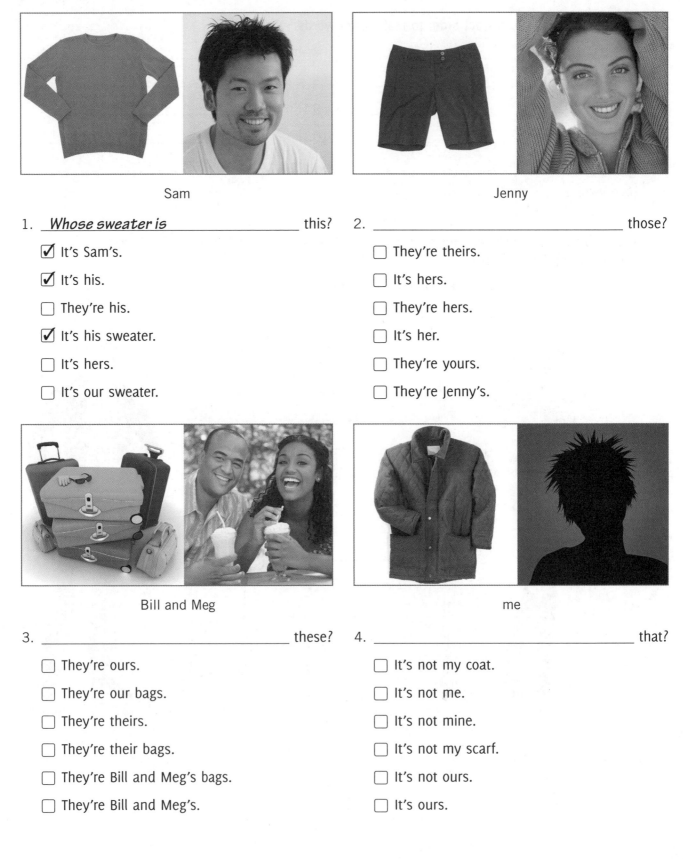

me

4. ________ that?

- [ ] It's not my coat.
- [ ] It's not me.
- [ ] It's not mine.
- [ ] It's not my scarf.
- [ ] It's not ours.
- [ ] It's ours.

4 Complete the sentences with the correct possessive pronouns.

1. They're Maria's jeans. They're ___*hers*___ .
2. This is not my T-shirt. This is not ______ .
3. Are those your sweatshirts? Are those ______ ?
4. These are the models' dresses. These are ______ .
5. Those are not our hats. Those are not ______ .
6. That's Adam's suit. That's ______ .

5 Whose are they? Write the sentence four different ways for each item.

Field Park
Lost and Found Log

Lost Item	Name
1. laptop	Peter and Kate Nelson
2. shoes	Linda Park
3. sunglasses	Ron Davis
4. flash drive	Neil and Jane Moore
5. wallet	Oliver Brooks
6. camera	Silvia Harris

1. *It's Peter and Kate's laptop.* *It's Peter and Kate's.*
   It's their laptop. *It's theirs.*
2. ______ ______
   ______ ______
3. ______ ______
   ______ ______
4. ______ ______
   ______ ______
5. ______ ______
   ______ ______
6. ______ ______
   ______ ______

D Favorite things

1 **Read the catalog page. Number the pictures from 1 to 4.**

a. ___

b. *1*

c. ___

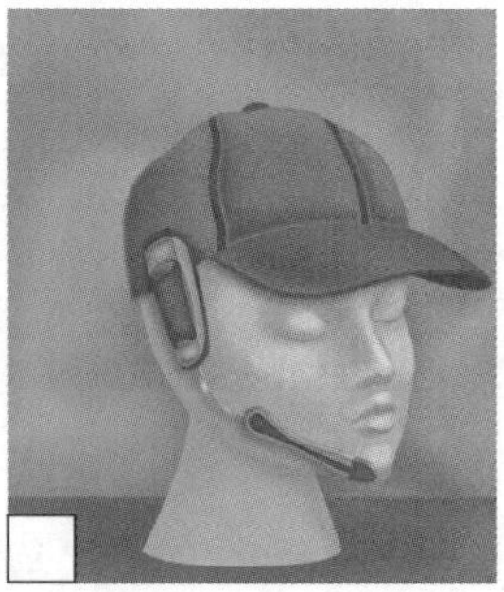

d. ___

Our Favorite Hats

1 Sca-hat
It's a scarf and a hat. This is Julianna Kora's design. Her *sca-hats* are very popular. The colors are blue, black, green, or yellow. Get one today!

2 Hat-brella
This *hat-brella* is in Roberto Pena's clothing line. It's his new design. It's a hat and an umbrella. The colors are blue, purple, or orange.

3 Pho-hat
Whose *pho-hat* is this? It's yours! Buy it today. The hat is red, brown, or white. The cell phone is in the hat! Talk to your friends and be warm.

4 Hat-glasses
Buy these *hat-glasses*. They're sunglasses with a hat. They are black, gray, or purple. They're great for skiing or snowboarding.

2 **Read the catalog page again. Then complete the chart.**

Product	Two items	Colors
1. *Sca-hat*	*scarf and hat*	*blue, black, green, or yellow*
2.		
3.		
4.		

Daily life

A Getting around

1 **Look at the pictures. Complete the puzzle with the ways of getting around. What's the mystery word?**

1. 

2. 

3. 

4. 

5. 

6. 

7. 

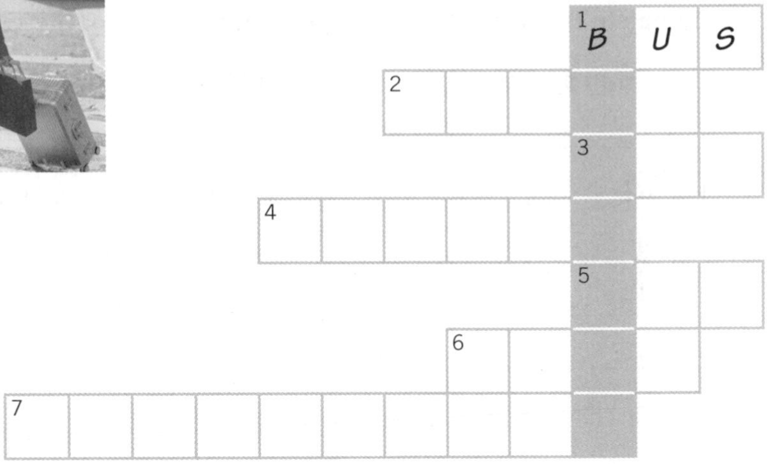

2 **Circle the correct verbs to make phrases. Then write the phrases.**

1. **have** / **take** / **walk** the bus — *take the bus*
2. **drive** / **ride** / **go** a car — ______
3. **take** / **drive** / **ride** a bicycle — ______
4. **be** / **take** / **ride** a taxi — ______
5. **work** / **walk** / **ride** a motorcycle — ______

3 Circle the correct answer to complete each sentence.

1. Molly ______ two cars.
   a. have
   (b.) has
   c. not have
2. Alex ______ his bike to work.
   a. ride
   b. rides
   c. to ride
3. We ______ to school.
   a. not walk
   b. doesn't walk
   c. don't walk
4. I ______ a motorcycle.
   a. doesn't have
   b. has
   c. don't have
5. You ______ the subway to work.
   a. take
   b. takes
   c. doesn't take
6. Simon ______ a cab.
   a. drive
   b. don't drive
   c. drives

4 Complete the text with the simple present forms of the verbs in parentheses.

I *don't have* (1) (not / have) a car. I ________ (2) (take) the train to work. My wife ________ (3) (not / take) the train. Her friend ________ (4) (have) a car, and she ________ (5) (drive) to work. So my wife ________ (6) (go) to work in her friend's car.

Our children Amanda and Brett ________ (7) (take) the bus to school. And they ________ (8) (ride) their bikes to their friends' houses. Our daughter Lisa ________ (9) (walk) to school.

Our son Jerry is 24, and he ________ (10) (not / go) to school. He ________ (11) (have) a motorcycle, and he ________ (12) (ride) it to work.

5 Look at the results of the survey. Then write sentences about the results.

We want to know how you get around!

How do you get to . . .	work?	school?
1. take the bus	13	1
2. take the train	7	4
3. take a taxi	3	1
4. ride a bicycle	1	3
5. drive a car	32	18
6. walk	1	5

1. *Thirteen people take the bus to work.*
   One person takes the bus to school.
2. ______________________________
   ____
3. ______________________________
   ____
4. ______________________________
   ____
5. ______________________________
   ____
6. ______________________________
   ____

6 How do you get to these places? Write your answers.

1. 
2. 
3. 
4. 

Example: *I drive.*

1. ______________________
2. ______________________
3. ______________________
4. ______________________

B What time is it?

1 **Look at the train schedule. Answer the questions. Write the times two ways, if possible.**

Departures

Time	Number	Train	To	Status	Gate
8:50 a.m.	2345	Silver Bullet	Boston	On time	12
9:30 a.m.	4567	Ace Express	Philadelphia	On time	4
10:45 a.m.	3456	NE Rider	Washington, D.C.	On time	9
1:00 p.m.	4522	Silver Bullet	Richmond	On time	7
2:17 p.m.	1029	Gray Line	Pittsburgh	On time	22
3:55 p.m.	3467	Ace Express	Raleigh	On time	15
4:40 p.m.	1259	Chicago Rail	Chicago	On time	6
6:15 p.m.	3050	Silver Bullet	Norfolk	On time	21

What time is the train to . . . ?

1. Boston *It's at eight-fifty a.m. / ten to nine.*
2. Philadelphia ______________________
3. Washington, D.C. ______________________
4. Richmond ______________________
5. Pittsburgh ______________________
6. Raleigh ______________________
7. Chicago ______________________
8. Norfolk ______________________

2 **Circle the correct words to complete the conversation. Use the train schedule from Exercise 1.**

A: What time **is it** / **it is**? (1)

B: **They're** / **It's** four o'clock. (2)

A: What **time** / **the time** is the train to Raleigh? (3)

B: At five **to** / **after** four. (4) We're **early** / **late**. (5)

3 **Write a conversation about the train to Norfolk. It's 6:00 p.m. Use the conversation in Exercise 2 as a model.**

A: ______________________

B: ______________________

A: ______________________

B: ______________________

C My routine

1 **Write the days of the week in the correct order.**

Monday ________ ________ ________ ________ ________ *Sunday*

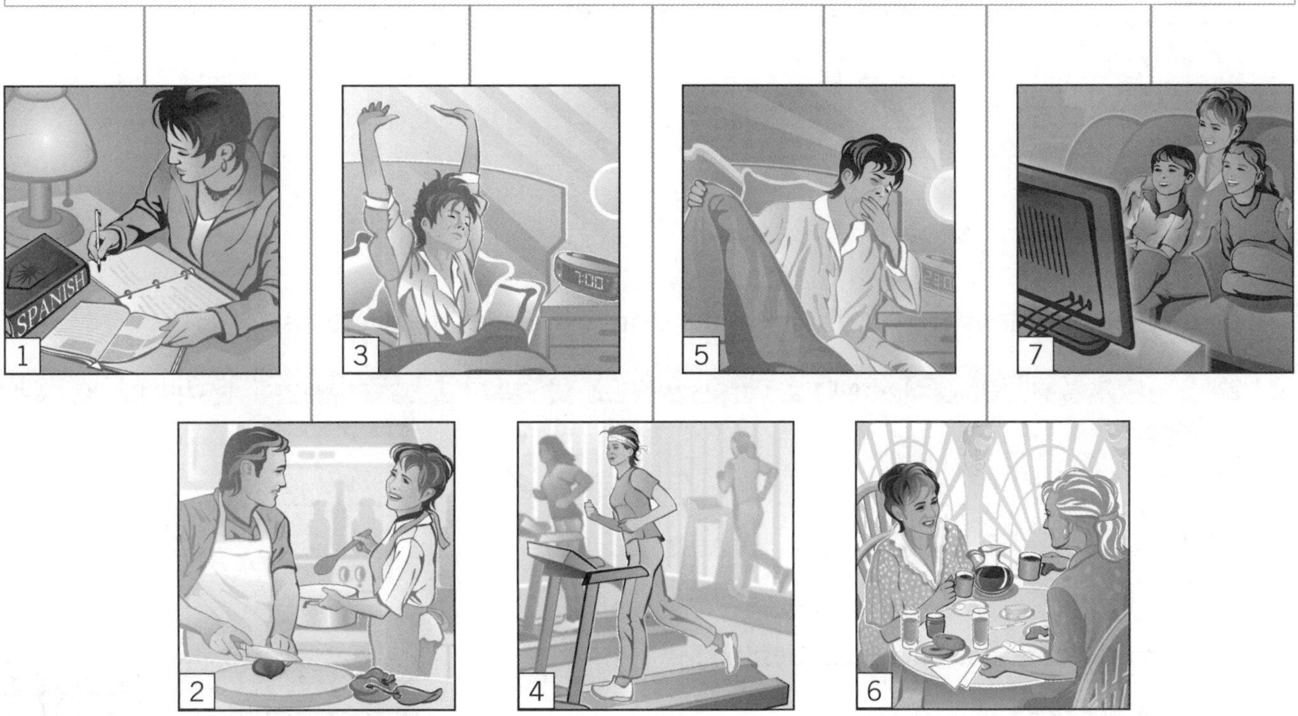

2 **Complete the sentences about Jackie's routine. Use the days of the week and the pictures in Exercise 1.**

1. Jackie *studies* Spanish *on Mondays* .
2. Jackie ________________ with her husband ________________ .
3. Jackie ________________ early ________________ .
4. Jackie ________________ ________________ .
5. Jackie ________________ late ________________ .
6. Jackie ________________ with her mother ________________ .
7. Jackie ________________ with her children ________________ .

3 Complete the chart with the correct words from the box.

8:15	midnight	the afternoon	the weekend
class	night	the evenings	Tuesday afternoon
✓Friday	noon	the morning	weekdays

on . . .	in . . .	at . . .
Friday		

4 Do they read the news every day? Look at the chart and answer the questions.

	Mondays	Tuesdays	Wednesdays	Thursdays	Fridays	Saturdays	Sundays
Bridget	✓	✓	✓	✓	✓	✓	✓
Paulo	✓	✓	✓	✓	✓		
Ava						✓	✓
Mike	✓						

1. Does Bridget read the news on Tuesdays?
   Yes, she does.
2. Do Paulo and Ava read the news every day?
   ____
3. Does Paulo read the news on weekdays?
   ____
4. Does Ava read the news on Saturdays?
   ____
5. Do Ava and Mike read the news on Wednesdays?
   ____
6. Do Mike and Bridget read the news on Mondays?
   ____

5 Put the words in the correct order to make questions.

1. on / study / weekend / Does / Andy / the / ?

   Does Andy study on the weekend?

2. day / eat / Do / every / they / breakfast / ?

   ____

3. at / to / work / go / Does / his / 8:00 / sister / ?

   ____

4. the / Do / coffee / in / evening / her / grandparents / drink / ?

   ____

5. weekdays / TV / Do / watch / on / Liv and Martin / ?

   ____

6. go / after / to / Does / midnight / Vanessa / bed / ?

   ____

6 Answer the questions from Exercise 5. Correct the information when the answer is "No." Use the words in parentheses.

1. No, *he doesn't* . *He studies on Mondays* . (on Mondays)
2. Yes, ____________ .
3. No, ____________ . ____________ . (8:30)
4. Yes, ____________ .
5. No, ____________ . ____________ . (on weekends)
6. No, ____________ . ____________ . (at 10:30)

7 Write five sentences about your weekly routine. Use the simple present forms of the verbs in the box and time expressions.

drink coffee	eat dinner	get up	go to school	study English
eat breakfast	exercise	go to bed	read the news	watch TV

Example: *I drink coffee every day.*

____

____

____

____

____

D My weekend

1 **Read the webpage. Check all the ways to go to each place.**

	Boston	Washington, D.C.	Coney Island	Orchard Beach
subway				
train	✓			
bus	✓			

TRIPS AROUND
NEW YORK CITY

BOSTON
Take the train from Penn Station. The trip is 3 hours and 35 minutes. Trains go to Boston all day and night.

Take a bus from New York to Boston. The buses go every hour from 7:00 a.m. to 10:00 p.m. every day. On Saturdays, buses are at 8:30 a.m. and 9:30 a.m., too. The trip is 4 hours.

WASHINGTON, D.C.
Take the train from Penn Station. You are on the train for 2½ hours. The times are different every day. Check the schedules.

Buses go every hour on weekdays and every 30 minutes on weekends. The first bus is at 7:30 a.m. The last bus is at 7:30 p.m. You're on the bus for 4 hours.

CONEY ISLAND
Take the D, Q, N, or F subway to Coney Island Terminal. The trip is 45 minutes to 1 hour.

Take a bus. The B36, B64, B68, B74, B82, X28, and X38 go to Coney Island.

ORCHARD BEACH
Take the number 6 subway to Pelham Bay. Then take the Bx12 bus to Orchard Beach. (You can take the Bx5 on weekends in the summer, too.) The trip is 1½ hours.

2 **Write B (Boston), W (Washington, D.C.), C (Coney Island), or O (Orchard Beach). Sometimes more than one answer is possible.**

1. The trains are at Penn Station. ___B___ ___W___
2. The number 6 subway goes there. ______
3. The first bus is at 7:00 a.m. ______
4. You take the B74 bus. ______
5. The subways from New York don't go there. ______ ______

Free time

A Online habits

1 **Put the letters in the correct order to make online activity words and phrases.**

1. c r s h e a h e t n t t l e e n r *search the Internet*
2. p s o h e n l n i o ______
3. l a p y m a g s e ______
4. p d u l o a s v d o e i ______
5. o p t s m m e c o n t s ______
6. c c e h k m l e i a ______
7. l o o d w n d a c i m s u ______
8. t c a h t i w h s r d f i n e ______

2 **Look at the pictures. Complete the sentences with the online activities from Exercise 1. Use the correct forms of the verbs.**

1. Do you *search the Internet* at work?

2. Helen ______ ______ every day.

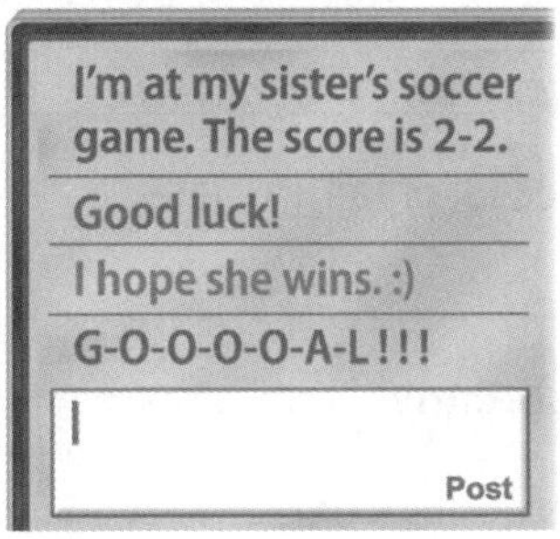

3. Di ______ on her friends' webpages.

4. I ______ ______ on Sundays.

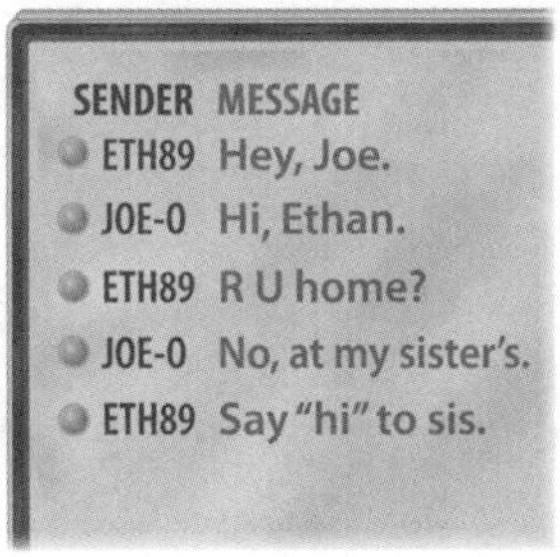

5. Ethan ______ ______ at night.

6. They ______ ______ of their cat every day.

7. Does she ______ ______ of her favorite singers?

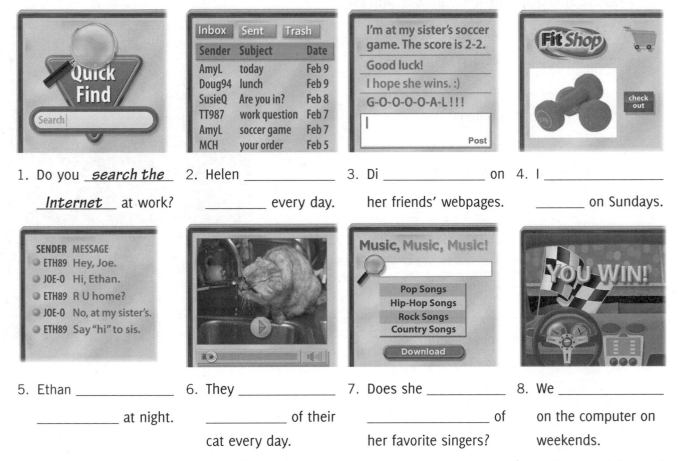

8. We ______ on the computer on weekends.

3 Write the adverbs of frequency in the correct order.

always	hardly ever	never	✓often	sometimes	usually

100%

1. ____________
2. ____________
3. *often*
4. ____________
5. ____________
6. ____________

0%

4 Put the words in the correct order to make sentences.

1. always / Robin / to school / walks / . *Robin always walks to school.*
2. games / sometimes / play / online / We / . ____________
3. work / you / on Saturdays / ever / Do / ? ____________
4. download / Sara and Toby / often / music / . ____________
5. to work / Fran / the bus / ever / take / Does / ? ____________
6. Keiko / with / hardly ever / chats / friends / . ____________

5 Read the answers. Write the questions with *ever*.

1. *Does she ever check email in class?*
   Yes, she usually checks email in class.
2. ____________
   No, he never gets up early.
3. ____________
   No, I never play games online.
4. ____________
   Yes, they often go to bed after midnight.
5. ____________
   No, they never shop online.
6. ____________
   Yes, we sometimes download music.

6 Look at Pam's answers to the quiz. Then answer the questions.

Are you addicted to the Internet?

How often do you . . .	often	sometimes	hardly ever	never
1. chat with friends online?	☐	☑	☐	☐
2. upload videos?	☐	☐	☐	☑
3. search the Internet?	☑	☐	☐	☐
4. check email?	☑	☐	☐	☐
5. shop online?	☐	☐	☑	☐
6. play games online?	☐	☐	☐	☑

1. Does Pam ever chat with friends online? *Yes, she sometimes does.*
2. Does she ever upload videos? ______________________
3. Does she ever search the Internet? ______________________
4. Does she ever check email? ______________________
5. Does she ever shop online? ______________________
6. Does she ever play games online? ______________________

7 Are the sentences true or false for you? Write T (true) or F (false). Correct the false sentences.

Example: I sometimes upload videos. *F*

I never upload videos.

1. I often play video games on weekends. _______

   ____

2. I never shop online. _______

   ____

3. I hardly ever search the Internet. _______

   ____

4. My father often checks email. _______

   ____

5. My mother sometimes posts comments online. _______

   ____

B How much is it?

1 Look at the pictures. Write the prices in words.

$62.50 **$600.25** **$42.45**

1. *sixty-two dollars and fifty cents*
2. ______________________
3. ______________________

$230.99 **$58.79** **$76.20**

4. ______________________
5. ______________________
6. ______________________

2 Complete the conversations with the correct words from the box.

✓can	fine	how much	it's	just	no	please	these	they're	yes

A. Salesperson: *Can* (1) I help you?

Jonathan: No, thanks, I'm ________ (2) looking.

B. Salesperson: Can I help you?

Yae Jih: ________ (1), thanks. ________ (2) is this wallet?

Salesperson: ________ (3) $24.50.

Yae Jih: Thanks.

C. Salesperson: Hello. Can I help you?

Mariana: Yes, ________ (1). How much are ________ (2) sunglasses?

Salesperson: ________ (3) $35.99.

Mariana: OK. Thanks.

D. Salesperson: Hi. Can I help you?

Christopher: ________ (1). I'm ________ (2). Thanks.

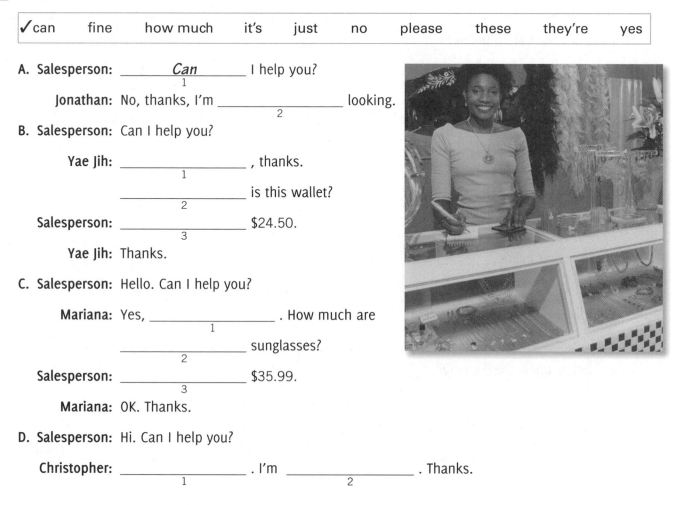

C What do you do for fun?

1 Write a sentence about each picture. Use a phrase from each box and the simple present forms of the verbs.

eat out	go dancing	go shopping	✓play soccer	watch movies

at Club Z	✓at Oak Park	at home	at restaurants	at the mall

Here's what I do for fun!

PHOTOALBUM

1. I *play soccer at Oak Park.*

2. I ______________________

3. I ______________________

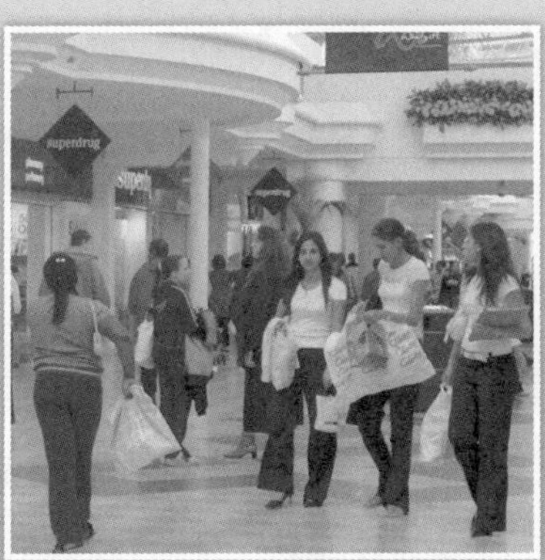

4. I ______________________

5. I ______________________

2 Match the questions and the answers.

1. What do you and your friends do for fun? ___e___
2. Where do you and your family eat out? _______
3. When do you hang out with friends? _______
4. Who do you go dancing with? _______
5. How do you get to school? _______
6. Why do you take the bus to work? _______

a. On weekends.
b. My wife.
c. I ride my bike.
d. Because I don't drive.
e. We download music.
f. At Terry's Restaurant.

3 Circle the correct words to complete each question.

1. (**Who**) / **Why** do you watch movies with?
2. **Why** / **How** do you get to your English class?
3. What **do your parents** / **your parents** do for fun?
4. **Why you** / **Do you** take English classes?
5. **When** / **What** do you usually go shopping?
6. Where **you do** / **do you** hang out with friends?
7. **When time** / **What time** do you usually get up on Mondays?
8. When **do you do** / **do you** eat out?

4 Answer the questions from Exercise 3 with your own information.

1. ______________________________
2. ______________________________
3. ______________________________
4. ______________________________
5. ______________________________
6. ______________________________
7. ______________________________
8. ______________________________

5 Complete the questions with the correct *Wh-* words, subject pronouns, and simple present verbs.

A. **Marta:** Hi, Jason. *Where do you go shopping* [1] ?

Jason: I usually go to the mall.

Marta: ______________________ [2] to the mall?

Jason: Because I don't shop online!

Marta: ______________________ [3] to the mall?

Jason: I drive.

B. **Jodie:** Hey, Sally. ______________________ [1] out?

Sally: I usually eat at The Blue Café.

Jodie: ______________________ [2] with?

Sally: I go with my husband and my children.

Jodie: ______________________ [3] usually ______________________ [4] there?

Sally: We usually go on Sundays.

C. **Justin:** Hey, Mark. ______________________ [1] for fun?

Mark: For fun? Well, I often hang out with friends.

Justin: ______________________ [2] out?

Mark: We usually go to the park or a club.

6 Complete the interview. Use the information in the notes.

Interview

Sandra Mill:

- works at Beth's Restaurant
- walks to work because she doesn't have a car
- watches movies with friends for fun

Reporter: Where *do you work* ?

Sandra: I work at Beth's Restaurant.

Reporter: How ______________________ work?

Sandra: ______________________ .

Reporter: ______________________ work?

Sandra: Because ______________________ .

Reporter: ______________________ fun?

Sandra: ______________________ .

Reporter: ______________________ with?

Sandra: ______________________ .

D Online fun

1 **Who goes dancing? Read the survey and check the correct boxes.**

☐ Group 1 ☐ Group 2 ☐ Group 3

What do you do for fun?

Here are the results from our survey.

GROUP 1 (age 13–19)
Teenagers always hang out with friends. They often go dancing at school dances. They go shopping at the mall. They sometimes watch movies at the theater or their friends' houses. They hardly ever eat out at restaurants. When they don't hang out with friends, they chat with their friends online and post comments on their friends' webpages. They also download music and play games online.

GROUP 2 (age 20–30)
People in this group hang out with friends, too. They never go to school dances, but they go dancing at clubs. They eat out at restaurants with their friends and family. They sometimes play sports in the park on weekends. They upload videos and download music at home.

GROUP 3 (age 31–40)
People in this group watch movies with friends and family. They check email and post photos of their family and friends online. They often eat at home on weekdays and eat out on weekends. They sometimes go dancing with friends or their husbands and wives. They are busy, so they often shop online.

2 **Read the results of the survey again. Then answer the questions.**

1. Who do people in Group 1 hang out with?
   They hang out with their friends.
2. What do people in Group 1 hardly ever do?
   ____
3. Where do people in Group 2 go dancing?
   ____
4. Who do people in Group 2 eat out with?
   ____
5. When do people in Group 3 eat at home?
   ____
6. Where do people in Group 3 often shop?
   ____

Work and play

A What does she do?

1 **Look at the things that people use for their jobs. Complete the puzzle with the jobs.**

Across

1. 

4. 

5. 

6. 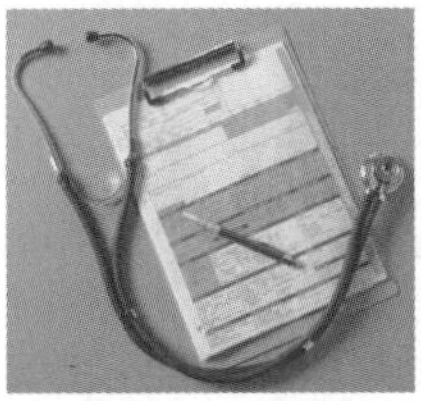

9. 

Down

2. 

3. 

7. 

8. 

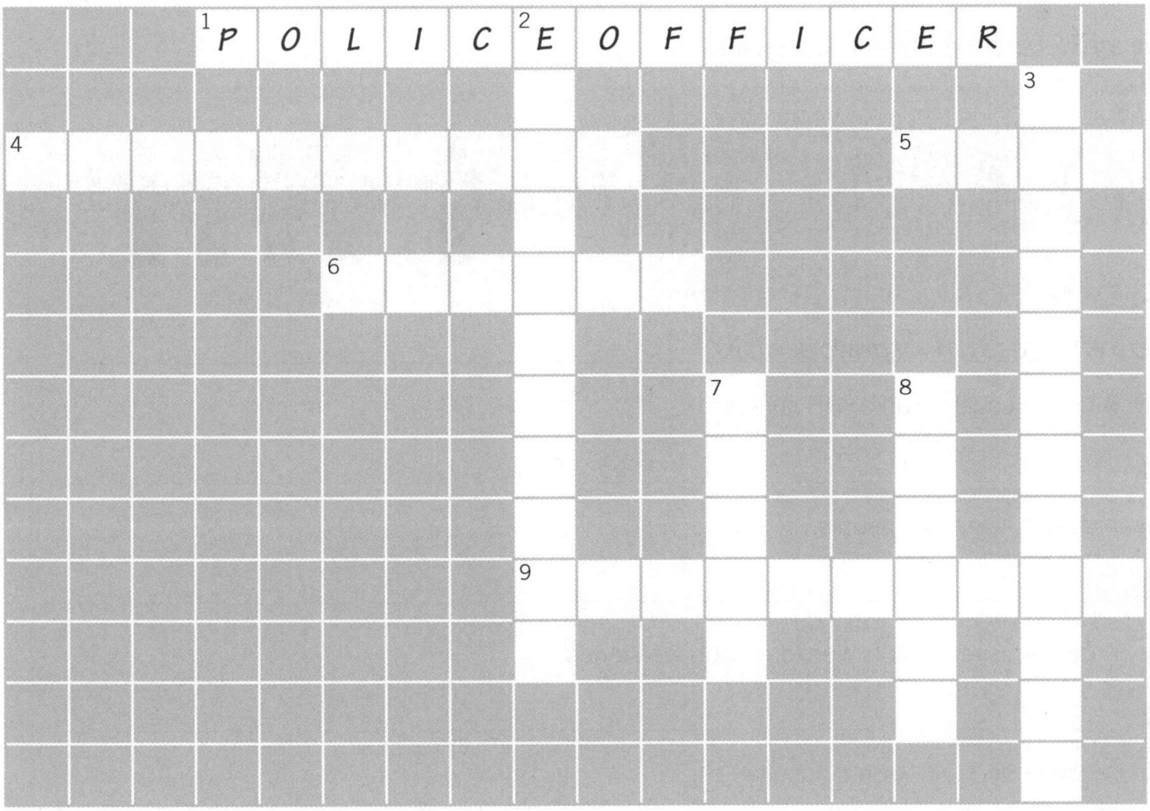

2 Put the words in the correct order to make questions.

1. does / brother / Where / work / your / ? *Where does your brother work?*
2. company / does / What / for / he / work / ? ______
3. he / does / work / When / ? ______
4. do / he / does / What / ? ______

3 Complete the conversation with the questions from Exercise 2.

Nick: Hey, Mindy. *Where does your brother work* (1)?

Mindy: He works in an office.

Nick: OK. ______ (2)?

Mindy: Oh. He works for Home Stop.

Nick: Really? My sister works there, too. ______ (3)?

Mindy: He's an accountant.

Nick: Cool. ______ (4)?

Mindy: He usually works from 9:00 to 6:00.

Nick: OK. I'll tell my sister.

4 Read the answers. Write the *Wh-* questions.

JOBFACTS

JOB: DOCTOR

Q: *Who does a doctor work with?* (1)

A: A doctor usually works with nurses.

Q: ______ (2)

A: A doctor helps sick people.

Q: ______ (3)

A: A doctor usually works weekdays and weekends.

Q: ______ (4)

A: A doctor often works in a hospital.

5 Read the text. Then answer the questions.

EMPLOYEE INFORMATION

Name: *Ted O'Neil*
Job: *electrician*
Company: *Mac Electrics*
Hours: *8:00 a.m.–5:30 p.m.*
Gets to work: *drive*
Leisure activities: *play soccer, watch movies*

EMPLOYEE INFORMATION

Name: *Sasha Powell*
Job: *flight attendant*
Company: *Go Air*
Hours: *They vary.*
Gets to work: *take a bus*
Leisure activities: *listen to music, go dancing*

1. What does Ted do? *He's an electrician.*
2. What company does he work for? ________________
3. When does he work? ________________
4. What does he do for fun? ________________
5. What does Sasha do? ________________
6. What company does she work for? ________________
7. How does she get to work? ________________
8. What does she do for fun? ________________

6 Answer the questions about a friend or a family member.

1. What does he / she do?

   ____

2. Where does he / she work or study?

   ____

3. When does he / she work or study?

   ____

4. How does he / she get to work or school?

   ____

5. What does he / she do for fun?

   ____

B Can I speak to . . . ?

1 Write the conversation in the correct order.

All right. Thank you.
✓ Good afternoon, TYA Air.
Hello. Can I speak to Jack Johnson?
It's Pam Davis.
One moment, please. . . . Oh, I'm sorry. Mr. Johnson is on another line.
Who is this, please?

Joe: *Good afternoon, TYA Air.*

Pam: ______

Joe: ______

Pam: ______

Joe: ______

Pam: ______

2 Look at the picture. Write a conversation with the expressions from the box. Use Exercise 1 as a model.

Just a minute, please. . . .   Could I please speak to . . .

A: *Good morning, TJ Accountants.*

B: ______

A: ______

B: ______

A: ______

B: ______

C Can you sing?

1 Look at the pictures. Complete the sentences with the simple present forms of the verbs from the box.

dance	fix computers	✓play the guitar	speak Spanish
draw	paint	sing	swim

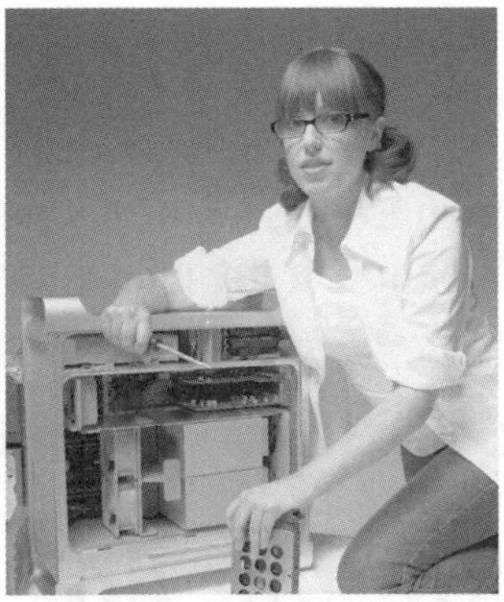

1. Don *plays the guitar* at the park.
2. Carlos ______________ with his father.
3. Vicky ______________ for her friends.
4. Eddie and Karen ______________ at a club on Saturdays.

5. Brian ______________ at the pool every day.
6. Mrs. Yamaguchi ______________ pictures on vacation.
7. Ricky ______________ at a restaurant on weekends.
8. Zoe ______________ pictures on the wall.

2 Read the answers. Complete the questions about the people from Exercise 1.

1. Where *does Don play the guitar*? At the park.
2. Who ______________ with? Eddie.
3. Where ______________? On the wall.
4. When ______________? On vacation.
5. Who ______________ with? His father.
6. When ______________? On weekends.

3 Write *yes* / *no* questions with *can* and the words in parentheses.

1. (Julia / speak French) *Can Julia speak French* ?
2. (Doug / play the guitar) ______ ?
3. (Doug and Evan / sing) ______ ?
4. (Emma / speak French) ______ ?
5. (Evan / swim) ______ ?
6. (Marcos and Emma / paint) ______ ?

4 Rewrite the questions from Exercise 3 with subject pronouns. Then answer the questions with the information in the online survey.

What can you do?

Can you . . .	sing?	play the guitar?	paint?	speak French?	swim?
Julia	No	No	Yes	Yes	Yes
Doug	Yes	Yes	No	No	Yes
Emma	Yes	Yes	No	No	Yes
Evan	Yes	Yes	Yes	Yes	No
Marcos	No	No	No	Yes	Yes

1. **A:** *Can she speak French* ?
   B: *Yes, she can* .
2. **A:** ______ ?
   B: ______ .
3. **A:** ______ ?
   B: ______ .
4. **A:** ______ ?
   B: ______ .
5. **A:** ______ ?
   B: ______ .
6. **A:** ______ ?
   B: ______ .

5 Look at the pictures below and the survey in Exercise 4 on page 46. Write sentences about what the people can and can't do. Use *and, but,* or *or.*

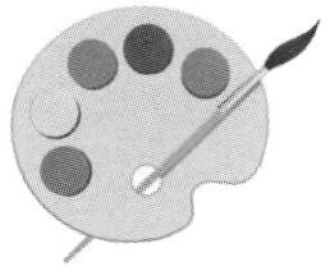 

1. Julia *can paint, but she can't play* *the guitar*.

2. Doug ______________________________ ______________________________.

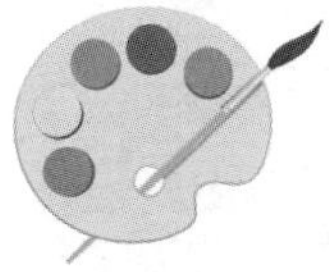 

3. Emma ______________________________ ______________________________.

4. Marcos ______________________________ ______________________________.

6 Can you do these things well? Check (✓) *very well, well, not well,* or *not at all.* Then write sentences about your abilities. Use *can* and the adverbs.

	very well	well	not well	not at all
1. dance	☐	☐	☐	☐
2. draw	☐	☐	☐	☐
3. fix computers	☐	☐	☐	☐
4. paint	☐	☐	☐	☐
5. play tennis	☐	☐	☐	☐
6. sing	☐	☐	☐	☐

Example: *I can't dance at all.*

1. ______________________________
2. ______________________________
3. ______________________________
4. ______________________________
5. ______________________________
6. ______________________________

D Work and study

1 Read the ads and answer the questions.

1. Who fixes computers? ____________________
2. Who is a teacher? ____________________
3. Who are musicians? ____________________

HAVEN COMMUNITY BOARD
POST YOUR SIGNS HERE

Writing Workshop

Can you write?
Do you want to write better?
Take my writing workshop.

Classes meet on Tuesdays from 6:00 p.m. to 7:30 p.m. in my apartment.

Call Josh at 659-3278 for more information, or email me at joshwrite@cup.com.

DRUMMER WANTED

The band 2Ds needs a drummer.

The 2Ds are Dana and Diego. Diego is the singer, and Dana plays the guitar. (She sometimes sings, too.)

We have drums, but we can't play them well. Can you play the drums?

Please email us at DD2D@cup.com.

Computer Help!

Do you often have problems with your computer? Help is here. I fix all kinds of computers. What kind do you have? A laptop? A desktop? Do you have trouble with software? I can fix it all.

Please call Susanna Morgan weekdays at 696-4215 or email me at susannatech@cup.com. Thanks.

2 Read the ads again. Check (✓) the true sentences.

1. ☑ Josh's classes are on Tuesdays.
2. ☐ Josh's classes are in the mornings.
3. ☐ Dana and Diego can sing.
4. ☐ Dana and Diego don't have drums.
5. ☐ Dana can play the guitar.
6. ☐ Susanna can fix laptops.
7. ☐ Susanna can't fix desktops.
8. ☐ Susanna doesn't have an email address.

Food

A Breakfast, lunch, and dinner

1 **Look at the pictures. Complete the puzzle with food words. What's the mystery word?**

1. 

2. 

3. 

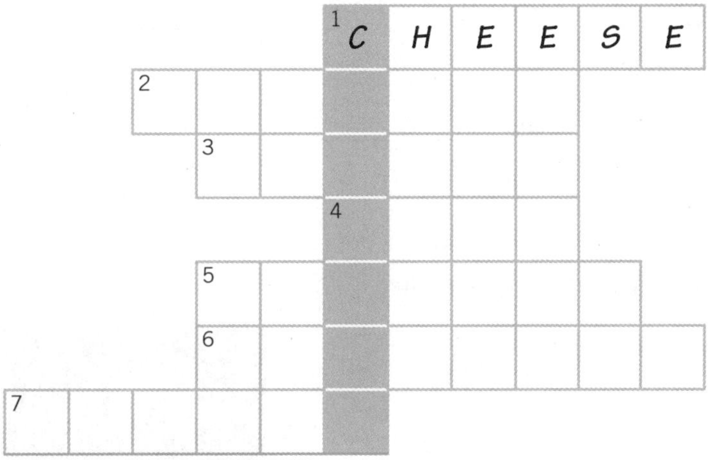

4. 

6. 

5. 

7. 

2 **Complete the sentences with the words from Exercise 1.**

1. Lynn usually eats ___*noodles*___ at her favorite Chinese restaurant.
2. I can't eat dairy. I never eat ________________ .
3. Carl's favorite food is fruit. He eats ________________ and ________________ every day.
4. I usually have milk and fruit with my ________________ in the morning.
5. ________________ and ________________ are my favorite vegetables.
6. Tanya's favorite grain is ________________ . She usually has it with beans.

3 **What food do you eat? Write two examples for each group or *I don't eat . . .***

Example: ___*I eat bananas and apples.*___ *or* ___*I don't eat fruit.*___

1. **Fruit:** ________________________________
2. **Vegetables:** ________________________________
3. **Meat:** ________________________________
4. **Dairy:** ________________________________
5. **Grains:** ________________________________

4 Are the food words count or noncount nouns? Write C (count) or N (noncount).

1. apple __*C*__
2. cheese ______
3. milk ______
4. tomato ______
5. meat ______
6. pasta ______
7. chicken ______
8. egg ______

5 Complete the answers. Use *some* or *any*.

1. Do you have any carrots? No, __*I don't have any*__________ .
2. Do you have any fish? Yes, ______________________ .
3. Do we have any apples? Yes, ______________________ .
4. Does Edward have any cereal? No, ______________________ .
5. Do they have any beans? No, ______________________ .
6. Does Lorena have any rice? Yes, ______________________ .

6 Complete the conversation with *a, an, any,* or *some*.

A: What do you usually have for breakfast?

B: I usually have __*some*__ (1) cereal.

A: Do you have ________ (2) milk with it?

B: Yes, I do.

A: And do you eat ________ (3) fruit?

B: Sometimes. I usually have ________ (4) banana or ________ (5) apple with my cereal.

A: Do you eat ________ (6) rice?

B: Not for breakfast. But I sometimes have ________ (7) rice for lunch. I make it with ________ (8) chicken or ________ (9) beef and ________ (10) vegetables. Oh, and sometimes with ________ (11) egg.

A: Really?

B: Yes. It's Korean food.

A: And what about dinner? What do you usually eat?

B: Well, I don't usually have ________ (12) meat for dinner. I often have ________ (13) pasta. It's my favorite!

7 Look at Andrea's food and her shopping list. What food does she have? What food doesn't she have? Write sentences with *some* and *any*.

1. *Andrea has some tomatoes.*
2. *She doesn't have any apples.*
3. ______________________________
4. ______________________________
5. ______________________________
6. ______________________________
7. ______________________________
8. ______________________________
9. ______________________________
10. ______________________________

8 Complete the lists with your own information. Then write sentences with *some* and *any*.

I have

____
____
____
____
____

Shopping List

I don't have

____
____
____
____
____

1. ______________________________
2. ______________________________
3. ______________________________
4. ______________________________
5. ______________________________
6. ______________________________

B I like Chinese food!

1 **Complete the conversation. Use the correct forms of the expressions from the box.**

love	really like	like	not like	not like at all	hate

Shelby: Let's make lunch. Do you like noodles?

Martin: No, I *don't like noodles* (1). 

Shelby: How about Mexican food?

Martin: Yes, I ______________ (2). 

Shelby: OK. How about rice and beans?

Martin: I ______________ (3). 

Shelby: OK. Rice and beans. We have some fish, too.

Martin: I ______________ (4). How about chicken? 

Shelby: I ______________ (5). How about beef? 

Martin: I ______________ (6). Let's have rice and beans with beef! 

Shelby: OK.

2 **Complete the conversation with your own information. Use some of the expressions from Exercise 1.**

Shelby: Do you like fish?

You: ______________, I ______________ fish.

Shelby: Do you like pasta?

You: ______________.

Shelby: How about eggs?

You: ______________.

Shelby: Do you like Chinese food?

You: ______________.

Shelby: How about Italian food?

You: ______________.

C Meals

1 Read the text. Then label the pictures with the correct underlined food words.

Sometimes it's difficult to eat out with my friends. Everybody likes different kinds of food! My friend Jon loves Asian food. He likes dumplings, and he really likes sushi. Sandy usually eats pasta. She loves spaghetti and noodles. Jake, her brother, likes American food. He usually has a hot dog or a hamburger. Louis likes tacos, but his favorite meal is breakfast. He loves cereal, eggs, and pancakes. And Kristen is always on a diet. She only eats soup and salad. It's terrible! How about me? Well, I eat anything. I love all kinds of food!

1. *hot dog*

2. ________________

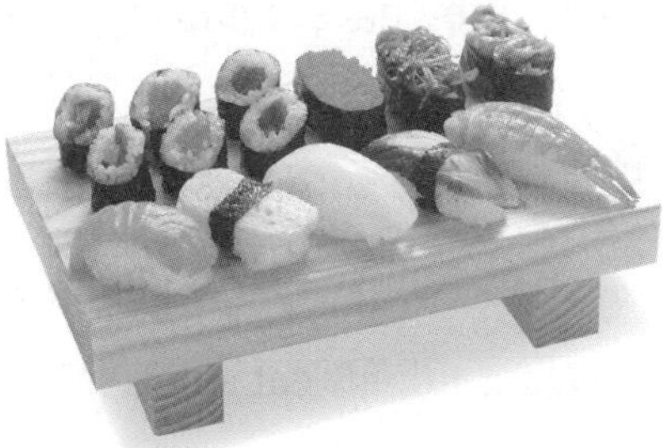

3. ________________

4. ________________

5. ________________

6. ________________

7. ________________

8. ________________

9. ________________

2 Cross out the word that doesn't belong in each list.

1. **On pizza:**	tomatoes	cheese	~~pancakes~~
2. **Italian food:**	pizza	hot dogs	spaghetti
3. **In a salad:**	carrots	cheese	soup
4. **Japanese food:**	tacos	sushi	rice
5. **In soup:**	noodles	salad	chicken

3 Correct the mistakes.

1. Brenda eats every day pizza. *Brenda eats pizza every day.*
2. Ahmed eats tacos once year. ______________________
3. We don't eat meat often very. ______________________
4. Andy eats cheese two a month. ______________________
5. Never Lydia eats vegetables. ______________________
6. They have dumplings four a week. ______________________

4 Circle the correct words to complete the conversation.

Pat: How **once** / **(often)**[1] do you eat sushi?

Alan: I don't eat sushi very **never** / **often**[2]. How about you?

Pat: I eat sushi **once** / **twice**[3] in a while. Kevin and I go to a Japanese restaurant **twice** / **three**[4] times a year.

Alan: My family **every** / **never**[5] eats out. We cook at home **every** / **often**[6] day.

Pat: Really? I don't cook **very** / **every**[7] often. Kevin cooks **often** / **twice**[8] a week, but we usually go to restaurants.

5 Match the sentences that have similar meanings.

1. Gary eats spaghetti every Sunday. *c*
2. Kyle doesn't eat spaghetti. _______
3. Marco eats spaghetti every Tuesday and Friday. _______
4. Mr. Lee eats spaghetti three times a year. _______
5. Victor has spaghetti once a month. _______

a. He eats spaghetti once in a while.
b. He eats spaghetti twice a week.
c. He eats spaghetti once a week.
d. He eats spaghetti 12 times a year.
e. He never eats spaghetti.

6 Look at Karen's answers to the quiz. Then answer the questions.

How international is your diet?

How often do you have . . .	every day	twice a week	once a week	twice a month	once in a while	never
Brazilian food?			✓			
Colombian food?						✓
Japanese food?		✓				
Korean food?				✓		
American food?	✓					
Italian food?			✓			
Greek food?					✓	

1. How often does Karen eat Brazilian food? *She eats Brazilian food once a week.*
2. How often does she eat Colombian food? ______
3. How often does she eat Japanese food? ______
4. How often does she eat Korean food? ______
5. How often does she eat American food? ______
6. How often does she eat Italian food? ______
7. How often does she eat Greek food? ______

7 How international is *your* diet? Answer the quiz with your own information. Then write sentences with the time expressions.

How often do you have . . .	every day	twice a week	once a week	twice a month	once in a while	never
Mexican food?						
Peruvian food?						
Thai food?						
Chinese food?						
Turkish food?						
French food?						

Example: *I never eat Mexican food.*

1. ______
2. ______
3. ______
4. ______
5. ______
6. ______

D Favorite food

1 **Look at the photo in Exercise 2. What kind of food is it?**

It's ______________________________ .

2 **Read the text. Then answer the questions.**

1. How often does Isabel eat at a Chinese restaurant? ______________________
2. Who makes Mexican food? ______________________
3. What's Isabel's favorite recipe? ______________________

HOME RECIPES TIPS BLOG CONTACT

EASY CHEF FORUM

What do you usually eat? How often do you eat out?
What's your favorite recipe? We want to hear from you!

Isabel

In my family, we usually have a well-balanced diet. We eat vegetables, fruit, and grains every day. We eat chicken about three times a week, and we eat fish once or twice a week. We hardly ever have beef. We eat it once in a while at restaurants, but we don't eat out very often. We do have some special days, though. Once a month, we eat out with our children at our favorite Chinese restaurant. The dumplings are delicious! And my mom comes over and makes Mexican food twice a month.

Here's my favorite easy recipe:

Veggie Pizza

Get some Italian bread. Put vegetables on top.
I use peppers, tomatoes, and onions.
Then add cheese, and cook it in the microwave for one minute. Delicious!

3 **Read the text again. Then write T (true), F (false), or NI (no information).**

1. Isabel has two children. *NI*
2. Isabel's family eats vegetables seven days a week. ______
3. Isabel's mother makes Mexican food for the family every week. ______
4. Isabel's husband sometimes makes veggie pizza. ______
5. Isabel's family never has beef. ______
6. Isabel can't cook Mexican food. ______
7. Isabel likes dumplings. ______
8. Peppers are vegetables. ______

In the neighborhood

A Around town

1 Label the pictures with the correct words from the box.

bank	coffee shop	newsstand
bookstore	gas station	subway station
bus stop	✓library	supermarket

1. *library*

2. ____________

3. ____________

4. ____________

5. ____________

6. ____________

7. ____________

8. ____________

9. ____________

2 Answer the questions. Use the places from Exercise 1.

1. Where can you usually get some coffee? *At a coffee shop, a bookstore, or a gas station.*
2. Where can you usually get a newspaper? ____________
3. Where can you usually get a book? ____________
4. Where can you get gas for a car? ____________
5. Where can you usually get some food? ____________

3 Look at the picture. Complete the sentences with the correct words from the box.

across from	between	in	next to	✓on	on the corner of

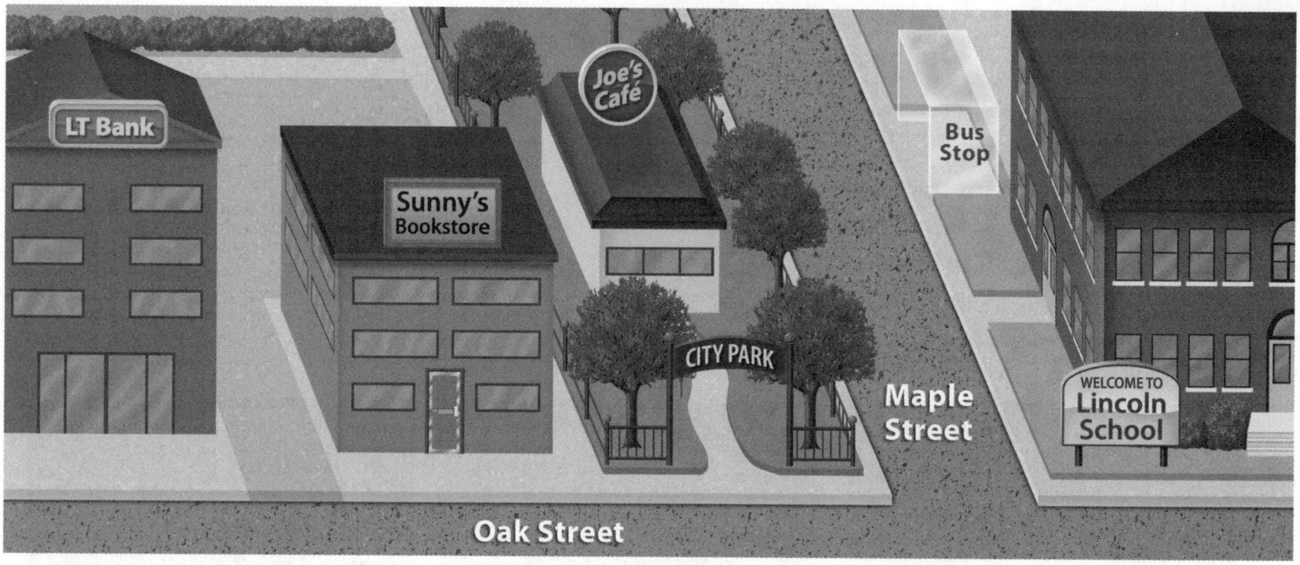

1. The bus stop is ___*on*___ Maple Street.
2. The park is ______________ Oak Street and Maple Street.
3. Joe's Café is ______________ the park.
4. The bookstore is ______________ the bank and the park.
5. The school is ______________ the park.
6. The bank is ______________ the bookstore.

4 Put the words in the correct order to make sentences. Sometimes more than one answer is possible.

1. is / The / supermarket / next to / the / post office / .

   The supermarket is next to the post office. / The post office is next to the supermarket.

2. The / Linden Street / department store / on / is / .

   ____

3. the / hotel / drugstore / across from / The / is / .

   ____

4. bookstore / café / in / the / The / is / .

   ____

5. the / library / The / bank and the school / is / between / .

   ____

6. First Avenue / The / hotel / is / on the corner of / and / Market Street / .

   ____

5 Read the clues. Label the places with the correct words. Then answer the questions.

A
- The supermarket is on the corner of Second Avenue and Prince Street.
- The coffee shop is between the bank and the hotel.
- The library is next to the bank.

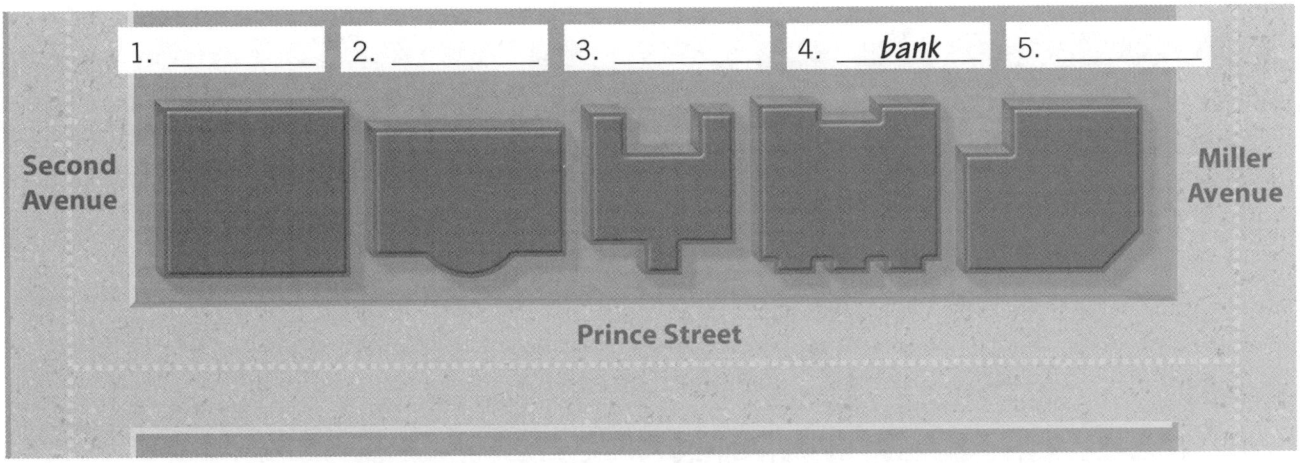

1. Is the hotel between the coffee shop and the supermarket? Yes, it is.
2. What is on the corner of Miller Avenue and Prince Street? ____________
3. What is next to the supermarket? ____________
4. Is the coffee shop next to the library? ____________

B
- The drugstore is across from the post office.
- The Internet café is next to the drugstore.
- The bookstore isn't on Oak Street.
- The newsstand is next to the bookstore.

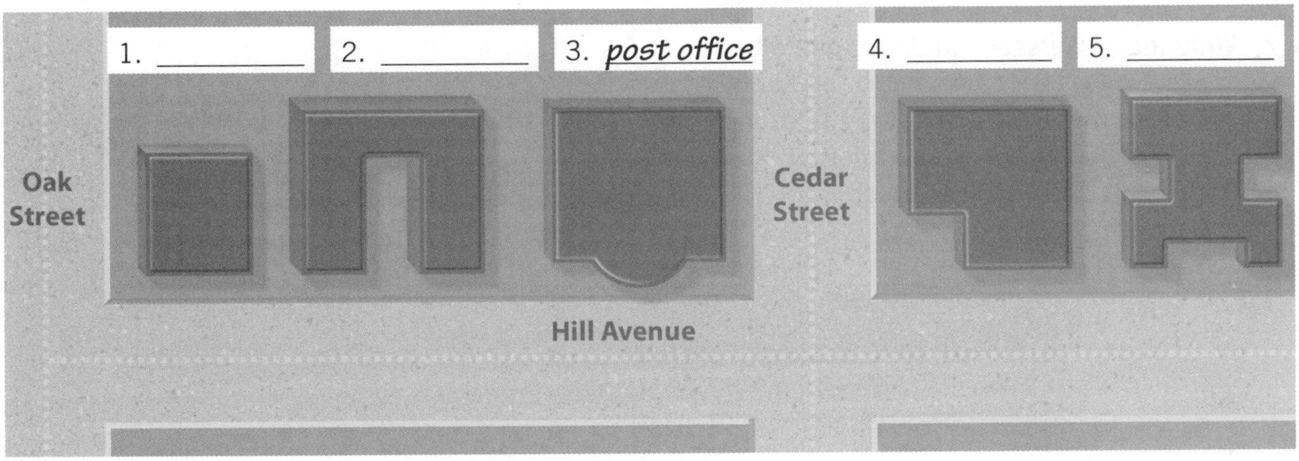

1. What is on the corner of Oak Street and Hill Avenue? ____________
2. What is between the post office and the newsstand? ____________
3. Is the Internet café on Hill Avenue? ____________
4. Is the bookstore across from the drugstore? ____________

B How do I get to . . . ?

1 Complete the directions with the correct words from the box.

blocks	left	take	turn	up	✓walk

Start: 150 York Street

End: 45 East Eighth Street

Start on York Street. ___*Walk*___ (1) to the corner of Elm Street.

Take a ______ (2) on Elm Street.

Go ______ (3) Elm Street.

______ (4) right on Fifth Avenue.

Walk four ______ (5) .

______ (6) a right on Eighth Street.

Go down Eighth Street. It's on the left.

2 Write the conversation in the correct order.

✓Excuse me. How do I get to the drugstore?
Go up Oak Street and turn left on First Avenue.
Great. Thank you very much.
Turn left on First Avenue?
Yes.

A: *Excuse me. How do I get to the drugstore?*

B: ______

A: ______

B: ______

A: ______

C Fun in the city

1 **Complete the puzzle and the sentences with the correct places to visit.**

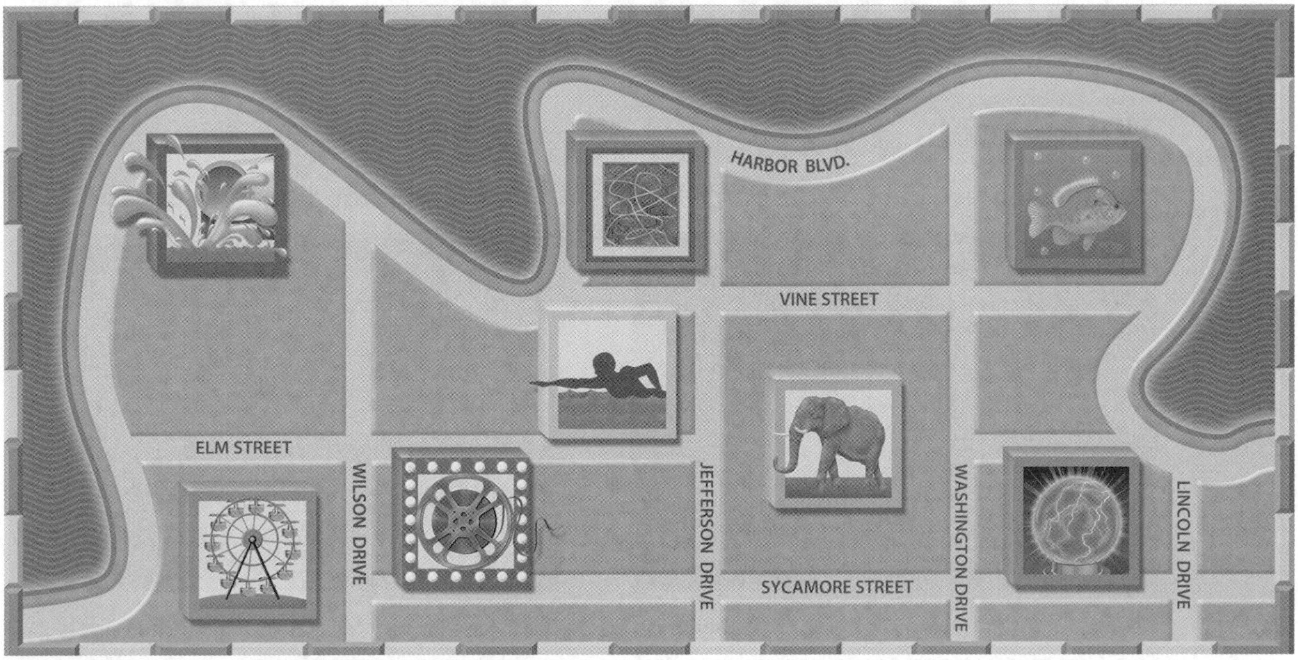

Across

2. Let's watch a movie at the ___*movie*___ theater.
3. My children can swim, and they love the ____________ park.
5. Do you like the fish in the ____________ ?
6. Is there a ____________ pool here?
7. Don works at the science ____________ .

Down

1. Let's see the animals at the ____________ .
2. I really like the art at this ____________ .
4. The ____________ park is fun! Wheeeeeeee!

2 Read the text. Then answer the questions.

GATLINBURG, TENNESSEE

Welcome!

There's a lot to do in Gatlinburg! Read about all of the fun places to visit here!

Indoor fun

We have a lot of museums. Go to the Hollywood Star Cars museum and see musicians' cars. You can see actors' and actresses' cars, too! Ripley's Believe It or Not Museum is also great. And Ripley's Aquarium has very unusual fish. We don't have a zoo in Gatlinburg, but you can see animals outside!

Outdoor fun

The Great Smoky Mountains National Park is in Gatlinburg. You can walk in it every day. We don't have a water park, but there are water slides at Ober Gatlinburg Ski Resort and Amusement Park.

1. Are there any museums in Gatlinburg? *Yes, there are.*
2. Is there an aquarium in Gatlinburg? ______
3. Are there any zoos? ______
4. Are there any parks in Gatlinburg? ______
5. Is there a water park? ______
6. Is there an amusement park? ______

3 Write sentences about Gatlinburg with *there is* / *are* / *isn't* / *aren't* and the information in parentheses.

1. (aquariums / 1) *There's an aquarium in Gatlinburg.*
2. (museums / 9) ______
3. (zoos / 0) ______
4. (movie theaters / 4) ______
5. (water parks / 0) ______
6. (amusement parks / 1) ______

4 Complete the conversations. Use the correct forms of *there is / are.*

A: Excuse me. *Are there any museums in this city* (1) ?

B: ______________ (2). The museums are on First Street.

A: Great. And are there any zoos here?

B: No, ______________ (3), but there's an aquarium. It's near the art museum.

A: OK. Thanks.

C: Excuse me. ______________ (4) near here?

D: A swimming pool? Yes, ______________ (5). ______________ (6) one in the park.

C: Great. ______________ (7) near the park?

D: No, ______________ (8). The library is across from the school, about ten blocks from here.

C: Thank you very much.

5 Complete the chart with the number of each place in your town or city. Then write sentences with *there is / are* and the information in the chart.

Place	Number
amusement parks	
aquariums	
movie theaters	
museums	
science centers	
swimming pools	
zoos	

1. *There* ______________ *in my town.*
2. ______________
3. ______________
4. ______________
5. ______________
6. ______________
7. ______________

D A great place to visit

1 **Look at the calendar in Exercise 2. Is the Ridgewood Community Center open every day?**

____

2 **Read the text. Complete the sentences with the correct days of the week.**

1. You can see a movie at the community center on *Friday* .
2. You can visit a museum on __________ .
3. There's an Italian dinner at the community center on __________ .
4. The swimming pool is open all day on __________ .
5. There is a book sale on __________ .
6. You can go to an amusement park on __________ .

RIDGEWOOD COMMUNITY CENTER
CALENDAR

Monday	Tuesday	Wednesday	Thursday	Friday	Saturday
Children's Art Tour 2:30 – 4:30 p.m. Tour the new Metro Art Museum with two guides. This is for children age 6-12 and their parents. ***$5 per person***	**Open Swim** All day Our swimming pool is open to everyone on Tuesday! ***It's free!***	**Italian Night** 6:00 – 8:00 p.m. There's an Italian dinner at our community center. Come and eat spaghetti! ***$8 for adults*** ***$6 for children***	**Bookstore** All day Bring old books to the center on Monday. On Thursday we have a book sale. ***All books are $1.***	**Movie Night** 6:00 – 10:00 p.m. Watch a movie at the center. There's a drama in Room B, and there's a children's movie in Room D. ***They're free!***	**Field Trip** 9:00 a.m. – 7:00 p.m. We take a bus to the Great Fun Amusement Park in Oakdale in the morning and come back in the evening. ***$45 per person***

NOTE: *We are closed on Sundays.*

Directions:

By bus: Take the Q62 bus to the Lamont bus stop. Walk down Lamont Street. Turn left on Orchid Street. We're on the corner of Orchid Street and Main Street.

By subway: Take the C train to Melvin Station. Walk up the stairs and turn right on View Street. Walk to Main Street and turn right. Walk two blocks to the corner of Main Street and Orchid Street.

3 **Read the text again. Then answer the questions.**

1. How much is the museum tour? *It's five dollars per person.*
2. What time is the Italian dinner? ______________________________
3. Is there a swimming pool at the community center? ______________________________
4. How do they get to the amusement park? ______________________________
5. Where is the community center in Ridgewood? ______________________________

What are you doing?

A I'm looking for you.

1 Complete the sentences with the correct words from the box.

at	behind	front	in	in	on	✓to	to	under

a. He waves __*to*__ Paula. She is _______ the children.

b. He runs _______ the movie theater.

c. Bob is _______ the bus. He's late.

d. She stands _______ an umbrella in the rain.

e. Paula stands in _______ of the movie theater.

f. The movie ends _______ 5:00.

g. She looks for Bob _______ the lobby.

h. The movie starts, but Paula isn't _______ the theater.

2 Match the pictures and the sentences from Exercise 1.

1. *e*

2. ☐

3. ☐

4. ☐

5. ☐

6. ☐

7. ☐

8. ☐

3 Circle the correct words to complete each sentence.

1. Calvin _______ at the bus stop.
   a. are standing
   (b.) is standing
   c. stand
2. Kate and Naomi _______ to Jen.
   a. aren't waving
   b. isn't waving
   c. don't waving
3. We _______ to our parents.
   a. talks
   b. don't talking
   c. aren't talking
4. _______ starting now.
   a. It's
   b. It doesn't
   c. It
5. _______ walking to school.
   a. I'm not
   b. I don't
   c. I
6. Lori and Ross _______ behind Jay.
   a. is sitting
   b. sits
   c. are sitting

4 Rewrite the email to correct the underlined mistakes.

Outspring Mail

Get Mail | New | Reply | Reply All | Forward | Mark Read | Defer | Next | Previous | Print | Delete | Junk | All | Search

Hello, Gwen!

We're haveing a great time in Spain. We're at a museum now. I'm writeing in the café. My husband is lookking for the Picasso paintings. My daughter are watching a movie about Spanish art. My son not watching the movie. He's play a video game here in the café. The baby isn't here. She's is sleeping at the hotel with my mother. Well, my mother's aren't sleeping. I think she's watch TV!

OK, now I need to look for my family and see some art!

Bye,
Stefanie

We're having a great time in Spain. We're at a museum now.

____

____

____

____

____

____

____

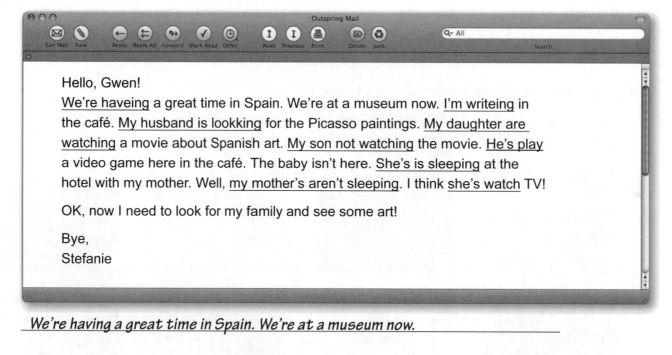

5 Write present continuous sentences with the words in parentheses.

1. (Matt / not drive / to work) *Matt is not driving to work.*
2. (We / play / soccer / at the park) ______
3. (Chloe / not sit / in the café) ______
4. (The game / start / now) ______
5. (They / swim / in the pool) ______
6. (Joan / not have / lunch right now) ______
7. (I / call / Audrey) ______
8. (You / not run) ______

6 Look at the pictures. What are the people doing? What aren't they doing? Complete the two sentences for each picture with the pairs of expressions from the box. Use the present continuous.

cook / eat at a restaurant	look for a book / hold a book
end / start	✓run / watch a movie

1. They *'re running* ______ .
   They *'re not watching a movie* ______ .

2. She ______ .
   She ______ .

3. The movie ______ .
   It ______ .

4. He ______ .
   He ______ .

B I can't talk right now.

1 **Circle the correct words to complete each sentence.**

Sally: Hello?

Jordan: Hi, Sal. It's Jordan. Do you have **good time** / **a minute**?
(1)

Sally: Oh, **sure** / **sorry**. I'm **busy** / **can't** right now. I'm cleaning.
(2) (3)

Can I **call** / **talk** you back?
(4)

Jordan: OK, **sure** / **sorry**. Talk to you **minute** / **later**.
(5) (6)

Sally: Thanks. Bye.

2 **Look at the pictures. Write conversations with the sentences from the box. Use the conversation in Exercise 1 as a model. Sometimes more than one answer is possible.**

Can you talk now?	I'm cooking dinner.	Is this a good time to talk?
I can't talk right now.	I'm doing my homework.	This isn't a good time.

1. **Jin Sun:** *Hello?*

Ivan: *Hi, Jin Sun. It's Ivan.*

______________________?

Jin Sun: __________. __________.

__________. __________?

Ivan: __________. __________.

Jin Sun: __________. __________.

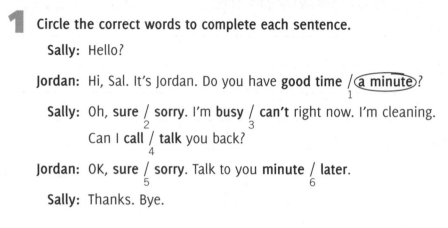

2. **Dan:** __________?

Marc: __________. __________.

______________________?

Dan: __________. __________.

__________. __________?

Marc: __________. __________.

Dan: __________. __________.

C These days

1 **Put the letters in the correct order to make activity phrases.**

1. e r l a n o t e v d r i — *learn to drive*
2. k e a t a c e d a n s s l a c — ______
3. e e c a t r a s t b e i e w — ______
4. o k l o f r o a b j o — ______
5. t s u d y t l i l a n a — ______
6. r t u t o a t u s d t e n — ______
7. e a k t n e t n s i l s o e s n s — ______
8. y t u s d r f o n a x m e a — ______

2 **Complete the text with the phrases from Exercise 1.**

The Idea Spot

Try something new! Here are a few ideas.

1. *Learn to drive* a car. You can learn at MPH Driving School.
2. ______ in Italy!
   You can take classes in Milan, Rome, or Florence.
3. Can you play sports? ______
   from Ralph Garvis at the Youth Gym.

4. ______!
   Baila has flamenco, tango, and salsa classes.
5. You can ______.
   Use your own computer. Tech Now teaches you online.

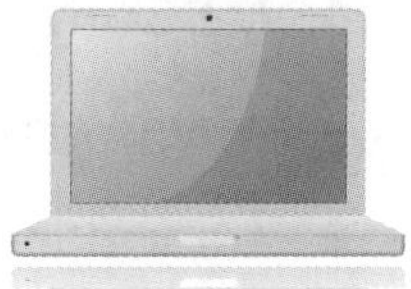

6. ______ with a friend.
   Go to the library or a café. Get an A on your test!
7. ______. Students at
   Byron Language School need help in Japanese and Chinese. Volunteer today!

8. ______ online.
   Find a job as a nurse, doctor, teacher, accountant, musician . . .

3 What are they doing these days? Read the clues and complete the chart with ✓ (yes) or ✗ (no). There is only one answer for each person.

- Carmen is taking a salsa class.
- Thomas isn't working these days.
- Megan isn't learning a language or looking for a job.
- Daniel is taking a language class.

Who is . . .	looking for a job?	taking a dance class?	studying Turkish?	creating a website?
Carmen	✗	✓	✗	✗
Thomas		✗		
Megan		✗		
Daniel		✗		

4 Answer the questions. Use the information in Exercise 3.

1. What's Carmen doing these days? ______________________________
2. What's Thomas doing these days? ______________________________
3. What's Megan doing these days? ______________________________
4. What's Daniel doing these days? ______________________________

5 Match the questions and answers.

1. What class is Debbie taking? ___e___
2. Where is Kathryn going? _______
3. Is Tonya creating a website? _______
4. Are Cindy and Mia tutoring students? _______
5. Why is Anna studying Italian? _______
6. Are you looking for a job? _______

a. Because she's looking for a job in Rome.
b. Yes, she is.
c. She's going to her dance class.
d. No, I'm not.
e. She's taking a Spanish class.
f. No, they're not.

6 Write present continuous questions with the information in parentheses.

1. (What / you / do / these days) *What are you doing these days* ?
2. (you / take / an art class) ____________________ ?
3. (Brad / take / the class) ____________________ ?
4. (Where / you / study / French) ____________________ ?
5. (What / you and Dave / do / these days) ____________________ ?

7 Complete the conversation with the correct questions from Exercise 6.

Erin: Hi, Fei. *What are you doing these days* ? (1)

Fei: Oh, I'm studying French!

Erin: ____________________ ? (2)

Fei: At the Bonjour Language School.

Erin: ____________________ ? (3)

Fei: No, he's not. He's taking tennis lessons.

Erin: Tennis? That's great.

Fei: He loves it. So, ____________________ ? (4)

Erin: We're painting and drawing a lot!

Fei: ____________________ ? (5)

Erin: Yes, we are! Oh, I'm late. Bye, Fei.

Fei: Bye, Erin. I mean, *au revoir!*

8 What are you doing these days? Answer the questions with your own information.

1. Are you taking any sports lessons? ____________________
2. Where are your friends studying English? ____________________
3. Is your English teacher studying a language? ____________________
4. Are you studying for an exam this week? ____________________
5. Is your mother or father looking for a job? ____________________
6. Where are you eating out these days? ____________________
7. Is your brother or sister taking guitar lessons? ____________________
8. What are you reading? ____________________

D What's new?

1 **Look at the photo in Exercise 2. What are the people doing?**

____

2 **Read the text. Write the names.**

1. Ron's son: ____________________
2. Ron's wife: ____________________

Outspring Mail

Get Mail New Reply Reply All Forward Mark Read Defer Next Previous Print Delete Junk All Search

Hey, Jeremy!

How are you? What are you doing these days? I'm finally taking a computer class! I'm creating my own website. I'm uploading a lot of pictures and videos, too. The pictures are of my kids, of course! Paul's ten now. He's helping me with my website! He's learning so much about computers at school. After school, he's taking soccer lessons at the park. His coach is Mr. Gonzalez. He is also tutoring Molly in Spanish. Is your daughter playing sports?

My wife and I are taking a Japanese class. Julie's also studying Spanish, and she's looking for a job. Are you and Beth cooking at home these days? We love your Greek salad and chicken! Are you still taking dance classes? Let's all go salsa dancing soon!

Write soon,
Ron

P.S. Here's a photo for you. We're eating sushi at your favorite Japanese restaurant!

3 **Read the text again. Then answer the questions.**

1. Is Ron creating a website? *Yes, he is.*
2. Who is helping Ron with his website? ____________________
3. What sport is Paul learning? ____________________
4. Who is tutoring Ron's daughter? ____________________
5. Is Ron's wife studying a language? ____________________
6. Is Ron's wife working? ____________________

Past experiences

A Last weekend

1 Complete the conversations with the correct present continuous forms of the verbs from the box.

listen	play	play	shop	✓stay	stay out	visit	watch

A. **Alan:** Hey, Mike. Where are you?

Mike: At home. I'm ___*staying*___ (1) home this weekend.

Alan: What are you doing?

Mike: I'm ______________ (2) an old movie. Are you home?

Alan: No. I'm ______________ (3) relatives.

B. **Tomas:** Hey, Clara. What are you doing these days?

Clara: Oh, I'm ______________ (1) in a band!

Tomas: Really? So are you ______________ (2) late on weekends?

Clara: Yes! Our band starts at 10:00 p.m. What about you? What are you doing on weekends?

Tomas: Oh, I'm ______________ (3) basketball on Saturdays and soccer on Sundays. That's all.

Clara: Hey, so come to one of our concerts!

C. **Bree:** Hi, Yoko. Can you talk right now?

Yoko: Yes. I'm just ______________ (1) to music. Why?

Bree: Oh, I'm ______________ (2) for new clothes and I need help.

Yoko: OK, I can help you. Where are you?

2 Complete the chart with the correct simple past forms of the verbs from the box.

chat	cry	dance	like	✓play	shop	study	visit

+ ed	+ d	y → i, + ed	double consonant + ed
played			

3 Look at the calendar. Write sentences about Vincent's activities last week. Use the simple past forms of the verbs.

MONDAY	
morning	exercise with Ray
afternoon	
evening	call Mom
TUESDAY	
morning	
afternoon	work at the bookstore
evening	
WEDNESDAY	
morning	play tennis with Ray
afternoon	
evening	upload the videos
THURSDAY	
morning	
afternoon	visit Grandpa
evening	fix Dan's computer
FRIDAY	
morning	
afternoon	study for the test with Lara
evening	shop for a new computer

1. *Vincent and Ray exercised on Monday morning.*
2. *Vincent* ____________________
3. ____________________
4. ____________________
5. ____________________
6. ____________________
7. ____________________
8. ____________________
9. ____________________

4 Complete Rachel's blog with the correct simple past forms of the verbs in parentheses.

LAST WEEK

On Monday, my sister and I ___*shopped*___ (1) (shop) for new clothes at the mall.

I ______ (2) (look for) a green dress for my friend's party. On Tuesday, I ______ (3) (search) the Internet for green shoes!

I ______ (4) (not / exercise) every day last week, but I ______ (5) (exercise) on Tuesday and Thursday.

On Friday, I ______ (6) (listen) to music with Jamie, and we ______ (7) (watch) a movie. We ______ (8) (not / watch) a new movie, but an old movie from 1927! The actors ______ (9) (not / talk) in the movie, and it was in black and white. We ______ (10) (love) the movie! We ______ (11) (laugh) and we ______ (12) (cry).

5 Write simple past sentences about you, your family, and your friends with the information in parentheses. Use time expressions.

Example: *My brother listened to music last weekend.*

1. (listen to music) ______
2. (stay home) ______
3. (stay out late) ______
4. (search the Internet) ______
5. (not / exercise) ______
6. (not / visit relatives) ______
7. (play soccer) ______
8. (not / play video games) ______
9. (watch a movie) ______
10. (not / download music) ______

B You're kidding!

1 **Complete the conversations with the correct words from the boxes.**

A. | not | ✓oh | yes | you're kidding |

Leo: I'm studying Japanese.

Amy: ___*Oh*___ (1) ?

Leo: ________ (2) , and I'm also studying Korean, Spanish, and Italian.

Amy: ________ (3) !

Leo: No. I'm ________ (4) . And I'm taking Chinese!

B. | know | oh, yeah | what | yes |

Chris: I have an English test on Tuesday.

Paul: ________ (1) ?

Chris: ________ (2) , and I didn't study.

Paul: ________ (3) ? You always study on weekends.

Chris: I ________ (4) , but I played soccer all weekend!

C. | at | for | really | yeah |

Ellie: I shopped for new clothes last weekend.

Pat: ________ (1) ? Where?

Ellie: ________ (2) the mall. And now I have a new suit.

Pat: ________ (3) ? You always wear T-shirts and jeans.

Ellie: I know, but I'm looking ________ (4) a job, and I have an interview.

2 **Match the conversations in Exercise 1 with the pictures.**

1. ☐

2. ☐

3. ☐

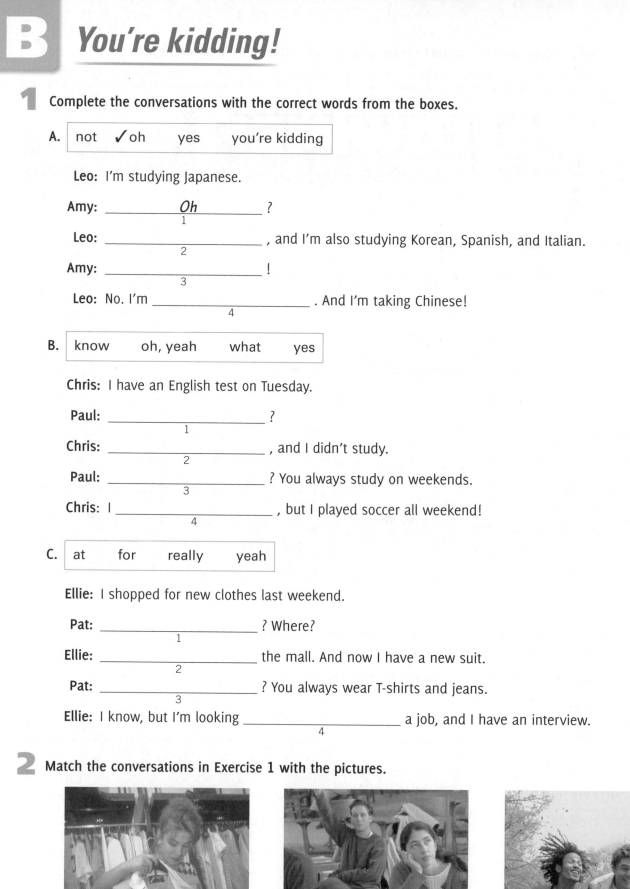

C Did you make dinner last night?

1 Circle the verbs that complete both expressions.

1. (have) / do:	a party	a car
2. **see / go:**	to work	grocery shopping
3. **go / make:**	breakfast	dinner
4. **get / make:**	a haircut	a job
5. **go / see:**	friends	a play
6. **make / do:**	the dishes	laundry

2 Complete the conversations with some of the expressions from Exercise 1. Use the present continuous forms of the verbs.

1. **A:** What are you doing?
   B: *I'm doing laundry.*

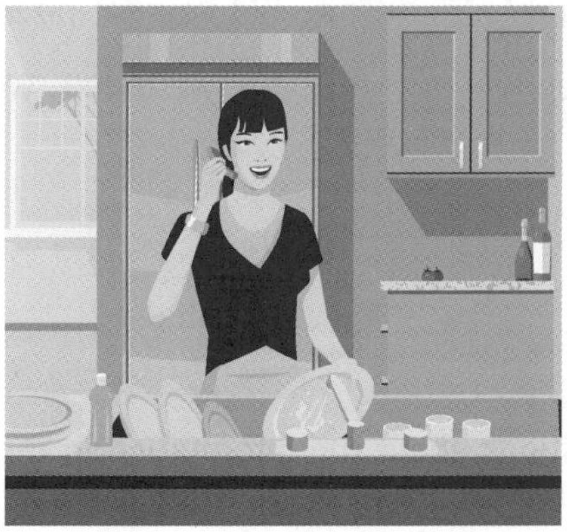

2. **A:** Do you have a minute?
   B: I can't talk right now. ____________________ .

3. **A:** Hi, Eva. Is this a good time?
   B: I'm sorry. ____________ ____________ right now.

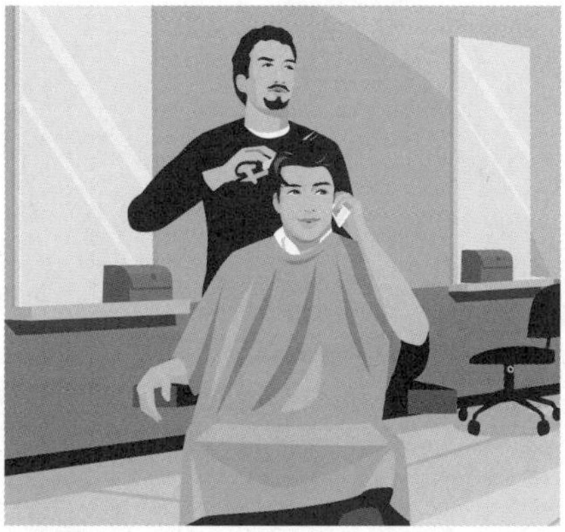

4. **A:** Can you talk?
   B: I'm busy right now. ____________________ .

5. **A:** What are you doing, Dan?
   B: ____________________ .

6. **A:** Can you help me with my computer?
   B: Sorry, mom. ____________ ____________________ .

3 Circle the correct words to complete the conversations.

1. **A:** ______ she get a haircut?
   B: No, she didn't.
   a. Does
   (b.) Did
   c. Do

2. **A:** Did you do laundry yesterday?
   B: ______
   a. Yes, I do.
   b. Yes, I did.
   c. Yes, I didn't.

3. **A:** Did you see Carol on Friday?
   B: No, I didn't. I ______ Wendy.
   a. see
   b. seed
   c. saw

4. **A:** Did Todd ride a bike to work?
   B: No, he didn't. He ______ .
   a. didn't drive
   b. drove
   c. drives

5. **A:** Did they ______ some water at the park?
   B: No, they didn't.
   a. drink
   b. drank
   c. drinked

6. **A:** Did you eat pizza at the restaurant?
   B: No, we didn't. We ______ tacos.
   a. eat
   b. ate
   c. eated

4 Write simple past *yes* / *no* questions about the information in the sentences. Then answer the questions with short answers.

1. Sue bought new clothes at the mall.
   A: *Did Sue buy new clothes at the mall* ?
   B: *Yes, she did* .
2. Ethan and Craig took a bus to Miami.
   A: ______________________________ ?
   B: No, ______________________________ .
3. He did the dishes last night.
   A: ______________________________ ?
   B: No, ______________________________ .
4. They went to work on Friday.
   A: ______________________________ ?
   B: Yes, ______________________________ .

5 Complete the text with the correct simple past forms of the verbs in parentheses.

David _____had_____ (have) a bad day
1
yesterday. He _____ (get up) late,
2
so he _____ (not / make) breakfast.
3
He _____ (run) to the bus stop,
4
but he _____ (see) the bus drive
5
away. He _____ (take) a taxi to work,
6
and he _____ (get) to work late. He
7
_____ (sit) at his desk and looked
8
at his computer. He _____ (read) the
9
note for Monday: "Martin Luther King Day. No work."
David _____ (go) home, and he
10
_____ (sleep) for three hours.
11

6 Answer the questions with the information from Exercise 5.

1. Did David get up late? _Yes, he did._____

2. Did David make breakfast? _____

3. Did David take a bus to work? _____

4. Did David get to work late? _____

5. Did David work yesterday? _____

7 Check (✓) the things you did last week. Then write sentences about what
you did and didn't do.

1. ☐ get up late _____

2. ☐ do laundry _____

3. ☐ buy new clothes _____

4. ☐ meet a friend _____

5. ☐ go to a play _____

6. ☐ get a haircut _____

7. ☐ read a book _____

8. ☐ eat at a restaurant _____

D I saw a great movie.

1 Read the text. Then circle the correct answers.

1. Jeremy went to ______ .

   a. Mexico b. Ohio c. China

2. He went with ______ .

   a. Beth and Ron b. Beth and Ron's daughter c. Beth and Brittany

3. He saw ______ .

   a. his friends b. his parents c. Ron

Hi, Ron,

We're on vacation in Sandusky, Ohio!

This vacation is all about our daughter, Brittany! We came to Ohio for Cedar Point. It's a great amusement park. We're staying with friends. They have a daughter, too. We went to Cedar Point on Tuesday. Thursday we went to Soak City. It's a water park. Brittany had a great time.

Beth and I are having fun, too. We liked Cedar Point and Soak City. Last night we saw a play. We aren't cooking at all! We had dinner at a Mexican restaurant and a Chinese restaurant. We're eating at a lot of cafés, too.

Right now we're relaxing – and writing postcards!

Jeremy

2 Read the text again. Correct the false sentences.

1. Jeremy and his family went to Cedar, Ohio.

   Jeremy and his family went to Sandusky, Ohio.

2. Jeremy and his family are staying with relatives.

   ____

3. Jeremy and his family went to the amusement park on Wednesday.

   ____

4. Jeremy and Beth liked Cedar Point, but they didn't like Soak City.

   ____

5. Jeremy and Beth saw a movie at night.

   ____

6. On their vacation, Jeremy and his family didn't eat out.

   ____

Getting away

A *Where were you?*

1 Complete the puzzle with the correct adjectives.

Across

3. This is a _____ party. We're having a great time.

5. Those hot dogs were _____ . I didn't eat them.

6. I went to an _____ soccer game last weekend! The players were very good.

8. This game is _____ . It's 0 to 0, and my favorite player isn't playing.

Down

1. That was an _____ book. I read it in 2005 and in 2007.

2. Can we watch a different movie? This is _____ !

4. The library is always _____ .

7. My brother's friends are very _____ . I can't study!

9. This food isn't great, but it's not bad. It's _____ .

			¹I			²	
³			N		⁴		
			T				
			E				
⁵			R				
			E				
			S				
			T				
	⁶		I		⁷		
			N				
⁸	⁹		G				

2 What do you think? Label the pictures with two possible adjectives from Exercise 1.

1. __*exciting*__ 2. _____ 3. _____ 4. _____ 5. _____

__*noisy*__ _____ _____ _____ _____

3 Put the words in the correct order to make sentences.

1. class / Lola / Was / in / Monday morning / on / ? *Was Lola in class on Monday morning?*
2. an / they / yesterday / amusement park / Were / at / ? ______
3. a / at / We / museum / were / . ______
4. was / fun and exciting / It / . ______
5. were / , / Yes / they / . ______
6. weekend / Jim's / How / was / ? ______
7. she / No / , / wasn't / . ______
8. you and Chris / on / Where / were / Friday afternoon / ? ______

4 Label the pictures with the correct questions and answers from Exercise 3.

1. *Was Lola in class on Monday morning* ?
______ .

2. ______ ?
______ .

3. ______ ?
______ .

4. ______ ?
______ .

5 Complete the text with the correct forms of the simple past of *be (not)*.

Did you read a good book?

TELL US WHAT YOU THINK!

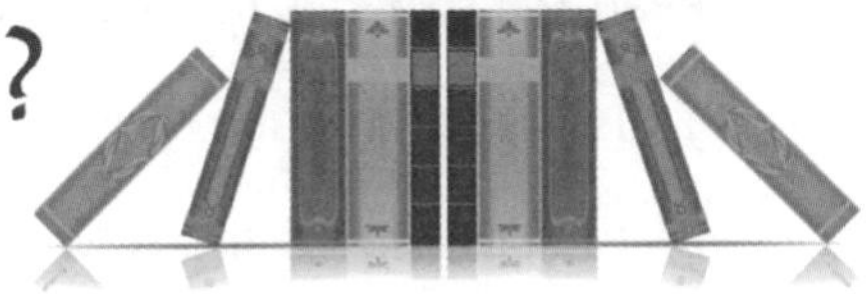

Gwennie

I read Moby Dick. It ____*was*____ (1) boring.

I didn't like it.

Dan91

No . . . Moby Dick ________________ (2) boring!

It ________________ (3) interesting! I loved it.

LukeMan

Wow, Dan91! You're kidding, right? Moby Dick ________________ (4)

interesting at all! It's 822 pages!

KatyG

OK, long, yes, but boring, no! Moby Dick ________________ (5) exciting. I

read four Herman Melville books, and they ________________ (6) all great!

TylerT

What? I don't think so. I read three of his books, and they

________________ (7) great. They ________________ (8) all terrible!

6 Answer the questions with your own information.

1. How was your weekend? ________________________
2. Where were you in 2010? ________________________
3. How old were you in 2006? ________________________
4. Was your last vacation interesting? ________________________
5. Were you in English class yesterday? ________________________
6. Where were you on Monday? ________________________
7. Where were your parents last night? ________________________
8. Were you and a friend at a concert last week? ________________________

B That's great!

1 **Read the news. Is it good or bad? Write G (good news) or B (bad news).**

1. I got a promotion. I'm so happy! ___*G*___
2. I missed my flight. Now I'm waiting for the next flight. _______
3. I was sick yesterday. My friends saw a great play without me. _______
4. I won a contest and got a trip to Mexico. It's so exciting! _______
5. I lost my new cell phone. I bought it last week, and it was $150! _______
6. I got a new job. It's very interesting! _______

2 **Write the conversation in the correct order.**

✓Did you have a good weekend? It was great. I went to a new club with friends. It was OK. I stayed home all weekend. I was sick. Thanks. And how was your weekend? That's nice! That's too bad.

A: *Did you have a good weekend?*

B: *It was OK.*

A: ______________________________

B: ______________________________

A: ______________________________

B: ______________________________

3 **Write a conversation with some of the sentences from the box. Use the conversation in Exercise 2 as a model.**

It was good. I saw an interesting play.	Oh, no!	That's awesome!
It wasn't great. I lost my wallet.	That's excellent!	That's terrible!

A: *Did you have a good weekend?*

B: ______________________________

A: ______________________________

B: ______________________________

A: ______________________________

B: ______________________________

C My vacation

1 Complete the sentences with vacation activities. Use the simple past forms of the verbs.

1. Tim s*hopped* in m*arkets* and b__________ s__________ in Tokyo.
2. Donna w__________ to a f__________ in Cuzco.
3. Eric w__________ to the b__________ and r__________ in Rio.

4. Tina t__________ p__________ of the Eiffel Tower in Paris.
5. Laura t__________ a t__________ of the Taj Mahal in Agra.
6. Rick and Lisa w__________ s__________ in San Francisco.

2 Cross out the words that don't make phrases with the verbs.

1. **go:**	to the beach	~~pictures~~	sightseeing
2. **take:**	a tour	to a festival	pictures
3. **relax:**	souvenirs	at home	at a hotel
4. **buy:**	new clothes	souvenirs	sightseeing
5. **shop:**	in a market	online	a tour

3 Look at the tour information. Then answer the questions in full sentences.

MEREDITH**TRAVEL** TOURS — MIAMI, FLORIDA

Last name	First name	Day	People traveling with	Getting to Miami by	Activities	Time
Arai	Hiro	Monday	wife	train	go sightseeing	11:00 a.m.–9:00 p.m.
Clark	Patty	Tuesday	–	train	take a tour of the Miami Science Museum	10:00 a.m.–12:00 p.m.
Hall	Lucy	Thursday	husband, two children	car	go to Miami Metrozoo	8:00 a.m.–8:00 p.m.
Vargas	Ricardo	Wednesday	wife, one child	bus	go to the Seaquarium	9:00 a.m.–4:00 p.m.
Young	Harry	Tuesday	–	bus	go to an art festival	2:00 p.m.–6:00 p.m.

1. Where did Patty go on vacation? *She went to Miami.*
2. What did Hiro and his wife do in Miami? ____________
3. Who did Lucy travel with? ____________
4. How did Harry get to Miami? ____________
5. What time did Patty's tour start? ____________
6. How did Ricardo and his family get to Miami? ____________
7. What time did the art festival end? ____________
8. What did Ricardo and his family do in Miami? ____________

4 Read the answers. Write the *Wh-* questions for the underlined part of the answers. Use the information from Exercise 3.

1. *How did Lucy and her family get to Miami?* They drove.
2. ____________ He traveled with his wife and child.
3. ____________ She took a tour of the Miami Science Museum.
4. ____________ He went to the art festival on Tuesday.
5. ____________ They took a train.
6. ____________ It started at 2:00 p.m.

5 Complete the conversation with simple past *Wh-* questions.

Holly: Hi, Grace. *How was your vacation* ?
(1)

Grace: My vacation was great.

Holly: ____________________ ?
(2)

Grace: I went to Costa Rica!

Holly: That's exciting! ____________________ ?
(3)

Grace: My brother and our friends Doug and Kim.

Holly: That's nice. ____________________ ?
(4)

Grace: We flew. We left at 6:00 a.m. We flew to Miami and then to San José.

Holly: ____________________ ?
(5)

Grace: We got to San José at 4:30.

Holly: Oh, that's not bad. ____________________ ?
(6)

Grace: We went sightseeing in San José, and then we went to the beach for four days and relaxed!

Holly: Awesome! ____________________ ?
(7)

Grace: Oh, the food was excellent. We ate a lot.

6 Think about the last time you visited relatives or friends in another city or country. Answer the questions.

1. Where did you go? ____________________
2. How old were you? ____________________
3. Who did you see? ____________________
4. Who did you travel with? ____________________
5. How did you get there? ____________________
6. What did you do there? ____________________
7. What did you eat there? ____________________
8. What did you buy there? ____________________
9. Did you get up early or late? ____________________
10. Was it exciting or boring? ____________________

D Travel experiences

1 Label the pictures with the correct headings from the text in Exercise 2.

1. *Make a Calendar* 2. ________ 3. ________ 4. ________

2 Read the text. Then answer the questions.

TRAVEL TIPS

Be safe when you travel. Here are some things you can do to have a fun vacation. Learn from our readers' mistakes!

GET A HOTEL
Plan your trip before you go! Leo took a bus to Salvador in Brazil. He didn't get a hotel before the trip. When he got to Salvador, he didn't find a hotel at first. He finally found one, but he paid a lot of money for it!

CHECK THE WEATHER
Search the Internet for the weather. Rachel went to Rome, but she didn't check the weather for Italy. She took only T-shirts and shorts, and she didn't take a coat. Brrrrrrr! She was cold.

MAKE A CALENDAR
Write down the days of your trip, and make a list of things to do each day. Ken and Lee went to South Korea, but they didn't make a list. The first two days of their trip were wasted. They didn't do anything fun because they didn't know where to go. They finally went sightseeing in Seoul, but they didn't go to the markets. They bought souvenirs at the airport!

REMEMBER YOUR WALLET
Don't forget your wallet and passport. Margot got to the airport for her trip to Sydney, Australia. Her wallet and her passport were at home. She missed her flight!

1. How did Leo get to Salvador? *He took a bus.*
2. What clothes did Rachel take to Rome? ________
3. Who did Ken travel with? ________
4. Did Ken buy souvenirs at the markets in Seoul? ________
5. Where was Margot's wallet? ________

Time to celebrate

A I'm going to get married.

1 Complete the sequences with the correct months.

1. January March ___*May*___ July
2. ______________ July August September
3. September October November ______________
4. January ______________ July October
5. ______________ May August November

2 Look at Kelly's birthday calendar. When is each person's birthday? Write sentences with words for the dates.

Birthday Calendar

Sort by: date

Makoto Saito
June 22nd

Kyle Brown
June 23rd

Lucia Ferrari
June 29th

Jack O'Dell
June 30th

Don Stuart
July 1st

Daniel Lucas
July 5th

Amanda Rivera
July 8th

Emily Simpson
July 12th

1. *Makoto's birthday is June twenty-second.*
2. ______________
3. ______________
4. ______________
5. ______________
6. ______________
7. ______________
8. ______________

3 Circle the correct words to complete each sentence.

1. Jacob's **going to** / **go to** visit relatives on Sunday.
2. Mr. and Mrs. Davis **are going drive** / **are going to drive** to work next week.
3. We're **are not going to** / **not going to** go to the beach.
4. Chet **is going to not take** / **isn't going to take** the train to work.
5. **A:** Are you **going to stay** / **go to staying** home today?

   B: Yes, **I am going** / **I am.**
6. **A:** **Is Sarah go** / **Is Sarah going** to study in Brazil?

   B: No, **she isn't** / **she doesn't.**

4 Look at the calendar. Write sentences about the people's future plans with *be going to.* Use the words in parentheses.

January	February	March
		22 – Ellie's trip to Ecuador
April	**May**	**June**
21 – Dana's 1st day at new job	*7 – Tim's graduation from college*	*2 – Willy's vacation (one week)*
July	**August**	**September**
23 – Jill and Lucas – skydiving!		*10 – Brian and Nicole's 1st day of college*
October	**November**	**December**
11 – Amy and Ken's wedding		*13 – Heather's big party*

1. (travel) *Ellie is going to travel to Ecuador on March 22nd.*
2. (start her new job) ______________________
3. (graduate from college) ______________________
4. (go on vacation) ______________________
5. (go skydiving) ______________________
6. (start college) ______________________
7. (get married) ______________________
8. (have a party) ______________________

5 Write *yes / no* questions with *be going to* and the information in parentheses. Then complete the answers.

1. (you / take / a taxi / to work)

   A: *Are you going to take a taxi to work* ?

   B: Yes, *I am* .

2. (they / get / married / next week)

   A: ______ ?

   B: No, ______ .

3. (he / create / a website for me)

   A: ______ ?

   B: No, ______ .

4. (we / eat out / on Friday)

   A: ______ ?

   B: Yes, ______ .

5. (she / look for / a job)

   A: ______ ?

   B: Yes, ______ .

6. (you / do / the dishes / tonight)

   A: ______ ?

   B: No, ______ .

6 Complete the chart with information about future plans for you, your family, or your friends. Use the events in the box or your own ideas.

get married	graduate	start a new job
go skydiving	have a big party	travel to [country name]

	Person	Event	Date
Example:	*Max and Leah*	*get married*	*August 3rd*
1.			
2.			
3.			
4.			
5.			
6.			

7 Write sentences with the information in Exercise 6 and *be going to*.

Example: *Max and Leah are going to get married on August 3rd.*

1. ______
2. ______
3. ______
4. ______
5. ______
6. ______

B Sure. I'd love to.

1 Complete the words with the correct letters.

Declining an invitation	Accepting an invitation
1. I'm s*orry*________ . I can't.	4. S________ . I'd l________ to.
2. I'm a________ I can't.	5. Yeah. That s________ gr________ .
3. I'm r________ sorry, but I can't.	6. S________ go________ .

2 Complete the conversation with phrases from Exercise 1. More than one answer is possible.

Sam: Hello?

Ty: Hi, Sam. It's Ty. Listen, do you want to go to a basketball game on Saturday?

Sam: Saturday? ________________ (1) .

Ty: Oh, OK. Well, do you want to go to the beach on Sunday?

Sam: The beach? ________________ (2) .

Ty: Great. I'm going to drive. Can we meet at your house at 9:00 a.m.?

Sam: ________________ (3) ! See you at 9:00 on Sunday.

3 Write a conversation about invitations with the phrases from Exercise 1 and your own ideas. Use the conversation in Exercise 2 as a model.

Marc: Hello?

Dina: ________________________

Marc: ________________________

Dina: ________________________

Marc: ________________________

Dina: ________________________

Marc: ________________________

C Planning a party

1 **Put the letters in the correct order to make party checklist phrases.**

1. h o s o c e h e t u s c m i — *choose the music*
2. d s e n h e t o s i i v t n i t a n ______
3. m k e a a e u s g t s l t i ______
4. l p a n e h t m n e u ______
5. k a b e a c e k a ______
6. t e d a e r o c e t h o m o r ______
7. y b u a f g i t ______
8. p p e e r r a h t e d o f o ______

2 **Look at the pictures. Complete the sentences with the phrases from Exercise 1 and *be going to*.**

1. Tonya *is going to make a guest list* .
   Danilo ______ .
2. Ben ______ .
   Mi Yon ______ .

3. Glenn ______ .
   Terry ______ .
4. Rodrigo ______ .
   Erica ______ .

3 Complete the chart with the correct object pronouns.

Subject pronouns:	I	you	he	she	it	we	they
Object pronouns:	*me*						

4 Rewrite the email to correct the underlined mistakes.

To: OliviaTaylor@cup.com
From: L.S.Taylor@cup.com
Subject: Mom's birthday

Hi, Olivia!

How are you? I'm busy with Mick and Susana. I'm going to take they to a soccer game at 12:00. Then we're going to go shopping. Susana has a concert on Friday. I'm going to buy it a new dress. Mick needs a new computer. I'm going to buy him at CompSave.

Listen, Mom's birthday is Sunday. What are we going to get him? Do you want to get she a sweater and a scarf? Look at the pictures. I can buy they online today. You can pay my later. Mom helps we all the time, so let's surprise hers with a party. Let's have a cake. Can you bake its? Dad is going to be here tomorrow. I can tell he about the party.

I'm going to call your after the soccer game. Are you going to be home?

Your sister,
Lisa

view download

view download

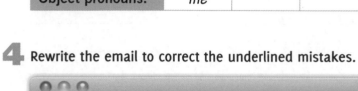

How are you? I'm busy with Mick and Susana. I'm going to take them to a soccer game at 12:00.

5 Put the words in the correct order to make sentences.

1. going / to / buy / you / What / are / Jen / ? *What are you going to buy Jen?*
2. help / going / Henry and me / Who's / to / ? ____________________
3. John / going / When / to / you / are / see / ? ____________________
4. to / is / going / How / Sonya / send / the invitations / ? ____________________
5. to / What time / Paul and Vera / going / is / he / call / ? ____________________
6. is / Where / going / she / meet / to / you and Jim / ? ____________________

6 Write conversations with the questions from Exercise 5 and the information in the pictures. Use object pronouns in the answers.

1. **A:** *What are you going to buy Jen?*
   B: *I'm going to buy her a hat.*

2. **A:** ____________________
   B: ____________________

3. **A:** ____________________
   B: ____________________

4. **A:** ____________________
   B: ____________________

5. **A:** ____________________
   B: ____________________

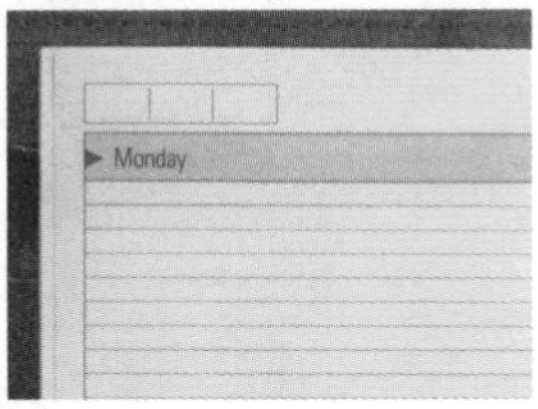

6. **A:** ____________________
   B: ____________________

D Birthdays

1 Look at the invitation. What are they going to celebrate?

Celebrate!

Host: Kelly
What: A party for Joe's birthday!
Where: Kelly's house
542 Maple Street
When: Saturday, June 14th
6:00 p.m.

It's Joe's birthday. Let's give him a great party! Shhh . . . don't tell him! I'm going to prepare dinner and bake a cake. Come early and help me decorate the house! Bring him a gift or a card. Are you going to come? Don't be late!

Are you going to come?

◯ Yes ◯ No

Guests: [_____]

Post a comment:

[_____]

🔵 **Yes**

RayS: Sure. I'm going to come!
Matt Blake: It sounds great. I'm going to bring my wife.
Dawn447: Josh and I are going to be there. See you on Saturday.
Ellie Smith: I'm going to bring my guitar and play him a song!
Paul Peters: I'm going to be late, but I'm going to be there!

🔵 **No**

Lydia: I'm sorry, I can't. My mother is visiting, and we are going to see a play that night.
Ali: I'm afraid I can't come to Joe's party. Tell him "Happy Birthday!"

2 Read the invitation again. Then write T (true), F (false), or NI (no information).

1. The party is at 6:00 p.m. on June 14th. ___T___

2. Guests are going to bring food to the party. _____

3. Kelly is going to bake a cake. _____

4. Matt's wife isn't going to come to the party. _____

5. Ellie can play the guitar. _____

6. Lydia is going to buy Joe a gift. _____

Credits

Illustration credits

Kveta Jelinek: 8, 29, 67; Andrew Joyner: 7, 18, 82; Greg Paprocki: 4, 14, 21, 44, 77; Garry Parsons: 10, 19, 65; Rob Schuster: 17, 24, 33, 51, 58, 59, 61, 88; Richard Williams: 12, 73, 93

Photography credits

1 ©Golden Pixels/Alamy; 2 *(clockwise from top left)* ©Fancy/Alamy; ©Photo Library; ©Jo Son/Getty Images; ©Ed Snowshoe/Getty Images; ©Media Bakery; ©Media Bakery; 5 *(clockwise from top left)* ©Courtesy Eddie Tucker; ©Soemo Fine Arts; ©AF archive/Alamy; ©Bill Olive; ©Michael Caulfield/Getty Images; ©Foto Arena/Getty Images; 6 ©Media Bakery; 13 *(Sophia, Felipe)* ©Media Bakery; *(Diego)* ©Image Source/Getty Images; *(all others)* ©Tetra Images/Alamy; 15 ©Alamy; 16 *(top to bottom)* ©Fuse/Getty Images; ©Media Bakery; ©DB Images/Alamy; 20 *(all)* ©Shutterstock; 22 *(clockwise from top left)* ©Shutterstock; ©Media Bakery; ©Shutterstock; ©Laurence Monneret/Getty Images; ©Shutterstock; ©Shutterstock; ©Alamy; ©Shutterstock; 25 *(top row, left to right)* ©Alamy; ©H. Mark Weidman Photography/Alamy; ©Jack Sullivan/Alamy; ©Andy Selinger/Alamy; *(middle row, left to right)* ©Alex Segre/Alamy; ©Media Bakery; *(bottom)* ©Photo Library; 26 ©Media Bakery; 27 *(left to right)* ©Media Bakery; ©Megapress/Alamy; ©ICP/Alamy; ©Photo Library; 30 ©Ian Thraves/Alamy; 31 ©Media Bakery; 32 *(clockwise from top left)* ©David Ball/Alamy; ©Photo Library; ©J. Schwanke/Alamy; ©Stacy Walsh Rosenstock/Alamy; 33 *(cat, barbells)* ©Shutterstock; 34 ©Media Bakery; 36 ©Silvia Otte/Getty Images; 37 *(clockwise from top left)* ©Anthony Pleva/Alamy; ©Mira/Alamy; ©Bubbles Photolibrary/Alamy; ©Media Bakery; ©Janine Wiedel/Alamy; 38 ©Alamy; 41 *(stethoscope)* ©Media Bakery; *(calculator)* ©Alamy; *(phone)* ©PhotoSpin, Inc./Alamy; *(menu)* ©Brand X Pictures/Getty Images; *(all others)* ©Shutterstock; 42 ©Vibe Images/Alamy; 43 *(both)* ©MBI/Alamy; 45 *(clockwise from top left)* ©Peter Dazeley/Alamy; ©Media Bakery; ©Media Bakery; ©Livia Corona/Getty Images; ©Fuse/Getty Images; ©Jupiter Images; ©Media Bakery; ©Upper Cut Images/Alamy; 47 *(all)* ©Shutterstock; 48 *(all)* ©Shutterstock; 49 *(all)* ©Shutterstock; 50 ©Alamy; 53 *(all)* ©Shutterstock; 54 ©Media Bakery; 56 *(left to right)* ©Alamy; ©Shutterstock; 57 *(top row, left to right)* ©Stuart Pearce/Alamy; ©Ian Dagnall/Alamy; ©Alex Segre/Alamy; *(middle row, left to right)* ©Media Bakery; ©Frances Roberts/Alamy; ©Imagic New York/Alamy; *(bottom row, left to right)* ©Vespasian/Alamy; ©David R. Frazier/Alamy; ©David R. Frazier/Alamy; 62 *(left to right)* ©Debra Behr/Alamy; ©Media Bakery; 63 *(left to right)* ©Peter Titmuss/Alamy; ©Alan Danaher/Getty Images; 68 *(top to bottom)* ©Photo Library; ©Fancy/Alamy; 70 ©Direct Photo/Alamy; 71 ©Lindy Powers/Alamy; 72 ©Media Bakery; 75 ©Media Bakery; 76 *(left to right)* ©Paul Doyle/Alamy; ©Media Bakery; ©Media Bakery; 78 ©Ei Katsumata/Alamy; 79 ©Mike Powell/Getty Images; 80 ©William Manning/Alamy; 81 *(left to right)* ©Media Bakery; ©Media Bakery; ©Media Bakery; ©Alamy; ©Photo Library; 83 *(top to bottom)* ©Media Bakery; ©Shutterstock; ©Alamy; ©Alamy; ©Media Bakery; 84 ©Mixa/Alamy; 85 *(clockwise from top left)* ©Image Source/Alamy; ©Eye Ubiquitous/Alamy; Media Bakery; Photo Library; ©Bill Bachmann/Alamy; ©First Light/Alamy; 87 ©Neil McAllister/Alamy; 89 *(all)* ©Shutterstock; 91 ©Media Bakery; 92 ©Photos India/Alamy; 94 *(both)* ©Shutterstock; 95 *(top to bottom)* ©Shutterstock; ©Media Bakery; ©Shutterstock; ©Patti McConville/Alamy; ©Shutterstock